Praise for Philip Dodd and *What's in a Name?*:

"There are wonderful gems here. Most fun are the very human aspects of Dodd's stories."   —*The Associated Press*

"This is the liveliest study of words and their origins since the work of Eric Partridge. Dodd offers a wonderful account of how some everything things got their names, from the saxophone to the sandwich."
      —Seth Lerer, Stanford University, author of
            Inventing English: A Portable History of the Language

"[A] very likeable chronicle of the lives of those whose names have been immortalized in the English language. . . . The book is one long glorious swerve."
                  —*The Guardian* (UK)

"It is the storytelling and the author's obvious affection for his subject that give a heart to this book. It's a quirky collection, concerned as much with people, history, and fate as with their eponymous associations."   —*Financial Times*

"Unstintingly and amusingly disrespectful."
                  —*Sunday Times* (London)

"A deft blend of substance and style."   —*Rolling Stone*

"Hard to beat when it comes to an infectious sense of excitement."   —*Daily Mail* (London)

"Phil is the Swiss Army knife of writers. And I don't mean the pathetic key-ring one, I mean the really good one that can do anything."   —Nick Mason of Pink Floyd

Philip Dodd developed a love of words and language as the son of dedicated crossword solvers; while studying French and Spanish at Jesus College, Oxford; and in a career as a book publisher and editor. His books include *The Book of Cities* (Pavilion, with Ben Donald), a tour d'horizon of the world's most intriguing metropolises, and *Musical Instruments* (HarperCollins), one of the Collins Gem series. He has also worked with the Rolling Stones, interviewing them for their 2003 autobiography *According to the Rolling Stones*, and with Nick Mason on his memoir *Inside Out: A Personal History of Pink Floyd*, and he is the editor of *Genesis: Chapter and Verse*. He lives in Rochester, Kent, with his wife, two daughters, and a tankful of guppies. Visit www.philipdodd.com.

What's in a Name?

FROM JOSEPH P. FRISBIE TO ROY JACUZZI,
HOW EVERYDAY ITEMS WERE NAMED
FOR EXTRAORDINARY PEOPLE

Philip Dodd

GOTHAM BOOKS

To Wan, Wan Mae and Mei Mae. We are family.

GOTHAM BOOKS
Published by Penguin Books (USA) Inc.
375 Hudson Street, New York, New York 10014, U.S.A.

Penguin Group (Canada), 90 Eglinton Avenue East, Suite 700, Toronto, Ontario M4P 2Y3, Canada
(a division of Pearson Penguin Canada Inc.); Penguin Books Ltd, 80 Strand, London WC2R 0RL,
England; Penguin Ireland, 25 St Stephen's Green, Dublin 2, Ireland (a division of Penguin Books
Ltd); Penguin Group (Australia), 250 Camberwell Road, Camberwell, Victoria 3124, Australia (a
division of Pearson Australia Group Pty Ltd); Penguin Books India Pvt Ltd, 11 Community Centre,
Panchsheel Park, New Delhi – 110 017, India; Penguin Group (NZ), 67 Apollo Drive, Rosedale,
North Shore 0632, New Zealand (a division of Pearson New Zealand Ltd); Penguin Books (South
Africa) (Pty) Ltd, 24 Sturdee Avenue, Rosebank, Johannesburg 2196, South Africa

Penguin Books Ltd, Registered Offices:
80 Strand, London WC2R 0RL, England

First published in Great Britain by Random House UK and in the United States as
a Gotham Books hardcover edition with the title THE REVEREND GUPPY'S AQUARIUM

Published by Gotham Books, a member of Penguin Group (USA) Inc.

First trade paperback printing, January 2009
1 3 5 7 9 10 8 6 4 2

Gotham Books and the skyscraper logo are trademarks of Penguin Group (USA) Inc.

ISBN: 978-1-592-40432-2

Printed in the United States of America

While the author has made every effort to provide accurate telephone numbers and Internet addresses
at the time of publication, neither the publisher nor the author assumes any responsibility for errors,
or for changes that occur after publication. Further, the publisher does not have any control over
and does not assume any responsibility for author or third-party Web sites or their content.

Contents

"As time goes on, we shall find out the more we learn how
infinitesimally little we really know."

Henry Caracciolo, president of the
Trinidad Field Naturalists' Club, 1893

"My dad said to me on his death bed, 'We never stop growing.'
That was the last thing he said, and then I closed his eyes. Nobody
stops growing, otherwise there's no point in doing the trip
in the first place."

Keith Richards, 2003

Introduction

"The name of a man is a numbing blow from which he
never recovers."
Marshall McLuhan

Sometimes—or in truth most times—ideas swim up and bop you between the eyes when you least expect them to. This was certainly the case with *The Reverend Guppy's Aquarium (What's in a Name?)*. One late spring evening I was watching a round of *University Challenge*, hosted with cheerful impatience by British TV's famously inquisitorial anchorman Jeremy Paxman.

He served up a question, a starter for ten, something along the lines of "What fish was named after a West Indian clergyman?" Nobody knew—and there is no smugness on my part, since I had no idea either. The quizmaster wearily provided the answer: "The guppy, named after the Reverend Robert Lechmere Guppy."

I lifted my eyes and looked to my left, where, in our modest tropical aquarium, a gaggle of colorful guppies—my and my then three-year-old daughter's favorite fish—were waggling their frilly tails, staring at the outside world, perhaps tut-tutting at the lack of general knowledge displayed by students today.

And I thought to myself, "I *never* knew that." It had never occurred to me that the guppy had been named after a person. Bingo! Eureka! Ker-ching! I suddenly realized that this was a story I wanted to pursue. In that fleeting moment of synaptic connection the basic idea of this book came to life. And over the next days I pottered, perused, Googled, goggled and mulled over its potential, sifting lists of people who had—not to put too pompous a varnish on it—had things named after them.

I came up with a selection of people whose names have become so much part of the language that when we hear them we think first of the object, not the person. And as I dug further, I found that the events of their lives provided a glimpse into their own fields of human activity and told us something about the nature of names, of identity and, in the era of 15-minute celebrity, about the true randomness of immortal fame.

These genuinely eponymous heroes also tapped into a current curiosity about word derivations—although I was not interested in creating a simple listing; there was more material to quarry here—and the ever-increasing fascination with family histories. From my days as a reference publisher, I had loved research and books about words. Now, as a writer and editor working with the likes of the Rolling Stones, I had learned not only to cut through thickets of myth and mystique but also that the narrative in every story came from people, their emotions and their high hopes or dented ambitions. My instinct was that there were intriguing, rarely told tales in the shadow of these names.

There is one thing I want to say straightaway. I really don't like the word "eponym." It sounds, for one thing, too earnest. It smacks of philological study, of codifying and cataloguing the world, of desiccating its variety and unpredictability, but that's a personal prejudice. I have tried to avoid the term, though not obsessively so, throughout the book.

I am also disposed against the use of "eponym" because the term has been co-opted by critics, amateur and professional, and the phrase "eponymous hero," to describe a character whose name gives a book, a film or a play its title—from King Lear and Jane Eyre to Ben-Hur or Jerry Maguire—has become hackneyed and repetitive.

What is an eponym? Let's start with a dictionary definition. I am a *Chambers* man (and boy), and it is always my first recourse in times like these. An eponym, my current edition tells me, is "a person, real or mythical, from whose name another name, *esp* a place name, is derived; the name so derived; a hero invented to account for the name of a place or people; a character who gives a play, etc, its title; a distinguishing title." It's from the Greek: *epi* upon, or on + *onoma* name.

Against that necessarily dry explanation—*Chambers* is not always so dry; its famed entry for "éclair" is "a cake, long in shape but short in duration"—my natural inclination was to veer toward real people, rather than the mythical. I thought it would be much more fun to find out about the true lives of the people who, often haphazardly, had bequeathed their names to enrich not only the English language but global vocabulary. There's a *New Yorker* cartoon that shows a Renaissance Frenchman saying, "You know, there's really no adjective to describe your sense of humor, M. Rabelais."

I put aside all objects named after characters. Farewell, the trilby, from George du Maurier's novel, and its neighbor on the milliner's shelves, the fedora, called after the tragic heroine— the eponymous heroine, no less—of a play by the 19th-century French playwright Victorien Sardou, one of whose other plays, *La Tosca*, formed the basis for Puccini's opera.

I discarded cities and countries named after people. There were simply too many of them—Wellington, Brisbane, Seattle, Washington, D.C., America itself (however, I did, for fun, plant in every chapter at least one toponym, a word derived from a geographical place or region). They also felt too intangible. I was drawn to the way a family name had become, to borrow a word from academia, objectified.

Another intuitive decision was to shy away from the profusion of brand names. To slap your surname on a product for com- mercial gain seemed far too obvious and, worse, smacked of hubris. I was attracted more by the stories of those people whose names had passed into the language frequently without their knowledge and sometimes against their wishes. As exceptions to my own rule, I liked the story of Mercédès Jellinek, whose father named his car after her, and I felt that the Jacuzzi had become so much the generic term for a whirlpool spa or bath that it effectively transcended its origin as a brand name.

Names are a movable feast, whether the reinventions of Marilyn Monroe, John Wayne or Elton John, or sports fans renaming themselves by deed poll after entire football teams. What I particularly appreciated were those names with which the heroes of this book had been born and that serendipity had played such a large part in molding our vocabulary.

As I drew up my short list, I also had to sieve out some spurious suggestions. Sir Oswald Binge, according to one culinary website, was an 18th-century Leicestershire squire whose weeklong feasts were notorious for their excess. My suspicions were aroused when the same site claimed that the avocado was named after an Argentinian explorer and botanist called Jorge-Luis Avocado and quoted his mother as complaining that she'd have preferred him to discover something rather more tasty, like baked Alaska.

Perhaps the most important element in my choice was a good story. "Never throughout history has a man who lived a life of ease left a name worth remembering," wrote Theodore Roosevelt, whose own nickname lives on, of course, in the teddy bear. When I read that the lack of certainty over the naming of the Oscar was "worthy of a Hollywood screenplay," I was naturally curious to know more, as I was when I learned that Joseph-Ignace Guillotin had supposedly tried to change the name of the machine that bore his name once it became the symbol of the Reign of Terror, and when that didn't work, had changed his family name instead.

Mysteries, loose ends, insights to odd corners and niches of life, that was the impetus. With my selection complete—and I did allow myself the flexibility to include one concept (mesmerism), one form of movement (the foxtrot), one location (though not geographical: the Gräfenberg spot) and those couple of brand names—I started contacting people whose memories and impressions would bring each chapter to life and, wherever possible, add a sense of place. Which is why I found myself variously on Broadway, in Walt Disney World and down in Buenos Aires, drinking a glass of Sax beer on the Franco-Belgian border and exploring a treasure trove of musical imagination opposite the Royal Free Hospital in Hampstead.

I don't know if I came away from these journeys with any universal truths. I did learn yet again, as so often in nonfiction, that the fact is an elusive being, but therein lies its beauty. I discovered that the connections and crossovers between these, on the surface at least, diverse lives were multiple and constantly surprising. And that, I guess, is the fascination of history, and of language, and proof that both of them are alive and swimming.

CHAPTER I

Joseph P. Frisbie and the Meaning of Pie

"When a ball dreams, it dreams it's a Frisbee."
"Steady" Ed Headrick

During an occasional moment of reverie, whenever I imagined a journey to discover the source of the Frisbee, my mind had most frequently projected images of long, sandy beaches on the coastline of southern California: maybe dusk in the shadow of Santa Monica Pier or hanging with some flaxen-haired beach bums in a secret surfing rendezvous, larking about with Frisbees while waiting for the next big wave. Sun-dappled pleasure was the overriding mood, lazy summer afternoons launching Frisbees across park lawns a dominant memory.

So, as the Metro-North train out of Grand Central Station trundled under a lowering sky and past the fading industrial glories and dilapidated warehouses of Bridgeport, Connecticut, and a keen wind from Long Island Sound whipped in a boringly persistent drizzle, my sense of dislocation was acute. Not a flaxen-haired hedonist in sight, only indistinct figures bent double, heads down, scurrying to keep out of the pin-sharp rain.

However, Bridgeport, and not Santa Monica, was my destination. For this is the home of the Frisbee—certainly as far as its name is concerned. One historian has even enthused that Bridgeport is "the Kitty Hawk of the Frisbee." For seventy years, on Kossuth Street, there stood the red-brick buildings of the Frisbie Pie Co., manufacturers and suppliers of some of the finest fruit pies in all of New England. Generations of deliverymen and consumers had discovered that you could idle away time by flicking the company's metal pie tins—each embossed with a Frisbie logo—and watching them fly.

The head of the company was Joseph P. Frisbie, a mainstay of the city's business community during the opening decades of the 20th century, when Bridgeport was in full boom, its motto *Industria crescimus* ("By industry we thrive"). There was even a rousing song about Bridgeport written by J. F. Smith and J. F. Ryan ("Bridgeport, I am longing for you, for you're a grand old town"), although I suspect the two songwriters probably dashed off similar ditties about any city that would pay them to sing its praises.

The downturn had come relatively quickly for Bridgeport. During the 1920s corruption scandals damaged civic confidence, and the Wall Street crash of 1929 and subsequent years of depression left severe stress fractures in Bridgeport's economic edifice. The residue of industrial decline is still visible. The train passed vacant lots next to abandoned factories with broken panes and fading signs and nudged into the station alongside unused jetties and rusting gantries. One urbane New York businessman had surprised me by telling me over lunch the day before to "be careful in Bridgeport."

I had never heard of Bridgeport until I needed to go there, but as often happens when a new name or word enters your consciousness, your eye and ear are attuned to spot it again shortly afterward. A couple of days later, I was walking along East 41st Street between Grand Central Station and the New York Public Library. I glanced down to find I was walking over a series of plaques carrying quotes from authors. This was Library Way, an installation promoting great literature. The selection of quotes was unpredictable and imaginative, from E. B. White to Gu Cheng and Marianne Moore, each one illustrated in bronze by Gregg LeFevre.

A couple of plaques along the word "Bridgeport" leapt out in a quote from Mark Twain's retro-sci-fi novel *A Connecticut Yankee in*

King Arthur's Court. After receiving a bash on the head in an armaments factory Twain's hero is transported back in time to A.D. 528. He comes round to be greeted by a knight on an armored horse and, not knowing he has shifted centuries, assumes the stranger is from a traveling show, maybe a circus, possibly an asylum. They set off together, and after an hour's journey fording brooks and crossing glades they spot a town by a winding river and a fortress bristling with turrets and towers. "Bridgeport?" asks our hero, pointing. "Camelot," replies the knight.

★

While Bridgeport's Camelot days were in full spate, Joseph P. Frisbie was building up his family's pie business. His father, William Russell Frisbie, had set up the company in the 1870s in the immediate wake of the American Civil War. He had been a manager for another baking enterprise in New Haven before moving to Bridgeport to set up his own company, which he ran out of the family's two-storey frame house. His sister Susan oversaw the baking, while William hustled their pies with a smart horse and trap and a nifty maxim: "Do one thing at a time, and do that well."

Joseph P. was born in the Kossuth Street house in March 1878. He helped out after school and in vacations and later applied a natural engineering instinct to make the family's life easier. In order to have the ovens at the right temperature for the start of the day, the ovens had to be turned on at two in the morning. Joseph P. rigged up an automatic timer that allowed his father to enjoy a few hours more of uninterrupted sleep.

He took over the company—in his mid-twenties—on his father's death in 1903 and steered its fortunes for the next four decades, expanding its output and its efficiency. The family house became the site of a factory with baking rooms, delivery bays and new machinery, much of it invented by Joseph P., who preferred to custom-design and build his own equipment: a pie rimmer using the principle of the potter's wheel, meat tenderers, a cruster that could process eighty pies a minute. Since there was no electricity for the bakery, he had a power plant constructed in the basement. In a questionnaire for the *American Dictionary of Biography*, completed by his staff after Joseph P.'s death, his colleagues wrote that these innovations and inventions were what he most wanted to be remembered by.

He had high standards of cleanliness and hygiene, a trait learned from his father. The deliverymen in their fleet of trucks and the factory staff wore snappy uniforms, the salesmen crisp jackets with bow ties and peaked caps. They had good wares to sell, up to thirty varieties of individual and family-size pies, delivered hot to a network of grocery stores. Apple was the best seller, with mincemeat second in winter, especially at Thanksgiving; you could also choose from pineapple, pumpkin, strawberry, huckleberry and blueberry.

Business was solid, and Joseph P. took to his role as a civic leader with aplomb. He was elected an Imperial Potentate of Pyramid Temple of the Shrine and was president of the Kiwanis Club, which he addressed in 1923 in a talk on the role of the pie. Despite his sober and punctilious demeanor, in the photographs that survive of him—in which he appears round-faced and slightly balding—he presents a genial expression. The transcript of his speech reveals a self-deprecation and some sly irony. "Pie is a modern institution," he said. "The fact that pie was not invented earlier in the history of man is one of the contributing reasons why the pathway of life has not been as smooth as it might have been." Eve, he suggested, should have made a pie with that fateful apple.

In the New Haven Historical Society I came across a directory of the Frisbie family in America, compiled by Nora G. Frisbie of Claremont, California. As genealogists like to do, she had logged each Frisbie with a reference number in chronological order. The family name (which, according to the U.S. Census Bureau, is the

7,277th most popular name in the United States—you never know when that information might save your life) has been spelled in various ways. As well as the Frisbie line, there have been Frisbys, Frisbeys, Frisbes and Frisbees—and at the time of the American Revolutionary War there was a total of fifteen variants. It probably hasn't escaped your notice that the plastic Frisbee ends in double e, while Joseph P.'s surname was the "ie" version. The reason for that we'll come to later.

The family's roots were in England, in the Leicestershire village of Frisby, and the most likely connection with the New World was the arrival in Virginia in the early 1600s of one Richard Frisbie. Edward Frisbie, possibly Richard's son, later settled in the Connecticut village of Branford, 20 miles or so along the coast from Bridgeport. Nora Frisbie (#3,799 in her own catalogue) was naturally biased in favor of her kinsfolk and proud of their energy, civic commitment and community spirit. "Frisbies have something unique," she wrote, not least among Americans their ability to trace a family line back to the early 17th century, and beyond that to England. She pointed out a high occurrence of twins in the family, noted that Frisbie characteristics include striking china-blue eyes, a streak of stubbornness, offbeat humor and a leaning toward civic duty, and reported that some 100 Frisbies had registered patents with the U.S. Patent Office.

Certainly Joseph P. (#3,793) fitted most of these elements of the family profile, and his inventions and determination helped boost output and sales of his pies. Under his leadership production rose from a couple of thousand pies to 200,000 a day in 1940, when he employed nearly 800 staff. New branches of the Frisbie Pie Co. were opened, in Hartford, the Connecticut state capital, Poughkeepsie, New York, and Providence, Rhode Island.

This upward swing slowed after Joseph P. suffered a minor heart attack in the 1930s. Thereafter his formidable energy levels were diminished, although his mind was still perky: a company Christmas card of 1940 contains a little doggerel rhyme he'd written telling the story of the company: "Dad and Peter, their efforts combined/Made tasty pies of every kind/Their little shop was soon too small/Big ones were added both wide and tall." He died the following year.

His widow, second wife Marion, took over the running of the company, but she was never as impassioned by the business, and in 1958—by chance the year that the Frisbee was first marketed—the Frisbie Pie Co. was sold. An auction that August was offering fifteen cake mixers, a pair of traveling ovens, a mechanical cow cream maker and ten pie rollers (assorted sizes). Twenty years later even the fabric of the red-brick factory was under attack.

A Frisbie relative, Peter C. (#7,374), researching his family roots in the mid-1970s, tracked down a former employee in Bridgeport who held a set of keys for the now abandoned factory on Kossuth Street. Inside the derelict, dirty building, he had a chance to rummage through the jetsam and found some boxes of photographs—including shots of the Frisbie Pie Co.'s baseball team—along with metal dyes and much of the pie-baking equipment. These massive machines were bolted to the factory floor, and Peter had no way of salvaging them. The time he next checked the machinery had gone, and shortly afterward the factory was demolished, its footprint at some point the parking lot of a jai alai court and later a dog track.

But though the fabric and the matériel of Joseph P.'s empire had been destroyed, the reputation of his pies lingered on. Those who had sampled them could still summon up a strong memory of their taste. Children taught down the road at the Kossuth Street School recalled the aromas that drifted through the open windows of their classroom; at the end of the day they would run down to the factory's garage doors, where lenient staff let them buy broken, burned or damaged pies for a snip.

*

Nancy Nickum Damtoft has more personal memories of Joseph P. Frisbie than most. She is his niece. Her mother's sister was the Marion who became Joseph P. Frisbie's second wife in 1927.

Had she known Joseph P. well? "Heavens, yes." If Nancy's parents were away she and her sisters would go up for the weekend to the Frisbies' clapboard home on Lookout Drive in Brooklawn Park, an upscale suburb of Bridgeport. The Frisbies were childless but had taken in—though never adopted in any formal way—a child named Betty, and they welcomed extra playmates for her.

Nancy remembered that Uncle Joe would come home from the factory at the end of the day, where Aunt Marion met him at the door with a smoking jacket. He often brought back a pie fresh from the ovens. While supper was being prepared he had time to sit and play with his nieces, amusing them with his gold repeater watch. "He was never robust after his heart attack, but he was very twinkly, warm, charming, lots of fun. His humor was dry. It just snuck up on you." No matter how twinkly, though, his eyes were not china blue, she said.

She also recalled that Joseph P. had a strong artistic side. He was a photographer who set up trick shots of himself and Aunt Marion apparently playing bridge against themselves, he was a painter in a self-taught Grandma Moses style and—appropriately for this book—he was a fair hand at the saxophone, as well as the clarinet, flute, xylophone and glockenspiel, all of which he played at home, though never in public.

Thanksgiving time was a special treat. "We would pile into the car and go to the factory. It was never terribly busy on Thanksgiving, so Uncle Joe would take us all around, show us the vats and the ovens, and then he'd give us a cookie. The pie company was a very large part of our lives." Nancy's favorite pies were the cherry and the mince. Like Joseph P.'s employees, she remembered him taking pleasure from his inventions. "He was very proud of his apple corer."

Would her uncle have enjoyed knowing that the family name, albeit in a slightly transmuted form, lived on? "Oh yes. He'd have thought the Frisbee was fun. He would have been very pleased."

Joseph P. did not leave any notes or Christmas ditties about his staff's habit of tossing the company's pie tins around, so we don't know if he saw them from his office window and allowed them to blow off some steam, or if they had to do it surreptitiously when the boss was away. But several former employees have confirmed that pie-tin tossing was a regular pastime, and rumor has it that if the river behind the factory were ever dredged, hundreds of old Frisbie pie tins would be delivered up.

*

The Frisbie pie tin came in three sizes: four, eight and ten inches across. These tins are much sought after by Frisbee collectors; they have a whole industry's worth of plastic Frisbees to amass, but the pie tins are particularly valued because of their rarity. A couple of examples are kept in the vaults of the Bridgeport Public Library—two 8-inch pie tins, pressed out of plain, now dull, metal, and each with a perforated F in the bottom and a ridged rim that added some basic level of aerodynamicism.

The transition from pie tin to plastic Frisbee does not follow a simple or direct line. The pie tins were certainly used for throwing or flipping, but so were many other objects. There are reports of Hollywood movie crews taking empty film canister lids and spinning them across the lot, of decorators using paint can tops, of cookie tin lids in flight. During the middle years of the last century there was a whole lot of lid-flippin' going on.

There are plenty of schools of thought about the true precursor of the Frisbee. A highly unlikely theory contends that a Yale student of the 1820s, one Elihu Frisbie, took a collection tray from the college chapel and discovered its flying potential. Frisbee historians refer to the natural inclination of mankind to throw flat, smooth, round objects, from skimming stones across a lake, to the discus and the Roman infantry under Scipio Africanus, who took on Hannibal's army at the Battle of Zama in 202 B.C. by flinging their circular shields at the enemy.

Nancy Nickum Damtoft is certain that as well as Frisbie Pie Co. employees, she knew of coastguards from New London, farther along Long Island Sound, who flung them off the fantail of their boats after eating the pies for lunch. Persistent claims to the origin of Frisbee throwing are also made by students from Yale, Princeton, Dartmouth, Williams—whose student body drew heavily on the Bridgeport area—and other colleges reached by Joseph P.'s delivery vans.

A statue of a dog catching a Frisbee was unveiled in 1989 on the campus of Middlebury, Vermont, promoting that college's claim as the true home of the idea: members of their Delta Upsilon fraternity said they had taken Frisbie fruit pie tins on a road trip in 1939 and learned the technique while a flat tire was being fixed. Mary Witkowski at the Bridgeport Public Library is dismissive of anyone else's attempts to muscle in. "Bridgeport," she told me defiantly, "is the rightful Home of the Frisbee!"

Wherever the pie tins *were* thrown, they could cause a nasty contusion if they connected with an unsuspecting head, so instead of "Fore!" the tin-chuckers would yell out "Frisbie!" to give anyone in the immediate crossfire time to take evasive action.

One of the Yalie Frisbie pie-tin throwers is Stephen I. Zetterberg, a lawyer now based in Pomona, who was at Yale Law School from 1939 to 1942. Yes, he remembered, he and his college chums had thrown Frisbie pie tins across the Yale Law quad, trying to avoid the attentions of the "elegant, but muscular" campus police, "the best-dressed persons in town," who were bemused by this habit. The space in the quad was too restricted for throwing baseballs, but a pie tin was perfect and provided light entertainment whenever he and his friend Phil Singleton, an engineering graduate from the University of Michigan, got tired of sitting in the library.

Returns

Returns of merchandise purchased from a Borders, Borders Express or Waldenbooks retail store will be permitted only if presented in saleable condition accompanied by the original sales receipt or Borders gift receipt within the time periods specified below. Returns accompanied by the original sales receipt must be made within 30 days of purchase and the purchase price will be refunded in the same form as the original purchase. Returns accompanied by the original Borders gift receipt must be made within 60 days of purchase and the purchase price will be refunded in the form of a return gift card.

Exchanges of opened audio books, music, videos, video games, software and electronics will be permitted subject to the same time periods and receipt requirements as above and can be made for the same item only.

Periodicals, newspapers, comic books, food and drink, digital downloads, gift cards, return gift cards, items marked "non-returnable," "final sale" or the like and out-of-print, collectible or pre-owned items cannot be returned or exchanged.

Returns and exchanges to a Borders, Borders Express or Waldenbooks retail store of merchandise purchased from Borders.com may be permitted in certain circumstances. See Borders.com for details.

BORDERS
BOOKS AND MUSIC
10-24 School Street
Boston MA 02108
(617) 557-7188

STORE: 0120   REG: 07/92   TRAN#: 3207
SALE   07/27/2009   EMP: 02043

ASST PENGUIN TRADE PAPER
9780681445688   IR T   4.00

Subtotal   4.00
MASSACHUSETTS 5%   .20
1 Item   Total   4.20
MASTERCARD   4.20
ACCT # /S XXXXXXXXXXXXX4325
AUTH: B81492
NAME: COBURN/COLLEEN M

07/27/2009 06:10PM

Zetterberg and his chums didn't claim to have initiated what they called pie-tin sailing, but they did try and apply some scientific principles to the art form. Another friend, Bill Platt, was at MIT and later worked on airplanes during the war. Together they examined the aerodynamic principles involved and tried to find ways to adapt the pie tins to improve their flight, fitting rubber extrusions to increase their gyrostability and going as far as contacting rubber companies to help their mission. "Had war and educational requirements not intervened," he said, "we might have taken it much further."

*

Stephen Zetterberg and his friends were not alone in considering the commercial potential of pie-tin sailing. Over in Long Beach, California, Fred Morrison, the son of an inventor, was drawing crowds as he threw his missile of choice—the lid off a five-gallon tub of popcorn—to his girlfriend. The spectators would ask them where they could buy one. Following a wartime stint in Stalag 13 he evolved the concept with an Army Air Corps colleague named Warren Franscioni, thinking that maybe there was a market for a plastic flying disc once peace was achieved.

There was serendipity in the timing of his idea. The 1940s was a decade when the knowledge and widespread application of plastics was rapidly evolving. The first man-made thermoplastic was Parkesine, a cellulose, unveiled at the London International Exhibition of 1862 by Alexander Parkes, a Birmingham metallurgist. An array of substances quickly followed: celluloid, rayon, cellophane, and then the first true plastic, Bakelite, the invention of a Belgian-born American chemist, Leo Hendrik Baekeland, which became available in 1907. Baekeland freely admitted his main aim had been to make money, and indeed he amassed millions from his plastic: Bakelite was used for telephone and radio casings, and later in weapons during the Second World

War. In the 1920s and 1930s, nylon, PVC, polystyrene and poly-ethylenes arrived, and in the immediate postwar years plastic became a viable option for any product designer looking for rigidity with lightness. Fred Morrison once remarked that the Frisbee was "perhaps plastic's finest form."

Other events combined to assist the marketing of Morrison's plastic disc. The Roswell UFO incident of 1947, the imminent prospect of space travel and the relatively recent discovery of Pluto (in 1930 by Clyde Tombaugh) helped introduce the idea of the flying saucer into postwar popular culture.

Morrison and his partner plugged into that and started perfecting what they initially called Morrison's Flying Saucer or the Pipco Flying-Saucer—other early names included the Whirlo Way and the Arcuate Vane—which they demonstrated at West Coast county fairs. Onlookers did not believe the pair could throw their saucer with such accuracy, so they pretended it was traveling on invisible wires.

Although Morrison and Franscioni made some progress, sales did not take off. The pair split, and Morrison continued producing what he now called the Pluto Platter. He made contact with Rich Knerr and Arthur "Spud" Melin, whose company, Wham-O, produced the hula hoop, a toy that equally captured another postwar interest—in this case in the South Pacific, when Hawaiian shirts looked cool and the ukulele was in vogue. Wham-O had clout and strong distribution channels, and in 1955 they struck a deal to market the Pluto Platter. Morrison retained a royalty on all future sales.

On January 13, 1957, Wham-O's first Pluto Platters were released. On the underside of each disc were the mantra-like instructions written by Fred Morrison's wife:

> Play catch—invent games
> To fly flip away backhanded
> Flat flip flies straight
> Tilted flip curves—experiment.

With David Waisblum, the current Frisbee product manager at Wham-O, I watched one of the company's earliest TV ads for the Platter, featuring a freckle-faced, all-American kid and majoring on the prevailing interest in sci-fi and space exploration. I liked one of the ad's taglines: "The sensational flying saucer that you command."

At some point shortly after the launch of the Pluto Platter, Wham-O sent out an advance team to conduct some direct market research on New England's university campuses to get feedback on how best to pitch the Pluto Platter. They reported that the successors of Stephen Zetterberg were still shouting out "Frisbie," and that at other colleges "frisbieing" was the common name of the sport. Wham-O took the word and with a deft tweak of the final vowels created a brand name that seemed to suit the toy's fizzing, whizzing flight combined with a suitably childish "whee." In 1958 the Pluto Platter was rereleased as the Frisbee.

The Frisbee was entering a toy market where brand names are—as far as I can tell—rarely named after real people. It is an industry in which the creation of an invented brand name is a vital part of the research and development process and commercially preferable, since all rights can be protected. (The honorable exception is Barbie, launched in 1959 and named after Barbara, the daughter of the doll's creator, Ruth Handler.)

*

Sales of the Frisbee were surprisingly and disappointingly sluggish. The hula hoop still reigned supreme and Frisbee production tailed off until the mid-1960s when a savior arrived, a recently appointed Wham-O employee who found a way to revive its fortunes.

This was Ed Headrick, who had joined the company as head of research and advertising. Ed had played some Frisbee and during a brief college career had dabbled in aerodynamics. He looked for ways to improve the Frisbee's potential. In those days he was very much the corporate man: in one trade press clipping he looks like a typical U.S. sitcom dad, suited and bespectacled. His daughter Valerie remembered him leaving for work at eight with his briefcase like everybody else. The difference was that he'd come back in the evening with a new prototype under his arm. "Hello, honey."

"How was your day at the office, Ed?"

"Just swell. I invented the Superball . . ."

Ed Headrick made one small but critical improvement to the Frisbee, adding a series of raised concentric rings on the top of the disc, later dubbed, though not by him, "the Lines of Headrick," like something out of Tolkien or J. K. Rowling. These rings proved performance-enhancing, stabilizing the flight of the Frisbee, which in earlier incarnations had a tendency to wobble midflight. Ed Headrick's other idea was to reposition the Frisbee, moving it out of the toy market and into the young adult and sports arena. And he added pizazz to the promotion. A natural showman, he appeared on *The Johnny Carson Show*, where he threw a Frisbee (or so he said) over the studio lights to curve around the audience and hit the sticks lying on the Carson band's snare drum.

By the end of the decade the Frisbee had been successfully relaunched and found a new role as a symbol of the counter-culture, the perfect accessory for hippies lounging in San Francisco's Candlestick Park. As Ed said, the Frisbee was "the emblem of the unruly," a lifestyle accessory allowing people who were "anti-everything" to be "pro-something."

That didn't prevent the U.S. Navy from running a research project, reputedly burning up $375,000 of taxpayers' cash, to produce a report called "Aerodynamic Analysis of the Self-Suspended Flare" to see if Frisbees could provide an alternative to parachutes for dropping flares to illuminate temporary wartime airfields. The conclusion was they couldn't.

Frisbee aficionados developed new sports. Up in Michigan a family of brothers called Healy created "guts," the aim of which was to line up and hurl the Frisbee as hard as possible at your opponent. A bunch of students from Maplewood, New Jersey, created Ultimate Frisbee, a non-contact alternative to American Football. It became a popular sport in schools because it teaches unspoken communication and since there are no officials the teams jointly determine any decisions. The philosophy of Ultimate is that consensus should prevail, not the person who screams loudest. It's hotly tipped as a future Olympic sport.

In the 1970s Ed himself invented Disc Golf, using the Frisbee as both driver, putter and ball. In place of holes he designed chain-link baskets. If you could hit the chain links accurately, the Frisbee would drop down into the basket, completing the "hole." There was some shrewd commercial calculation behind his game. Whereas a single Frisbee used for catch could last for years, Disc Golf required a range of discs, which would get scuffed and chipped and need frequent replacing.

By the time Ed Headrick left Wham-O, sales of the Frisbee had reached 100 million and rising. And sure enough, where money is involved, the claims and counterclaims of who really came up with the idea began to rumble.

I talked about this with David Waisblum at the Wham-O building in Emeryville, just outside Oakland, California. It was another dank day; I wasn't having much luck pursuing the California dream. We discussed the tectonic clash between the Frisbee and big business. The spirit of Frisbee, the grassroots view, said David, was "Spread the love. Just believe in it." He is still an active Frisbee player, who understands the mentality. "Who wants to get the crap kicked out of them on a football field? Not me." But some of his friends, he thought, would consider he had sold out by joining Wham-O, which in recent times has been bought in turn by larger corporations—Mattel, Charterhouse

Group and Cornerstone. Commercial envy and greed, say the purists, taint the spirit of the Frisbee.

As late as 2006 Fred Morrison, the Pluto Platter inventor, was publishing a book called *Flat Flip Flies Straight* (the title based on those original Pluto Platter instructions) because he was unhappy with versions of Frisbee history being put about, which he felt diminished his role in its evolution. It's always the way.

★

To pursue the spirit rather than the greed, I visited the headquarters of Ed Headrick's Disc Golf Association. This turned out to be an anonymous building in Watsonville down in the fruit orchards of Monterey County next to a row of abandoned greenhouses. Inside I met Farina Headrick, Ed's widow, and the association's general manager, Scott Keasey.

They were in the final stages of preparing plans for a museum in Ed's honor due to open not far from the U.S. Masters golf course in Augusta, Georgia. The museum would contain a quantity of Joseph P. Frisbie memorabilia—not only some pie tins, but an even rarer pie cabinet, and the collector's Holy Grail, a brick salvaged from the Frisbie Pie Co. building on Kossuth Street.

I think I would have enjoyed meeting Ed, who died in August 2002, after suffering a stroke at a Pro Disc Golf Championship in Florida. It was a surprise to everyone, as he had always been fighting fit. In the Second World War he had been in Europe with the 87th Cavalry of the 7th Armored Division, taking part in the Battle of the Bulge, riding shotgun with a bazooka on a jeep. He'd had a stint as a deep-sea diver, a water heater salesman and as an executive for a program described as TV's *Good Housekeeping*, before finding his niche at Wham-O.

Farina explained that she had met Ed in her native El Salvador. In answer to my question about what had attracted her to him, she took me to see a huge black-and-white photo of her and Ed.

He was handsome, tanned, taut biceps under a white T-shirt, level eyes (his nickname was "Steady Ed"). "That is why I fell in love with him!"

Farina had brought some of Ed's archive for me to look at. Ed clearly had an impish, boyish sense of humor. One of his business cards was tiny, with the inscription: "The lack of business from your firm forces me to use this economy size card." Another concluded his career highlights with "Handsome & Humble." A Wham-O annual report featured Ed in drag as Miss Steady Eddie, 1973 hula hoop national champion.

Scott told me that beneath Ed's humor there was a steely core. He could be fusty and difficult on occasion. He defended the patents of his Disc Golf targets ferociously. And he wore a medallion that he told everyone was the only gratitude—plus $50 in consideration—he had ever received from Wham-O.

It was time to throw some Frisbee. I headed outside with Scott, who nipped to his car to fetch his personal disc collection. The putters looked like traditional Frisbees, slow floaters intended for close-controlled approaches to the target. These were relatively easy to use, though it still took a while to master the action. The drivers were a different matter—like plastic sawdiscs, designed to cut through the air. At full pelt, they travel like a Harris hawk in attack mode. The world record long-distance throw is around 800 feet, the length of two and a half NFL football fields.

Scott decided to go out on the open road and let rip. His first disc exploded into flight a foot or two off the ground and continued to rattle up the road. The second was fighting a slice all the way, but didn't quite clear a neighbor's chain fence. Barking erupted. "Holy shit, there's a German Shepherd in there. It's gonna frigging chew my disc." An initial parley with the dog was not promising, and Scott decided to retrieve it later.

It was my turn to let a driver loose. It shot away in a massive arcing hook, skimming the top of a greenhouse and disappearing round the corner of dirt. This was like a golf novice on the first tee being given a Callaway driver, to be handled with care.

Scott explained that the beauty of Disc Golf was that it was organic. Courses were set out on public land, and once the targets had been installed anyone could pull up with their discs and play. Unlike traditional golf the course did not need to be cultivated, in fact its rawness was part of the sport's charm, an at-one-with-nature experience—his own favorite course overlooked the Pacific at Monterey—and free courses meant no economic barriers.

Here was a sport that suited the spirit of Frisbee. And the spirit of Ed Headrick. In later life Ed let his hair grow long, sometimes sported a gray ponytail and an earring and rode a motorbike. Although he had successfully played the corporate game and knew the value of his patents he was a compassionate humanitarian. Farina told me that even when he was in the hospital after his stroke, he said he wanted to create an MRI body scanner that was less forbidding, so that patients who were scared would feel relaxed.

In the files of the Bridgeport Public Library was a letter from Ed, sent after he left Wham-O, to Huntley Stone, the lawyer for Marion Frisbie, Joseph P.'s widow, offering her the chance to earn some money by trademarking the Frisbie name, as compensation for the original pie-pan flying by the company's drivers. "While there may be no legal requirement for this effort," he wrote, "I personally feel it is time the Frisbie family had some fun also."

"Steady Ed" had a name for Frisbee freaks. He dubbed them Frisbytarians and playfully created an imaginary religion. After his death, he said, he wanted his ashes to be used in a limited edition set of golf discs. After some discussion among his relatives his wishes were met. Sitting on top of my bookshelves as I write this are a driver and a putter from that limited edition, each containing a little piece of Ed. As he was fond of saying: "When we Frisbytarians die, we don't go to purgatory. We just land on the roof and lie there."

CHAPTER 2

In Pataphonia with Adolphe Sax

"Don't play the saxophone. Let it play you."
Charlie Parker

There was a time when the game of Ten Famous Belgians was a demanding test of general knowledge and imagination. If you have never enjoyed its charms the name of the game is a perfectly concise summary of its ridiculously simple aim: to list ten Belgians—not one more, not one less—of significant renown.

I used to play it driving across Belgium from the ferry port of Ostend to the German border en route to the annual Frankfurt Book Fair, an ideal way to idle away the monotony of the lowlands. The rules were surprisingly strict. Nominees had to have been alive after Belgium's independence in 1830 (no Flemish painters to boost the numbers) and to have staked a legitimate claim to fame outside Belgium. As the proud and quite possibly the *only* British owner of not one, but two albums by the singer Raymond van het Groenewoud, the latter was a stipulation I found particularly irksome. Gradually the celebrity ten would coalesce around Tintin's creator Hergé, Jacques Brel, Georges Simenon, the cyclist Eddie Merckx, jazz guitarist Django Reinhardt and painter René Magritte. At a pinch Audrey Hepburn—by virtue of having being born in Brussels—could pass muster.

And then it all changed. The Belgian tennis world served up a couple of superstars in the Walloon Justine Henin and the Flemish Kim Clijsters, their rivalry on—and off—court a symptom of the schizophrenic makeup of their country. The fashion business kicked in with designer Dries Van Noten and the Antwerp Six. Well, between the tennis duo and the rag-trade sextet, the game was virtually done and dusted before you could pull out of Ostend docks. I've since tried playing Ten Famous Luxembourgers. Early indications are that this may keep me going for some while yet.

There was one name permanently inked in on my personal list of famous Belgians: Adolphe Sax, the music instrument inventor and visionary. He fulfilled the necessary criteria. Born in Dinant in 1814, he had spent his adult life as a full-fledged Belgian, and even the toughest adjudicator could hardly argue that his name did not resonate throughout the world.

Sax. What a name. What a perfect name for the instrument Adolphe Sax invented. There is no clear-cut reason why certain eponyms should take hold in the language, although some kind of mellifluous easiness on the ear is an obvious advantage. But Sax: I don't believe you could invent a better name for the instrument even if you sent out a thousand market research teams to focus group the ideas to extinction. That initial S, as curvaceous as the body and bell of a tenor. The A, a single, open, breathily vulnerable vowel. And the whole rounded off with a smacker of a smoochy late-night X, the shimmer of a ride cymbal dissipating the name into the air of a smoky basement club. With apologies to Kim, I can't help feeling that the Clijstersphone might have been struggling to establish an enduring presence in the pantheon of musical instruments.

★

Dinant is a small town (population: 13,000) straddling the broad River Meuse in the south of Belgium a few miles from the border with France. Over millennia the Meuse has dug a wide, deep valley into the surrounding countryside. I was being chauffeured there by one of my oldest friends, Jacques Devos, a bona fide

Belgian, though not yet, alas, a famous one. As we approached Dinant through fertile fields and coppices of fir trees, Jacques told me we were about to experience "one of the steepest descents in Belgium." Hills are clearly at a premium in Belgium; it felt like a gentle slope. Down on the riverside, though, the cliffs above the town were impressive, and a *téléphérique* stood ready to whisk passengers up to a citadel mounted high above Dinant's iconic onion-domed church and the house where Adolphe was born.

Considering that Adolphe Sax is by some way Dinant's most famous son, it's not at all surprising that the main road has been renamed rue Adolphe Sax. A life-size bronze Adolphe relaxes on a bench, cradling a tenor sax. The local baking delicacy—the *couque*, a kind of hard, crunchy slab of biscuit sculpted with decorative pictures—comes, of course, in an Adolphe Sax version. The town council's logo is based on the shape of a saxophone. After a morning's exploration, Jacques and I retired to the Bar Sax just off the rue Sax for a glass of Sax beer, but despite that, Adolphe's presence was, in fact, pleasantly low key and not yet theme-parked out of existence.

As well as paying my respects to Sax's birthplace, I had wanted to visit the Maison de la Pataphonie, housed in an old cleric's house in the heart of Dinant. The Maison is neither museum nor conservatoire, but a resource created by the Belgian luthier Max Vandervorst (he calls it an "instrumentarium") for visitors, especially schoolchildren, to explore music and let their imaginations run free. Pataphonia, says Vandervorst, does not yet exist on any known map. It is a state of mind, a landscape on the outer edge of creativity.

One room in the Maison is dedicated to Adolphe Sax and, in particular, a rare example of his contrabass saxophone. The family of saxes starts with the sopranino, the highest and smallest of the clan, and descends via the two most familiar—alto and tenor—to the baritone and occasional bass saxophone. The contrabass is one deeper, a monster sax taller than a man. On a chill December day when the Maison was shut to the general public, Michel, one of the *animateurs* who runs it, offered to let us in. The contrabass was a fearsome beast, caged in a glass box. With a little encouragement and some lung-bursting puffing, Michel started to warm its acres of metal out of their winter lethargy, and suddenly the noise of the contrabass was unleashed: a full foghorn of sound juddering the bass of my spine. If the band of the *Titanic* had had the presence of mind to boost their brass section with a couple of these, the ice floes a-bow would have crumbled. As it was, the sound waves from Sax's Brobdingnagian sax rumbled and rippled out into his birthplace.

By the time Adolphe, or Antoine-Joseph as he was christened, was born—on November 6, 1814, the first of eleven children—the Sax family had been in Dinant for at least five generations. Adolphe's father, Charles-Joseph, was a manufacturer of instruments, and Dinant was an appropriate choice of workplace: one of the town's local industries was dinanderie, a technique for hammering metals, especially tin, copper, silver and brass, to create decorative objects. Today, a giant dinanderie saxophone sits just down the road from his house.

Charles-Joseph left Dinant the year after Adolphe's birth, although the family stayed behind. He had been appointed by King William I of the Netherlands as a *facteur de la Cour*, making instruments for the royal army's military bands. Charles-Joseph was an adept craftsman and possessed the inventive bent his son inherited, filing a raft of patents, including those for a keyboard-harp, a few lyres and guitars, and the Piano-Sax of 1853.

Many of Adolphe Sax's biographers (hagiographers would be a more apt name) have portrayed the lad as a full-scale prodigy. They have him joining his father in the workshop as a toddler, learning how to bore a clarinet body or fine-tune flute keys at the age of six, studying flute at the Brussels Conservatoire and at sixteen presenting an ivory clarinet and a pair of flutes at the Brussels industrial exhibition. They also relate a catalogue of potentially fatal incidents—one near-drowning, a gunpowder explosion, the inadvertent swallowing of a dose of vitriol water—and quote his mother's tribute, "He was a child condemned to unhappiness."

The truth, the saxologist Malou Haine believes, is more prosaic. Adolphe did attend a class or two at the Royal School of Music, a precursor of the Conservatoire, but there are no records of him exhibiting at the industrial shows so young—quite probably he was helping his father out while learning the trade.

*

Not only was Adolphe's father a talented instrument-maker, so were a number of his siblings. Many of their original instruments are on display at the Musée des Instruments de Musique, known as MIM, in Brussels. In the same way that on any journey I am always prepared to make a significant deviation for a decent cemetery, I also enjoy dropping into musical instrument museums wherever they crop up. Many are disappointingly dry or fusty and have drained the instruments on display of any vitality. Hushed rows of serpents, tambours and fifes under glass cabinets can be sumptuous to the view, but there's not much point if you can't hear how they sound. I much prefer those museums that allow their instruments space to breathe and time to be played, either by the public—though rarely—or by visiting professionals.

I remembered MIM as falling into the fusty category, but in the ten years since I had first visited it the museum had moved to occupy the light, spacious and elegant floors of the former Old England department store, an art nouveau treasure, just down the road from the Royal Palace. Géry Dumoulin, one of the museum's librarians and a Sax specialist, escorted me around. Before we headed to the Sax collection, Géry suggested that we meander through the rest of the museum, where other epony-

mous instruments were on display, each strange and beautiful,
some ephemeral husks lost to oblivion, others still in use.

In the wind and brass section of the museum, we came across
the sarrusophone, commissioned by regimental bandmaster
Pierre-Auguste Sarrus in the 1870s in collaboration with the
Gautrot company. It used the same conical tube as a sax but
added an oboe's double reed to create a more nasal sound
intended to provide an alternative to the oboe and the bassoon
and offer more oomph for brass bands. There's a hard-to-find
recording of Sidney Bechet playing a sarrusophone on a track
called "Mandy, Make Up Your Mind" with the Clarence Williams
Blue Five alongside Louis Armstrong on trumpet.

The rothphone, invented by the Milanese Ferdinando Roth,
was a sarrusophone bent into the shape of a sax—as its alternative
name, the unwieldy saxsarrusophone, suggests. Popular in their
native Italy, the rothphones were more slender than the
saxophones, and the ones I saw looked like spaghetti draped
round an invisible fork. The heckelphone, designed by Wilhelm
Heckel, is a rare wind instrument from the 1900s, sitting somewhere between the oboe and bassoon, created partly in response
to a request by Richard Wagner for an instrument to do just that:
his brief was actually for something that combined the sound of
an oboe with the beef of an Alpine horn. The mullerphone is even
more obscure: a double bassoon created in Lyons in 1850 or there-
abouts by Louis Muller.

Clearly this period from the mid-1800s to the end of the century
was an era when brass and wind instrument design was in a state
of flux and innovation, but few found more than a handful of
composers to write for them, and most remain curios. Perhaps
the only other instrument from this burst of activity to have
broken through into the mainstream was the sousaphone. Géry
Dumoulin apologized for the lack of one in the MIM collection,
but everybody knows the shape of that extraordinary boa
constrictor of brass enfolding its player, which was developed by

the Philadelphia-based J. W. Pepper and dedicated to the march king John Philip Sousa, who had suggested the idea of a more practical tuba. The sousaphone's portability gave it a perfect niche providing the oompah for marching bands to underpin the hip thrusts of cheerleaders, with an occasional cameo appearance in the humorous end of the rock business, namely the Bonzo Dog Doo-Dah Band.

The museum contained most of the other instruments named after their creators. The Franklin armonica or glass armonica was a mechanized contrivance, devised by Benjamin Franklin, which reproduced the old party trick of rubbing a finger round the lip of a wineglass to create a note. The armonica used forty-six glass hemispheres turned by a treadle to automate this effect; Franklin and Anton Mesmer used it to set the mood for their spirit gatherings. A Belgian version was called the mattauphone. Joseph Mattau was a *maître des bals*, a kind of official party planner, in the mid-1800s, and his "instrument" was a table covered with glasses, looking like the morning-after remains of an elegant though seriously heavy cocktail party.

Just as brass and wind instruments had once focused the minds of instrument-makers, there was a flurry of instruments named after their inventors in the 1920s and 1930s, a flurry that coincided with the new frontier of electronics. MIM contained examples of the theremin, the ondes martenot and the trautonium. I had been waiting to see a theremin close up for some while. If you think you have never heard the sound of a theremin, you have, believe me. Its quavery wobble runs through "Good Vibrations" by the Beach Boys, and in concert Brian Wilson still flutters his hands above his keyboard at the appropriate moments. The sad truth is that for the recording the group used a synthesized version, but the sound is spot on.

A wonderful feature of the theremin is that the player never actually touches the instrument. To visualize it, imagine a ghetto blaster from the 1980s with two turrets, one topped by an antenna, a clothes hanger sticking out from the other; these two antennae are linked to a couple of oscillators. The player moves his or her hands around the antennae to alter the nature of the instrument's supernatural whine—the right hand usually affecting pitch, the left hand volume.

This was the brainchild of a Russian radio operator named Lev Termen, known in the West as Léon Theremin. Lenin was a fan; he took lessons and sent Theremin out on tours to spread the word. Dedicated supporters have since kept the theremin alive, a diverse bunch including Robert Moog (whose own Moog was one of the first practical synthesizers), sci-fi movie composers, Marilyn Manson, Half Man Half Biscuit, and Lothar and the Hand People, a trippy late-1960s act from Denver: Lothar waved his hands about while the Hand People, a bunch of groovy dancers, gyrated around him. Thomas Harris's Hannibal Lecter also named it as one of his two favorite instruments; the other was the harpsichord.

Géry Dumoulin had dug out a teach-yourself theremin book, which essentially instructed aspiring thereminists to "wave your hands around the antennae." In a section called "Tuning the Etherwave" I found a piece of advice its author had lifted from *Castañuela Olé*, a castanet tutor written by "Tabourot," because he felt they were wise words for anyone trying to learn the theremin. He called this Tabourot's Law: its central message was that if you are having problems trying to achieve something difficult and are convinced you will never make any progress, then at the very point you are about to give up in frustration, that is precisely when you are going to make a breakthrough. It's an excellent law, which I recommend applying to most human endeavors.

Theremin was a pioneer in the field of electronic instruments along with Maurice Martenot, who had been a radio operator for the French army during the First World War and was a keen cellist. He developed a parallel idea to Theremin's—in fact the two did meet—also using a vacuum tube oscillator. But to alter the pitch of the note Martenot attached a ribbon to the oscillator with a ring on the end for the player to pull back and forth. He added a dummy keyboard to act as a guide. The sound was routed through a loudspeaker. There's a great photo of Martenot standing at a little console with some volume controls a few feet away from the instrument, his finger tugging on his ribbon. The composers Varèse, Milhaud and Messaien were very taken with the ondes martenot, which found a small hardcore of revivalist enthusiasts in the 1970s Quebec band Harmonium and Radiohead's Jonny Greenwood, although it was never used, as has occasionally been suggested, to create the female vocals on the *Star Trek* theme tune.

Another variant was the trautonium, developed by the German electrical engineer Dr. Friedrich Trautwein, again in the 1920s. He relied on electric wires, which the player touched to complete a circuit and produce the note. This instrument, which was developed by Trautwein's associate Oskar Sala and for which Hindemith composed, was used by Sala as part of Bernard Herrmann's score for Alfred Hitchcock's *The Birds,* creating those scary representations of avian anger.

Up on the museum's second floor a set of cabinets showcased the talents of the Saxes: a two-piston B-flat cornet made by Charles-Joseph and an absolutely exquisite clarinet fashioned by him out of grenadille, a hard African ebony. Adolphe's brother Alphonse was represented by an overelaborate Daliesque cornet with seven pistons, a crazy conglomeration of valves and tubes. Géry Dumoulin told me it was theoretically perfect but totally impractical, "a little silly," he said.

And that was the key to big brother Adolphe's success. Although he occasionally went off down a fantastical route—I noticed a trombone he'd made with seven bells—the majority of his instruments were carefully crafted and scientifically conceived. In Sax's time each element of an instrument was constructed in a separate atelier with different workmen responsible for the valves, the mouthpiece, the bell, the tube connecting the mouthpiece to the first valve. Like a production-line car, the whole was fitted together at the head workshop, providing plenty of scope for inconsistency. But Sax had a reputation for irreproachable construction. He applied mathematical equations to the tubes and valves. He rethought existing instruments: one of his earliest successes was improving the playability of the bass clarinet. Yet although he expanded the scope of wind instrument thinking, his creations were eminently playable, and so they found a practical, commercial market.

★

To learn more about Adolphe's impact I visited the London shop of Tony Bingham, who has been dealing in old musical instruments since the 1960s when he started selling antiques in the Portobello and King's Roads, where Keith Richards would occasionally drop by to look for a new sound. "Keith would come in and say, 'I'll take that. Make me out a bill.' It was to do with curiosa rather than scholarship." Now in Hampstead, Tony's shop is a heady cabinet of curiosities, jam-packed with temple drums, bassoon bodies, serpents—I thought I also spotted a psaltery—and a broom cupboard of original Adolphe Sax saxes in various stages of repair. "Sax," said Tony, "was a great bloke," whose first major achievement was designing a concerted family of instruments: the saxhorns.

Sax developed the saxhorns when he was in his twenties, a fine-tuning of various existing instruments into a coherent whole, which are still at the heart of the kind of brass band music played by the Black Dyke Mills and Brighouse and Rastrick bands. I had heard of the name saxhorn, but never really understood what they were until I encountered the complete set in Brussels; seeing them all together I realized that these were variations on the euphonium, the cornet and the flügelhorn. And, joy of joys, I recognized the tenor saxhorn as the slender tenor horn, which, as a catastrophically, cataphonically bad teenage trumpet player, I had always slyly lusted after.

As well as rationalizing his instruments and improving the quality of their manufacture, Sax turned on its head the traditional thinking that the material from which a wind instrument was constructed was what gave it a distinctive timbre. Sax realized, and articulated, that this was not the critical factor: an instrument—a flute, a trumpet, a clarinet—could be constructed not just from wood or brass but from ebony, silver, even glass, as long as the material was not porous, so sound could not escape.

Tony Bingham has republished a chatty Victorian book called *Talks with Bandsmen* by Algernon S. Rose, and he pointed out a pertinent paragraph. "To prove that the tone of an instrument depends less upon the density or thickness of its metal or the substance of which it is made than the proportion of its parts, Messrs Besson sent me a bugle of plaster and one of gutta-percha, and a cornet of paper. All of these could be easily sounded, and they retained, to some extent, the tone-quality associated with instruments of the same form but made in copper or brass. Messrs Mahillon of Brussels," claimed Rose, "have even constructed instruments of cheese." Tony Bingham's bulging display cabinets contained some delicate glass bugles made for fun by craftsmen at the end of the workweek.

The key element is the shape, the bore of the instrument. If it is the same diameter throughout (like a trumpet right up until its flared bell), the sound, shriller and more piercing, is significantly different from a conical bore, where the width of the tube increases throughout the length of the instrument, as in a French horn, producing a softer, rounder note. Equally Adolphe Sax understood that it is the length of the tube that determines the high or low pitch of the sound. Bending it back on itself or twisting it around had no impact on pitch or timbre. The third element is the way the column of air in the instrument is vibrated—

its "insufflation." Trumpeters and trombonists blow directly into an open mouthpiece (the embouchure I was so lacking in); a flautist blows across an open aperture. The clarinet uses a single reed; oboes and bassoons a double reed. Each method affects the nature of the sound coming out the other end.

These principles, among others, Sax applied to the development of his lasting legacy, the saxophone. He developed it over a number of years, seeking the right combination of factors. Although Adolphe patented the saxophone in June 1846, he had been working on it since the end of the previous decade, certainly according to his father, adjusting, tweaking, experimenting. This was no overnight inspiration.

Essentially, although the reality is far more subtle, Sax took the conical bore of the French horn and applied it to a longer, thinner instrument. He selected a single reed, like the clarinet's, to vibrate the air. He adapted the fingering of the oboe and the flute. And he made the whole instrument out of brass, because of the malleability, the ductility of the metal—leading to the apparent anomaly that the saxophone, a woodwind instrument, is often counted as a brass instrument and has become a central character in any "brass section."

Why Sax set off on this route is not certain, but looking at a copy of the original *brevet d'invention*, the patent he filed in 1846, his first version of the saxophone is clearly a variant on the now-forgotten ophicleide, which was a 19th-century brass version of the old wooden serpent, played with a cupped brass mouthpiece. It seems likely that Adolphe was trying to improve on, and add more power to, the ophicleide and ended up with a brand-new instrument. On the same patent document there is also a drawing of what anyone would recognize as a tenor sax.

Sax had created a new sound, a new sonority, a tonal hybrid— Wagner dubbed it a *Racenkreuzungsklangwerkzeuge*, or mongrel musical instrument. Despite the best efforts of Sax's many detractors, who claimed he lifted all his best ideas, nobody was ever able to present as evidence any precursor to the saxophone.

One of the strongest impressions of Sax is that he inspired controversy, stoutly defended by his admirers, savaged by his rivals. There is a wonderful phrase in one of the biographies by Léon Kochnitzky. "Sax," Kochnitzky notes, "like Beaumarchais in the 18th century, like Whistler in the late 19th century, had exceptional gifts for the gentle art of making enemies." (Both the others had gained a similar reputation for acting as magnets of hostility.) Another biography is titled *La Vie tourmentée d'Adolphe Sax.*

In June 1842 Hector Berlioz had trumpeted—or perhaps more accurately saxophoned—Sax's skills and his new instrument in a column in the pages of the *Journal des débats*, the paper for intellectuals published weekly in Paris, where Adolphe had re-located, *"riche d'idées, mais léger d'argent,"* as his contemporary biographer François Joseph Fétis wrote. "He is a calculator, an acoustician, and when required a smelter, a turner and embosser. He invents and he accomplishes," proclaimed Berlioz, who composed a piece for the saxophone to be performed at the Salle Herz in 1844. Sax played it himself, bringing along an instrument jury-rigged with sealing wax and string—it was still a work in progress. He was constantly fiddling with the shape of the bell, the fingering, the internal dimensions of the mouthpiece. Rossini said that the saxophone had the most beautiful palette of sounds he had ever come across. Auber and Meyerbeer were in his corner. These composers formed a kind of Praetorian guard to defend their hero.

Sax's opponents were equally committed. At the lower end of the scale, jobbing orchestra members did not take kindly to the newfangled instruments he was coming up with, hence the reason Sax often had to perform himself. That was simply human nature, and orchestral journeymen have always been notorious for resisting any change that might threaten their turf. As a result, no matter how beautiful the sound that sent Berlioz or Rossini into excelsis, the addition of the sax to the classical music repertoire was disjointed. And so it has remained something of an outsider in the orchestral arena.

Luckily, Sax had another outlet for his inventions: the military brass band market. This was a much sought after opportunity as hefty government contracts were on offer. Sax had one glorious moment of triumph in a face-off with one of his primary competitors, Michel-Henri Carafa. Sax had written to the minister of war suggesting that his instruments could beef up the nation's ailing military bands, and a competition on the Champs de Mars was arranged for April 22, 1845, according to reports a gorgeous spring day. In front of an invited audience of 20,000, the two combos did aural battle: first the traditionalists, then Sax's cutting-edge lineup featuring a phalanx of saxhorns. The competition was characterized by the satirical newspaper *Le Charivari* as the battle between the Saxons and the Carafons, and Sax was victorious. His instruments were easier to play, richer in tone and more portable.

But these lucrative deals meant that his rivals were more vindictive than the mere obstreperousness of the orchestras. At one point a symposium of other manufacturers ganged up together—quite formally, with a president, Marcel-Auguste Raoux, a treasurer and secretary—to trash Sax's reputation, accuse him of plagiarizing their designs and generally tie him up in legal wrangling. They even went to the lengths of sending examples of his saxes out of the country to be returned with false predated patents, although it was the success of the saxhorns (and doubtless the fact that they had been outdone by a Belgian) that had really put their noses out of joint. Things got rather nasty. There was an unexplained fire at his workshop, even a failed ambush attempt.

Sax never shirked the challenge. He would go *mano a mano* with all comers. "Aggressive," "nit-picking" and that most damning of charges, "arriviste," are among the adjectives they hurled at him. He was equally litigious. He sued the singer Marie Sasse to stop her using the stage name Sax and repeatedly issued writs against Ferdinando Roth, the rothphone's inventor. And he directly attacked his cabal of opponents. One morning, just after Christmas 1854, he gathered a squad of bailiffs, police and clerks in a Parisian café, who, at ten o'clock sharp, headed off in fourteen coaches in a lightning raid on the factories and offices of his rivals, scooping up evidence for the courtroom. No wonder he had a reputation for being caustic.

The picture is lopsided. Sax had a philanthropic streak. He helped raise funds for Berlioz to visit Russia and also set up a workshop in the central prison in Melun to provide work for its inmates, although it seems the cons were unimpressed and tried to rip him off. Personal letters I came across in the Dinant municipal archive are those of a gentle father concerned to keep in touch with the children he'd sent back to Belgium when life in Paris got a little too crazy, not because of his business ructions, but because of the physical dangers of life in the Commune of 1871.

In Coblenz, during a series of celebrations in honor of Beethoven, Sax found himself in Franz Liszt's apartment making small talk with one of his greatest rivals, Wilhelm Wieprecht, Musikdirektor of the German 10th Army Group and inventor of a contrabass clarinet called the batyphon. The two affected a rapprochement, but Liszt observed that they would not be *"d'accord"* for very long.

Germany was protective of its instrument-makers, who must have been annoyed that, because of its name, some people thought the sax came from Saxony. As a side note, back in Dinant, the local archivist uncovered for me a clipping, undated, from a French newspaper during the Nazi occupation: *"Le saxophone est naturalisé allemand"* was the headline. Joseph Goebbels had previously banned all jazz as contrary to the German spirit. The music retailers and instrument-manufacturers were up in arms and had sent a deputation to the minister of national economy, who had referred it up the food chain to Goebbels. Three weeks later he delivered his judgment. Well, well, the saxophone, it now appeared, had the necessary requirements for Germanism, according to Goebbels, as it had been invented by Adolf (*sic!*) Sax, who, the article claimed, was "blond, blue-eyed and dolicoce- phalic, as befits a German."

When Sax died in 1894, his fortunes were still volatile. As late as his eightieth year, just before his death, Chabrier, Massenet and Saint-Saëns were lobbying the minister of arts to help Sax. Napoleon III remained a benefactor throughout Sax's later years, bestowing the *Légion d'honneur* on him, and parliament excep- tionally extended the term of his patents. But the saxophone was yet to find a solid place in music history. Struggling in the traditional orchestra, though establishing itself within the brass band, its toehold was precarious. Salvation through jazz was close at hand, however.

*

Sax's instruments began to infiltrate the United States. The Distin family, a father-and-sons group of English brass players who per- formed on saxhorn, were, in Tony Bingham's words, "the Beatles of the 19th century," playing thousands of concerts and offering their own range of merchandised portrait jugs. The family had become Sax's commercial agents, and one of the clan, Henry Distin, relocated to Philadelphia, promoting his products. Another early adopter was Patrick Gilmore, an Irish Bostonian bandleader, whose tagline was "the salesman of musical thunder" and who added eight saxes to his lineup. As the saxophone took a leading role in the marching bands of New Orleans, it accompanied funeral wakes and Mardi Gras celebrations and escorted the journey of jazz north. During the dance band era of the 1920s and 1930s orchestras featured an ensemble of saxes taking on the role of the strings, interspersed with solos. It wasn't until after the Second World War that the sax became a lead instrument in the jazz quartet, for me the quintessential jazz forum.

From then on the sax found its voice, or rather voices. Because the saxophone responds so closely to the character and tone of its player, there is an honest immediacy about the instrument. A pianist can hide behind the mechanical transfer of energy from key to hammer to string, but a sax player is in direct contact with that column of air. Consequently, the saxophone is a wonderful communicator of a saxophonist's emotion, able to reflect pain, euphoria, loss, celebration, romance, ennui. There are thrilling jazz trumpeters—Dizzy, Satchmo, Clifford Brown—all with distinctive voices; I saw Miles Davis a couple of times toward the end of his life, and although he spent much of the time with his back turned to the audience, playing intermittently, when he nailed a single note you knew it could only be Miles. But saxes have so many moods and facets.

From my own anthology I can hear right now the tumbling dexterity of Charlie Parker's alto, the stomp of Dexter Gordon's tenor, the township spunk of Dudu Pukwana and the Nordic intensity of Jan Garbarek's tiny curved soprano. The sax is as suited to the breathy, umber hues of Stan Getz or the romantic gush of Coleman Hawkins and Ben Webster's *Blue Saxophones* duets as it is to the balls-out energy of Sonny Rollins. It allowed John Coltrane to take the cloyingly sentimental—though beautifully written—mush of "My Favorite Things" and recast it as a journey into the inner soul.

The sax in jazz offers more than a lifetime's worth of listening and emotion, but its flexibility and adaptability have given it a platform in most popular music forms. It has found a place in rock 'n' roll: Bobby Keys letting rip on the Stones' "Brown Sugar," Clarence Clemmons powering the E Street Band in Springsteen's "Born to Run," the solo by Dick Parry on Pink Floyd's "Money." It's been at the heart of great pop hits—Gerry Rafferty's "Baker

Street," George Michael's "Careless Whisper"; ABBA paid homage to the twin sax sound of Billy Vaughn on their "I Do, I Do." There are pumping baritone saxes at the root of "Good Golly Miss Molly" and the James Brown riffs. Everywhere the sax turns up it leaves its mark.

I was introduced to the saxophone via Archie Shepp, a sometime hard bopper, part of the generation of John Coltrane and Ornette Coleman, a politically committed musician who once described the sound of his sax as the "machine-gun fire of the Vietcong." My first foray into jazz, at sixteen or seventeen, had been to try listening to a Charlie Parker collection, but I simply couldn't connect. My palate was not yet ready for such brilliant and demanding fare. Disappointed at my inability to respond to Bird, but unfazed, I returned to my local record store and its jazz section and picked out Archie Shepp's *Montreux Two*, a live album, purely on the basis of two magnificently moody black-and-white photos by Giuseppe Pino gracing its cover.

Back home, I dropped the needle and experienced an instant conversion listening to Shepp's quintet, with sax and trombone, playing his own composition, a flowing waltz-time number called "Stream." Only recently did I discover that the album cover had misspelled the name of the track: it's actually called "Steam," but it's still a hell of a number. And I was hooked straightaway.

A couple of years later I was in Paris as a student. Archie Shepp played in the city frequently, and I went to see a few of his shows. I hustled a request through his manager asking Archie to grant me an interview for a student magazine I'd set up. He agreed, and on a drizzly January evening I trekked to the Hôtel Lutetia, just by Sèvres-Babylone, an art deco hotel with a jazzy vibe: Josephine Baker used to live there. Over beers in a deepening gloaming, Archie took the trouble to spend an hour or more with this callow kid and educated him in the origins of jazz, the griots of West Africa and his personal philosophy of the sax. Which reminds me of a quote from Emil Cioran, the Romanian-born existentialist

essayist and philosopher. In his *Syllogismes de l'amertume* of 1952 he
wrote: "What's the point of spending time with Plato when a
saxophone can equally well give us a glimpse into another
world?" The conversation with Archie Shepp opened the door
and lit my imagination.

Adolphe Sax never stopped imagining. He continued spewing
out ideas in all directions throughout his life. He wanted to set up
a school of inventors. He thought a steam-powered organ should
be set up on the highest hill in Paris to fill the city with music and,
in Berlioz's words, broadcast "the joys and sorrows of a metro-
polis." He designed an acoustically enhanced ovoid concert hall.
He improved the whistle on railway engines by increasing its
intensity. The *goudronnière sax* was a tar box to impregnate the
bedrooms of consumption sufferers with antiseptic creosote. He
devised a gigantic cannon to lob out equally gigantic mortars
(which I was glad to see he had dubbed the "saxocannon").
Remembering the creations of Theremin and Martenot, what if
Sax had lived to enter the electronic era?

Whitney Balliett, the esteemed jazz critic of *The New Yorker*,
writing about Ben Webster, has left a suitable epitaph for
Adolphe, his imagination and his sax. "As the years went by, he
would close certain phrase endings by allowing his vibrato to melt
into pure undulating breath—dramatically offering, before the
breath expired, the ghost of his sound."

Chapter 3

The Whirl According to Roy Jacuzzi

"'It's nothing like a goddamn bath,' said Lovelear.
He clutched the curved sides and lay flat. 'This is godly.
This is terrific. This is enlightenment right here.'"
Zadie Smith, The Autograph Man

Roy Jacuzzi lives in Happy Valley, California. For the man who created the whirlpool bath, an address that combines contentment and the suggestion of flowing water seems highly appropriate. But there is more to Roy's choice of residence than a neat piece of word association, as I learn while his top-of-the-line Mercedes AMG eases us effortlessly up through the valley's gentle winds.

There is more than one Happy Valley in California; Roy's particular one lies northeast of Berkeley, off Highway 24. The terrain on either side is soft and soothing: farmland, fruit trees, houses tucked back off the road. As we rise up, I get an impression of a lush European landscape, almost Alpine at times, and Roy tells me that both his grandfather and great-uncles used to own farms out here fifty or more years ago, before the residential homes moved in. He points out one of the family's farm buildings, half hidden behind the foliage.

Up a final slope we reach Roy's own house. He slows the car so we can see the gates that stand at the entrance. They are tall, of wrought iron, with a flourish of metal sunflowers twining up, as if alive, through the gates' slender bars. The gates came from the house that his family owned in Italy before they began their migration to the United States.

"Seven brothers and six sisters came over from Valvasone, in Friuli," he says. "Their parents—my great-grandparents Giovanni and Teresa—had gardens and fruit; Giovanni was a carpenter and craftsman. They raised their thirteen kids, and then the children headed to America because it was the land of opportunity. They believed in the American dream." In what was a typical pattern of the time the elder brothers made the journey first and worked to earn enough money to bring over their younger siblings, and so on. "The oldest Jacuzzi brothers were Rachele, Valeriano and Francesco; my grandfather Giuseppe was the fourth oldest. They were followed by Gelindo, Giocondo and Candido, all great Italian names."

During construction work at the Valvasone house in the 1970s the original gates of Giovanni and Teresa's house were unearthed. They had been buried deep in the grounds to avoid discovery during the Second World War, when all metal was at a premium, but never dug up again. Roy had them excavated and shipped over to the States, where, cleared, cleaned, renovated and polished, they announce the threshold of his driveway. Equally they declare, by virtue of the care and attention lavished on them, that the story of Roy Jacuzzi and the Jacuzzi is rooted in the origins, the journeys and the adventures of the Jacuzzi clan. It is a neat circle, because replicas of these very same gates still frame the entrance of the original house in Friuli.

Roy's home in Happy Valley is an expansive, but not ostentatious, Italianate villa. The only showiness is the handful of Ferraris carefully parked in glass-doored garages. We settle into a den above one of the wings, next to a pool table and some guitar amps—it's where his kids have licence to party—and where he has, in advance, laid out documents and photos drawn from his personal archive. "I've got hoards of material downstairs, things from my grandfather on how he came to the United States, who came over, how they came over. And there are thousands of photos: they were photography fanatics, man." He is engaged on the lengthy task of collating and writing a book detailing the history and achievements of the Jacuzzis.

Or of the Iacuzzis, to be precise. Back in Friuli the family's surname was spelled with an initial I. When, in 1907, the first brothers to make the Atlantic crossing (Valeriano and Francesco) arrived in New York harbor, they entered the portals of Ellis Island, those "front doors to freedom," and prepared to trudge through a maze of corridors and anterooms for processing by doctors, clerks and tallymen. One of the immigration officials, out of misunderstanding, weariness or lack of attention, entered the family name in the records as Jacuzzi with a J. Through such a slip of the pen is history made.

Roy settles back into the narrative. He is a natural storyteller, an upbeat, friendly-faced guy with curly, now graying, hair, an open-necked plaid shirt, totally relaxed in his own environment— where he guards his privacy with great care—and within his own tradition. I can feel him warming to this story of Italian immigrants leaving behind the poverty-line grind and adapting their family skills to the needs and demands of their new life, moving westward like a river finding its natural course, settling into the meanders of opportunity that America had on offer.

"They worked on the railroads. They came across country. And eventually they all landed in northern and southern California. Coming from agricultural ground in Europe and always wanting to put food on the table, they worked on anything to do with the earth, with food, with plants, with trees. Fundamental things."

It is clear that the Iacuzzi brothers, now proud Jacuzzis, possessed plenty of the spirit that life as recently arrived immigrants demanded. They were conscientious workers—"incredibly hardworking people," says Roy—that sine qua non of basic survival. And as more and more of the brothers and sisters arrived, they began to operate as a close-knit unit, working together to support the extended family. Giovanni and Teresa finally joined their children in the late 1910s.

*

So far, this is a good, but not untypical, tale of Italian immigrants making their way in America. But the Jacuzzi brothers had an extra dose of imagination and ingenuity that generated the kind of ideas that not only solved immediate problems but offered a glimpse of potential riches.

Within a few years of arriving, the Jacuzzis started designing airplane propellers. This apparently sudden sideways shift into what was then a genuinely cutting-edge technology grew out of work odd-jobbing in the citrus groves of California. The owner of one of the estates they were working on was also the founder of a pioneering airplane company—Wilbur and Orville's Wright Flyer had left the soil of North Carolina only in 1903—and it landed a contract to supply engines to the U.S. government.

The brothers saw an opening. Back in Friuli they had survived by coming up with pragmatic solutions and building their own equipment as and when required. Relying on their well-honed, practical engineering skills, they offered to create propellers for the engines. They not only supplied the propellers but added— literally—their own twist, calculating that a curved, or pitched, propeller would add more horsepower per revolution than the flat propellers currently in use. Testament to the fact that this was a significant step forward in aviation design are the examples of those first Jacuzzi "toothpick" propellers donated to the Smithsonian Institution in Washington, D.C. Here was a new direction for the Jacuzzis. In 1915 they set up a plant fabricating hand-finished, laminated propellers in a workshop on San Pablo Avenue in downtown Berkeley, California.

From the outset they displayed the curating mentality that preserved the documents and photographs that now form the basis of Roy Jacuzzi's archive. "Every one of the propellers they made they logged, they put serial numbers on. I have a book of every single one of them. Their attention to detail was unbelievable."

At the same time the citrus groves offered another route forward. At night there was always a danger that the fruit crops might freeze. Traditionally estates used large windmills to disperse a heavy liquid mass like oil over the area to keep the crops warm. The Jacuzzis proposed a way of avoiding having to hoist heavy drums up to the top of the windmill. Their solution combined a pump and a venturi system. "Pretty much the same thing," explains Roy, "as an injector you might have in your car. It introduces air into a liquid mass via an orifice and as it explodes it provides thrust."

The Jacuzzi business was heading in two different directions. "They were experimenting with pumps and screwing around with propellers. Then they started fooling around with building airplanes." With another surge of energy and imagination, the brothers developed a tiny, one-person plane, and then a larger, closed monoplane, the Jacuzzi J-7, which could accommodate passengers in its small cabin, one of the first passenger planes ever produced (and with room for a few extra bags of mail). The whole family pitched in: Roy remembers his grandmother's fingers callused and bent from the effort of sewing fabric onto the wings of the plane. They organized day-trip flights back and forth from Berkeley to the Yosemite National Park, 100 miles to the east, and secured a contract to deliver mail. "You can imagine, a bunch of crazy Italians building homemade airplanes, but they were doing pretty good." Their work on pumps and planes cross-fertilized; they put injectors from their agricultural pumps into a Model T Ford engine for use on the planes, to help keep the aviation fuel running even when the plane tilted.

At this point the Jacuzzis had the potential to become major players in the aviation industry. But a fatal accident in 1921 abruptly halted their progress. One of the planes flying over to Yosemite crashed, killing the passengers onboard, including one of the brothers, Giocondo. There were various theories about what happened. Some observers claimed the wing of the plane had cracked and fallen off, others that the engine had exploded in midair or that the plane had hit bad turbulence. Roy uncovered a different truth after reading his grandfather's account. He believes that the pilot that day wanted to visit a girlfriend who lived in Modesto, halfway between Berkeley and Yosemite, and that he maybe flew low over her house to show off to her, did a roll, got too close to some telegraph wires, clipped them and took the plane down. "Long story short, the brothers being so close, the grandparents said, 'Jeez, God obviously didn't want us to fly, this is crazy. You have to stop flying.' "

There was also a hard-nosed practical reason for getting out of the aviation business: to avoid any potential claims from the victims' relatives bankrupting the airplane part of the business. So the family turned all their attention to selling pumps off the back of a truck, schmoozing the maintenance guys on the farms, who were often fellow Italians. Over the decades their pump business continued expanding. "Deep well, shallow well, swimming pools, filtration systems, every kind of pump you could think of."

When he was young Roy took his turn helping out in the family workshop; he and his parents lived in the house belonging to his grandfather Giuseppe (now known as Joseph), and on weekends and after school he spent time in the plant and the foundry. He was given "the nicest, dirtiest jobs you could find" and along the way received—"I call it through osmosis"—a solid grounding in and understanding of hydraulics, mechanics and engineering.

Candido, the youngest of the original brothers, had a son named Kenneth, who suffered from rheumatoid arthritis. This was in the 1940s, when Candido lived up near where Roy lives now, and visiting the hospital for treatment meant a tiring round trip into Berkeley. Treatment for rheumatoid arthritis involved hydrotherapy, circulating warm water and air around the patient, who was sitting in a stainless steel tank, to ease the pain in his joints. The brothers suggested developing a pump to save Candido's wife the trek back and forth, a pump that could fit into a standard bathtub.

Roy shows me an original of this pump downstairs. It looks like nothing else than an outboard motor, a pretty basic piece of mechanical engineering—and a long way from what we know as the Jacuzzi—but it is a direct precursor. Having created a version for Kenneth to use at home, the brothers' entrepreneurial spirit kicked in. If they could make a cosmetically more agreeable version they could sell it to hospitals and schools and door-to-door to private homes as a therapeutic aid for anyone suffering from muscle aches and pains. By the mid-1950s this prototype whirlpool bath was on sale, with endorsements from Jack Benny, George Burns and Jayne Mansfield.

A decade later Roy was at college in Berkeley, still working in the family plant on weekends and experimenting to find ways of bringing together his studies in engineering and design. As he talks about his passion for "design that has a purpose," the word "imagineer" comes into my mind. Roy Jacuzzi, I realize, is an imagineer. And he is about to tell me how he transformed this outboard motor circulating bathwater to ease aches and pains, how he took that frankly uninviting and ungainly piece of machinery and bewitched, bubbled and beautified it into something with a whole unstoppable life and lifestyle of its own.

*

Just at that moment, as Roy is trying to open up an example of the invention he patented, Roy's wife, DeeAnn, pops up to see how we're doing. "Have you reached the 1970s yet? The 60s, oh my gosh." DeeAnn is a tall Scandinavian foil to Roy's Italian-ness. To fuel our conversation she has provided, along with coffee, a plate of divine slim ginger biscuits. I ask her what they are—they are *pepparkakor*, Swedish gingersnaps, which she has found locally and buys for the holiday season: Christmas is only ten days away. (Later she brings up a tin for me to take away, which fuels me for months afterward.)

Roy looks up. He is still struggling with the prototype jet he wants to show me. "Honey, can you get me a Phillips screwdriver?" he asks DeeAnn.

"OK, where do I find that?" There is a pause.

Roy sighs, "Oh, Jesus."

"In your toolbox?" suggests DeeAnn.

"You can't go there," says Roy. DeeAnn and I look at each other and simultaneously we remember: Christmas is *only* ten days away.

"Ooh," she says, "I know why I can't go there, I'd be happy to. You can keep talking all day, now I know."

Roy has managed to prise apart the jet he's been working on and picks up the story. During the time he was at college, the family were actually winding down production of the therapeutic pump. But they let Roy see what he could do with it. He developed the first of his whirlpool baths while he was studying; bringing it to completion took the best part of four years.

He approached the pump with a new sensibility, the attitude of a third-generation Jacuzzi. "That pump had a lot of problems. Imagine getting into a bathtub and straddling this pump with your legs. In those days a conventional bathtub was five feet by twenty-six inches and no deeper than ten inches. It was a birdbath. So the whole experience was not at all comfortable. What I was trying to do was to develop the whole idea of taking water and putting air into it by creating jets, but at the same time I also made the bathtub much deeper and got it so you could circulate the water around your body with air." And therein lies the essence of the Jacuzzi. The water feeding it was circulating faster and frothier, and because the jets were set into the wall of the bathtub and the sides of the tub were contoured, you could actually lie back and enjoy the experience.

Roy's Jacuzzi jet employed the same venturi principle his grandfather and great-uncles had used to push fluid up the citrus grove windmills forty years earlier. Venturi was another Italian

imagineer—Giovanni Battista Venturi, born in Bibbiano, southeast of Parma, in 1746. A professor, initially of geometry and
philosophy, and later of physics at the University of Modena, he
created the venturi tube, in which the tube narrows, forcing any
liquid to pass through at increased speed and creating a vacuum.
A side tube allows air to be sucked in by the vacuum, pushing air
into the liquid and giving it thrust.

Venturi was applying the Bernoulli principle developed by the
Dutch-born, Basel-based Daniel Bernoulli. With his colleague
Leonhard Euler (Euler missed out on the name check) Bernoulli
established the principle that when air or liquid passes over a
curved edge it speeds up to avoid a vacuum, the principle
traditionally used to explain how an airplane wing gives lift or
how an FI car's airfoil provides downforce. Venturi, Bernoulli—
it's like a Russian doll of eponyms. In science subjects you can't
move for the things: it's a welter of volts, amps, watts, newtons
and joules, of fahrenheits, curies and becquerels.

In the standard venturi air would come into the back of the
orifice and force the water through. What Roy changed was the
way the air and the water entered. He tells it better than I ever
could. "I needed a high volume of water. I was also trying to
move it and to compress it with a lot of air so that when it hit your
body the bubbles exploded all over you. I had a two-inch pipe
feeding an inch-and-a-half pipe, like rush hour with twenty
million cars trying to get through one tunnel. We're forcing this
mass of water into the backside of the venturi, this huge, beautiful
elliptical orifice. And what is unique is we allow air to be pulled in
not just from one side but two, top and bottom, and the vacuum
pulls it through. If you see the water explode, the water is just
incredible, it's gangbusters, spinning at an incredible rate."

His other innovations were to create a chamber in which the
jet could move and rotate and to allow the diameter of the tube,
the tunnel, to be gradually reduced, giving higher and higher
pressure. This meant that a bather could dial in the velocity for

the jetstream and control where and how the bubbles would hit.

Roy brings me a copy of his first patent, U.S. patent 3,571,820, file date June 6, 1968. The core description reads: "A hydromassage bath installation wherein a jet assembly is mounted in a vertical wall of a bath tank in spaced relationship to the drain opening with all flow passages in the circulatory system being above a drainline valve to assure a sanitary isolation of the drain line from the circulatory system during use and further assure complete emptying of the bath water to the drain line opening of the drain valve." I think I prefer the way Roy tells it.

Luckily Roy had a feel for the language of sales and marketing that the rigors of patent descriptors belied. He had picked up on the nascent interest in health and physical fitness, well-being and body concerns that was starting to emerge as a side effect of affluent consumerism in late-1960s America: California was an especially good epicenter to be in.

He was "infatuated" with the Italian culture of the Roman baths and called his first tub "the Roman." The Whirlpool brand name was already taken. So a Jacuzzi tub it was. I tell him it's the perfect name. Like Sax or Frisbie, it seems to suit the object. The Italian surname automatically evokes *la dolce vita*. And the fizzing sizzle of its double z suggests the water enticingly bubbling and breaking.

With the basic whirlpool design in place, Roy went out to market and sell that first tub. Like his forebears selling agricultural pumps off the back of their truck, he took his tubs to fairs and county shows, gleaning immediate public feedback. When a builder was working on a house, Roy would be out there selling him a bathtub, finding out new information to put back into future designs and acquiring what Roy thinks of as his street smarts. "You could be a genius, come out of Harvard Business School, but if you don't have common sense, good street smarts, if you don't listen to what people would really like and see where the trends are going, you can't sell crap."

"People think, 'Oh, yeah, Jacuzzi, overnight.' BS. There are so many designs that never make it past the drawing board, that die in the guy's garage. I spent a lot of time building the product and then going out and selling it. You have to continuously understand what the customer wants, keep working with it, keep making changes."

The difference between Roy's tubs and his family's pumps was that he was selling the Roman with a price tag, in 1968, of $838.00, at a time when a standard bathtub might fetch $75.00. This meant that for every 12 pumps the family sold, he made the same on one tub, with serious profit margins to boot. He started building up his own customer base among the plumbing fraternity, back then often extended families, Irish or Italian, just like the Jacuzzis. He headed to the Home Builders' Show in Dallas, where all the major builders would congregate, took a small booth, popped a couple of tubs on display and sold 3,400 of them, each order secured by a $50 deposit.

He was on the road for the best part of five years and admits he missed out on the early life of his older children. But he was driven. He expanded the whirlpool bath, added more jets, created deeper and larger tubs (as affluent girths expanded) and designed two-person tubs. Eventually a standard hot water heater could not handle the water delivery requirements. He designed a whirlpool bath with its own heaters and filters, a complete package that could be used outside the house. The Jacuzzi created its own market.

"I'm credited as one of the pioneers of re-innovating the bathroom, making it more luxurious. In 1968 there was one bathroom to a house; if you had two, you were really wealthy. The idea of a master bathroom was absurd. I'm not trying to brag. I'm not Pininfarina," he says, referring to the great Italian car stylist. "But I am recognized in the plumbing world as the designer of the whirlpool bath and in the swimming world as the designer of the whirlpool spa." And it's true, he is honored in the Hall of Fame of America's National Kitchen & Bath Association.

This is perhaps the moment to mention another bathroom legend, Thomas Crapper. Every time I have ever talked about this book, I have been asked "Are you writing about Thomas Crapper?" Well, apart from this paragraph, no, but to put everyone's mind at rest, there was a Thomas Crapper, a London-based Victorian plumber. He was not the inventor of the flush toilet, but he did have a flair for publicity and was successful enough for the future Edward VII to hire him to kit out Sandringham with his wares. The word "crap" predated Thomas by several centuries, although it was out of use by the late 1800s. Somewhere along the line it returned to common parlance, possibly, but only possibly, reinforced by Thomas Crapper's relatively high profile. The truth is that a tongue-in-cheek 1969 biography of Crapper by Wallace Reyburn called *Flushed with Pride* gave credence to the link, but most lexicographers view the connection as a verbal urban myth.

*

I have been trying to find a moment when all the effort, imagination and dynamism that Roy pumped into his Jacuzzis moved to a new level, when the word itself—Jacuzzi—was propelled beyond the status of a brand name for some forward-thinking whirlpool tubs. I don't know if Roy would agree with me, but I believe one of the critical tipping points came in 1975, with the release of *Shampoo*. This was a movie that projected the hedonistic lifestyle of California, with Warren Beatty bedhopping through Beverly Hills as George Roundy, hairdresser to the ladies of the canyon, in a pre-AIDS era of free love and sexual liberation; the film is set in late 1968, just before Richard Nixon takes office as president.

One of the key sequences in the film takes place at a groovy party in the mansion of "Sammy," a reclusive, Gatsbyesque character. George arrives and is almost immediately accosted by red-haired twins, who invite him to "Come on down to the Jacuzzi." "What, right now?" he says. He declines—he's concentrating on making it with Julie Christie—but the twins and the Jacuzzi feature throughout the rest of the sequence, the twins lounging naked in the Jacuzzi, a babbling pleasure-pit lit by underwater lights underneath a wooden bridge. That is my Jacuzzi moment, when the word was planted fair and square in the English language and established as a symbol of a sybaritic lifestyle.

In the late 1970s the Jacuzzi family company was sold to the Kidde Corporation. Roy was one of the few Jacuzzis who elected to stay. Most of the others decided to leave, taking the opportunity to make some money and retire. The original family of thirteen brothers and sisters was several generations down the line. "There were 279 family members," says Roy. "Can you imagine what a family organization was like? There was inevitably some friction when you have that many people. I was a maverick because they didn't know what to do with me. I was very much in favor, along with a couple of the other second generation, to sell the business, because when you start to get so many individuals and all of them have votes and all of them have different ideas about what you should and should not do, it gets to being a little bit gamey. It could be a zoo."

He became chairman, oversaw the company's growth to sales of $1,200 billion worldwide and brought his own business philosophy to the fore. "I love competitors, and I love to be friends with them because they're good, they're smart, creative thinking people. They push you, they help you. I bought a lot of my competitors. I would buy them and leave their name alone, run it through my factory, like Chevrolet, Cadillac and Pontiac all coming out of the same plant. Different people, different skews."

Despite the demands of his job, the imagineer imagined on. There were Jacuzzis for boats, Jacuzzis in planes. One customer, a sheik, wanted a tub in his Boeing 747. The company had to work out how to stop the water flooding the cabin at takeoff and landing. The answer: a secondary tank in the hold containing heated water that could be pumped up after takeoff and then drained off to another holding tank. A Japanese corporate boss asked for a stainless steel tank to heat the water to lobster-boiling temperatures. Roy played with acrylics, laminates, TVs in the Jacuzzi, showers, programmable jets, waterfall effects. He redesigned the shower as the J-Dream, complete with seats, hydrotherapy jets, CD players and waterproof closets. It's clear he will be inventing and designing and dreaming for the rest of his days.

*

Roy's mention of the replica sunflower gates back in Italy had stayed in my mind, and I determined to go and see the family's home. I had an instinct that visiting Valvasone might complete the picture.

Three months later I was heading toward the Italian Alps, the snow-frosted mountains that form a backdrop if you look north from Venice's Fondamente Nuove. Valvasone is a small town on the plain of Friuli, which stretches north of Venice, flat, flat countryside. A good friend, Luigi Caporal, who lives in Venice but was born not far from Valvasone and knows the area well, was driving me there.

Agriculture is still a significant part of the economy, vineyards and orchards on either side. In the small towns we passed through were small factories. Luigi explained that the farmers, used to solving technical problems by constructing their own equipment, often set up family-run businesses to create high-quality, specialized parts, which they could supply, for example, to the major car manufacturers in Milan or Turin. There was also a local tradition of *maiolica*, glazed pottery, and many of the factories produced porcelain bathroom furniture—indeed right at that moment we drove by a storage lot piled high with bidets and basins. I recalled that Roy had told me the company sold as many, if not more, bathtubs in Italy than in the United States.

Valvasone is a quiet town with a gorgeous ice cream–striped duomo and helpful residents, the newsagent keen to introduce us to the head of the tourist office, the municipal clerk pointing out the direction to the town library. Roy had given me pretty clear instructions for finding the family home, on a two-lane highway running south of the town away from the built-up center. It lies not far from an industrial estate that includes the offices and factories of Jacuzzi's Italian operation, sited here out of respect for the origins of the family. The house stands a couple of minutes' walk away, close up by the road, which sliced through the original grounds. And just in case we miss it there are those sunflower gates to tell us we've arrived.

Sure enough, the gates are immediately visible, next to the three-storey stone farmhouse. The gates are open, so Luigi and I stroll in wondering if anyone is there. We find a black-clad figure sweeping up leaves and some blossom that have fallen from a magnolia tree just inside the entrance. It is early spring, and there is a bright calm about the place. Luigi approaches the sweeper and plies some Friulian charm. She is Ida Galluzzo (that double z again), 95 years old, the mother of one of the current owners. She chats about the neighborhood, the fruit trees that were part of the farm, points out the ancient *gelso*, a mulberry tree, which dominates the courtyard. Ida says her daughter will be back later. Would we like to come back? Of course we would.

We took a break for lunch in the La Torre Restaurant, built into the old castle in nearby Spilimbergo, hometown of Eduardo Paolozzi's family. Fortified by Friulian wine, "the best white wine in Italy, probably the world," said Luigi, and a glass of high-octane grappa, we returned to the house and found Silvana Mulotti in situ, wondering who the *due signori* who had been befriending her mother might have been. She showed us around the house, pointing out in a dining room the wall that had once supported a giant Jacuzzi propeller. Upstairs there is an original example of Roy's first Roman tub. Roy and DeeAnn held their wedding reception underneath the mulberry tree.

Silvana also told us that in the church in Casarsa, the next-door town, was a painting by a Iacuzzi. We went to look for the church. It was tiny, a *glesiut* in Friulian dialect, rebuilt after wartime bomb damage and locked. As we turned away, a middle-aged woman walked out of a neighboring house. When would the church be open? "Oh," she said, "no problem, my cousin has the keys." A minute later the keys were in our hands. And inside the church we found fragments of frescoes, with a plaque revealing that one of the painters had been a Iacut in 1588.

These were deep roots, deeper even than the mulberry. This was where the Iacuzzis came from. Somehow it all fitted together. The gates at the house, the originals now resident in Happy Valley. The factory built on the land across the road. The tradition of small family-run businesses, applying technical expertise and creativity. The family working the earth, tending their fruit trees—cherries, peaches and apples, Ida had said—arriving in the States and gravitating naturally toward the fruit farms of California, a fertile ground for their natural talents.

*

After our conversation Roy had dropped me and my tin of *pepparkakor* back at my hotel in Lafayette, a fifteen-minute drive from his home. There was a gigantic Christmas tree in the lobby, muted carols in the background. Before happy hour I went out to the hot tub next to the swimming pool. It was mid-December, twilight, a chill night drawing in. The steam was inviting, gently drifting off the top of the tub. I padded out in the hotel's robe and slippers and lowered myself in. I was feeling exhausted, imagineered out. A touch of jetlag, too. I lay back and looked straight up: beyond the fir trees overhead, the night sky was sumptuous, marbled indigo.

I felt good. I felt really good. I snuggled back against one of the jets. Any tiredness evaporated with the steam. And I offered up a silent prayer of thanks to Signor Jacuzzi. *Tanti auguri*, Roy.

CHAPTER 4

A Hungarian in Buenos Aires: A Brief Birography

"All a writer needs is a cheap pad and a 10-penny biro."
George MacKay Brown

There is a small permanent display of original ballpoint pens in the CAI, the Argentinian Centre for Engineers, one of those august professional institutions that like to base themselves in a solid, imposing edifice. The CAI's grand mansion overlooks the Avenida 9 de Julio, a fourteen-lane boulevard that scythes through downtown Buenos Aires.

The exhibit is tucked away a little, mounted on a wall in a dim corner of one of the mansion's large foyers. In fact, when I asked the receptionist on duty where the display was, she knew nothing about it and denied its existence. Only the intervention of a more clued-up colleague allowed me to find the pens, which were the remnants of a much larger retrospective exhibition that had celebrated the life of their inventor.

There are four ballpoint pens, each produced in the early 1940s, vertically positioned in a row and balancing like ballet dancers up on their points. It seems strange to see them on show as artifacts. They look unremarkable because they are so familiar, such everyday objects: the mass-produced granted iconic status.

Each of the pens—slender and quite short—has a retracting button on top and a pocket clip. They all have a metallic sheen except for one, which has an all-black finish. I noticed that they have the mature design of a ballpoint that would last. These are

not throwaway plastic tubes, but more substantial, more sophisticated pens, the kind I remember being given when I was a child
as part of stationery sets sent as Christmas presents.

These were pens for professionals, pens that were fit for a pilot,
a doctor, a scientist or an engineer. They were the very first
ballpoint pens produced by their Hungarian inventor, László
József Biró, the earliest examples of the biro.

*

I had landed in Buenos Aires early one May morning, mid-
autumn in the southern hemisphere. It was my first visit to
Argentina, my first time in Latin America. Shreds of wispy mist
wreathed flat scrubland. Occasional puddles of pampas grass
emerged under a thin white sun. There was an air of distant
calm about the landscape. I tried to capture the moment and to
set it alongside other first impressions of new continents, each
after an overnight flight: a snow-muffled Beijing, a damp but
cheerful Melbourne, the 1950s-retro color and commotion of
Trivandrum.

Buenos Aires might seem an unusual destination for tracing
the life of a Hungarian inventor, but the city, as the whole of
Argentina, was one of the great immigrant magnets of the mid-
20th century, attracting communities from across Europe,
including substantial pockets of Italians—the familiar farewell in
Buenos Aires is *"¡chau!"*—alongside English and Welsh
incomers, the latter settling communities in the south toward
Tierra del Fuego, as documented by Bruce Chatwin in the pages
of *In Patagonia*. There were Basques and Ukrainians, and from
further afield immigrants from the Middle East, including the
parents of the country's onetime president Carlos Menem, who
had come to Argentina from Syria.

As a consequence the city is noticeably European in aspect and
outlook, and there is a well-preserved and patina-polished Old

World feel, from the wood paneling in its cafés to the business-suited genteel gentlemen who escort their elegant dates to a lunchtime liaison.

By the middle part of the last century there was, as there still is, a Hungarian community in Buenos Aires—maybe 30,000 or so now—but László Biró, who arrived in 1940, was not a traditional immigrant coming to join other family members who had previously made the journey. He had been invited to relocate to the city by some Hungarian businessmen, who were already based there and who offered him the chance to continue working on his ballpoint pen invention without the disruption of the war, which was engulfing Europe.

László Biró had always been an inventor. Like Adolphe Sax, he spewed out ideas across a wide range of activities. In 1930 he had designed and manufactured a "cheap, useful and convenient" washing machine. A couple of years later he produced what he claimed was the first automatic gearbox. He traveled to Berlin with the mechanic friend who had helped him design it, riding a motorcycle and sidecar fitted with the gearbox, and demonstrated the device to the local agents of General Motors. They acquired the design and then, he said, told him that they had done so only to stop anyone else acquiring it and that they had absolutely no intention of putting it on the market.

By 1940 he already had a résumé that included stints of experience as a journalist, sculptor, painter, art critic, racing driver, stockbroker, hypnotist (weirdly), car salesman and, of course, inventor. It was during his time as a journalist, working on the science and future magazine *Elöre* (the word means "go ahead" in Hungarian) that he had the moment of inspiration that led directly to the development of the biro.

László would frequently get frustrated by the fountain pen he used at work. He said that when he was conducting interviews the pen would quite often dry up, so he would have to ask to borrow one, which he found both annoying and inconvenient.

On a visit to the print works that produced the magazine, he later wrote that he saw a " 'mechanical monster,' a rotary press, with its characteristic 'plac, plac, plac' printing the newspapers without leaving horrible spots, and using an ink which dried as soon as it hit the paper. So I asked myself, would it be possible to simplify this piece of machinery so it could be held in the hand?"

His solution was simple in principle, although it would take years to perfect: a quick-drying ink fed by pressure or gravity onto a small ball rotating in the tip of the pen, providing a constant flow of ink. It was genuinely revolutionary.

Since the origins of writing—marks daubed by fingers dipped in plant juices or animal blood, most probably—there had been only a few critical improvements, though each of those was in itself hugely important. The writing surface had moved on from cave walls to clay and wax tablets, which could be scratched with a stylus. These were in turn superseded by the arrival of papyrus and, later, paper. As far as pen technology was concerned, the quill had reigned supreme for a millennium or more, with all its disadvantages: the constant re-inking it required, the high level of wastage, the lack of any kind of consistency. No wonder the finest calligraphers were so highly regarded.

Little changed until the mid-19th century, when metal pens and nibs were introduced. The first steel nib patent was taken out in 1808 by a British engineer, Bryan Donkin, who later developed canned food and gas industry technologies and whose own name lives on in a range of gas safety valves. In the 1880s Lewis Waterman, a New York–based insurance broker, developed an ink reservoir to feed the nib, thereby offering a longer gap between refills, and in the 1920s and 1930s the Waterman company evolved the self-contained ink cartridge. The fountain pen was a vast improvement on what had gone before, but—as László Biró found—nibs could still get clogged up, the fiddly business of changing cartridges often left stains on fingers, hands or clothes, and ink blots remained an irritating problem (other than for Hermann Rorschach).

★

László Biró had first developed his ballpoint idea in Hungary, but initially moved to France to look for the funding he needed to take it further. He had had a number of offers to finance his invention, but with the prospect of war none came to fruition.

However, a chance encounter from his days as a journalist provided the means to take up the offer from his Buenos Aires contacts. During a reporting trip to a holiday resort in Yugoslavia, László had been using an early version of his ballpoint pen to write out a telegram. Next to him a short but distinguished, bespectacled gent stood waiting, accompanied by a young woman—László said he had not really paid much attention at all to either of them, and that if he had, it was the woman who had caught his eye.

Shortly afterward the concierge at the hotel called him over and told him that the gentleman in question wanted to meet him. A date was arranged, and the young woman—who it transpired was the older gentleman's secretary—translated from Spanish to German. He was an engineer, he explained, and had been very interested in the writing implement he had seen László using. He asked if László had ever considered moving to Argentina to produce the pen and suggested that, if he ever did, he should get in contact as he would give him his full support. He signed and handed over a business card. László tucked it away, noting that his new acquaintance was the president of some company or other.

A little later, László happened to bump into the secretary in one of the hotel's corridors and asked her which company her boss was the president of. "Company?" she said. "Don't you know who he is? He's the president of the republic of Argentina." This was Agustín P. Justo, who had trained as a civil and military engineer and who was indeed president of Argentina between 1932 and 1938.

When the opportunity arose for László to go to Argentina and pursue his R&D on the ballpoint, it was extremely difficult for Hungarian citizens to obtain visas to travel to Argentina. However, he had wisely hung on to Agustín P. Justo's business card, and when he turned up at the Argentinian consulate and flourished the former president's card, the paperwork was shooed through.

László was on the point of setting sail from Barcelona when he discovered that another László Biró—a cousin, as it happened, and born in the same year—was an anti-Franco rebel who was being persecuted by the Spanish government. Having eventually established that he was not the Biró in question, László ran up against another problem with the Spanish customs officers: his detailed blueprints for the ballpoint pen caused some consternation because to the untrained eye they looked remarkably like the plans for a torpedo. He finally made it out.

As a business partner he invited a fellow Hungarian, János György Meyne, to join the company he was setting up in Buenos Aires. The two had met in Paris, when László was sitting chatting with friends in the Café de la Paix on the boulevard des Capucines. Meyne had come up to them to say he had overheard them speaking in Hungarian and how nice it was to hear the language—could he join them? The pair became firm friends, and, because Biró never considered himself a businessman, Meyne took over the commercial side of the business. The two only ever had a gentleman's agreement, but László always made sure that the correct percentage of his earnings, which he had promised to Meyne, was paid across to him, an uncontracted arrangement they continued to observe throughout a further 45 years of friendship and partnership. The company they formed, along with László's brother Georg, was called Biro-Meyne-Biro, and in Argentina the biro is still called a *birome*, from an abbreviation of the company name.

The ambience of Buenos Aires appealed to László Biró. He appreciated the courtesy and the friendliness of its inhabitants, and he particularly liked the sense of *yapa*, a word from the indigenous Inca language *quechua* that was used to describe a shopkeeper's habit of throwing in a little something at no extra cost and as a gesture of goodwill (the Cajun equivalent *lagniappe* comes from the same root). In the bars of Buenos Aires the waiters still add an extra splash of *whisky nacional* to top off the standard measure. As I was to discover, the spirit of *yapa* was very much part of László Biró's approach to life.

*

László Biró's daughter, Mariana, was nine when the family moved to Buenos Aires. I met her at the Escuela del Sol, the school that she founded with her late husband in 1966, drawing on the inspiration (and financial backing) of her father. In the lunch-time sunshine the gleeful playground squeals of the schoolkids—there are 400 in total, from kindergarten to secondary-school age—provided a constant accompaniment to our conversation.

Outside Mariana Biró's office hung a poster with the message: "All children are inventors. Because they are not afraid of getting their hands dirty. Of eating pasta. Or of using a hammer as if it were a brush. Of breaking something up just to see how it works. And to begin with the impossible, which is when adults usually give up."

I asked Mariana what, if anything, she recalled of her family's life in Budapest. "We lived in Buda, up on the hill, and ever since I can remember there were test tubes and rubber pipes running throughout our house." She was an only child. "I don't even have cousins. My father was one of two brothers, Georg and László, and my uncle Georg never had any children." The Biró family.

profession was medicine: Mariana's grandfather was a dentist, her uncle a doctor, dentist and biochemist. Her father studied medicine and engineering but never really wanted to go to university. "He would say, 'Once you know what something is like, you can't imagine it differently.' He wanted to be free of that. Yet he was a very studious man, especially when he required information for his inventions. When he wanted to know about something he studied and studied and studied until he was satisfied that he had the knowledge he needed to do something else."

Was he a good parent? "I don't think he realized he was a parent! Every so often he would say, 'Ooh, I have a daughter.' But there was no doubt about our love for each other. I never thought I didn't have a father, but he was away traveling a lot, and I think my mother translated my father to me."

She says László was not a conventional man, very mischievous when he was a child (he described himself as an "enfant terrible"), the antithesis of her uncle Georg, who was tall, thin, dark-haired, "very formal, but an extremely kind man. My father was shorter, was blond when he had hair—when I knew him he was already bald—and he had big blue eyes, very, very blue, very expressive. I was always interrupting his work, but he would say, 'Come in, come in,' and he meant it. 'I'll take it up later.' The most important thing for him was people. If a human being wanted to talk to him, everything else could wait."

And Mariana's mother, Isabel? "My mother was a very pretty woman, but very frail. When I was about nine months old she had to go to hospital because she had contracted tuberculosis, which was the disease of the time. She was in hospital for a year and a half; I went to live with my grandmother. And then she was cured by the latest thing, injecting air in the lung which had collapsed. The doctor sat by her bed one day and said, 'Do you want to live?' 'Yes I do, I have a baby.' 'Well, live.' 'But what about the bacillus?' The doctor said, 'Leave that to us. All you have to do is want to live. Be interested in what we doctors are doing to you. And if we say we are going to inject air in your lung, receive that air.' " She survived and lived to the age of eighty-three.

Her mother's family had been against the marriage to László: "'He's not going to feed you,' they said. 'You'll have to eat test tubes.' My father and my mother were completely different. If one thought something was white, the other thought it was black, but they never had an argument or a fight." If there was a social engagement, László would try and stay behind to tend his experiments. "My mother would go in and say, 'Now, go and dress. We have to go out tonight.' I remember my father's face, looking up, saying, begging actually, 'Do I have to go?' And my mother would say, 'Yes, this time you have to come.' 'Oh, all right,' and he would head upstairs, get changed and go out. This scene happened a thousand times. But sometimes my mother would think it over and say, 'No, actually you can stay. I can make your excuses.' And he would be so grateful."

Mariana's mother was tolerant of her husband's desire to invent. Later, when they were living in Buenos Aires, her mother noticed some women in white coats and aprons wandering around the house. She asked who they were, and László explained they were chemists helping him with an experiment that had to be monitored for twenty-four hours a day and that he had set the experiment up in their personal bathroom so he could be close by. "How long are they staying?" she asked. "About a week," he said. They stayed for three years. Mariana much later met one of these ladies, who told her she had received a wonderful welcome in the Bíró home, but the best thing of all was her mother's Hungarian goulash.

Food was not a high priority for László. It was a necessity: what he wanted was fast delivery of food to fuel his work. Whenever he ate he always had piles of books around him; even the dining table was piled high with them. "He never knew what food was. At the time we had a cook and maid at home. I don't think he ever went into the kitchen. One day after I had got married there was no help at home that day. My mother was out somewhere and she went back home because she thought he was going to die of hunger. He didn't care if he ate or not. He never realized the space that food occupies in some people's life."

Mariana tells a favorite family story. "He loved pancakes, very thin Hungarian pancakes. You put nuts or chocolate in them and rolled them up. He was eating some of these and looked up at my mother to say, "When are we going to have pancakes?" She looked at him in astonishment. He was on pancake number six! Something had reminded him of pancakes . . . It was because he was eating them!"

László would focus intensely on the project of the moment to the exclusion of everything else. When he took time out to work on his hobbies of painting and sculpture he would concentrate entirely on that for weeks at a time, and then—when the art was finished—move on and not touch a brush or a knife for years. "Painting and inventing are not opposite poles of my personality," he wrote. "They are complementary, stemming from the same root. The same excitement, the same challenge, to accomplish something." He was also a keen entomologist. "He knew an awful lot about ants, because he was fascinated by their social structure," recalled Mariana. Whatever he took on, creating a painting or designing a pen, he did it with intensity and passion.

Ah, passion. That reminds me of a passage from *What a Carve Up!*, the novel by Jonathan Coe. His character Michael Owen, commissioned to write a history of the dysfunctional Winshaw family, is also working on a book review. Michael is searching for an elusive word to describe the quality the author is missing, but he can't quite find the mot juste. His mental thesaurus has failed him. He wants to say that the author lacks, not intelligence, not technique nor ambition, but brilliance, bravado, grace, esprit. At last Michael has a flash of retrieval—the author lacks *brio*—and sends his copy off. When the review is published an acquaintance tells Michael he doesn't quite understand the last line. "There's obviously some clever metaphor or figure of speech that I've missed out on . . . What are you trying to say, exactly? That this bloke is never going to write a really good novel, because he doesn't own a pen?" Michael snatches the review back, only to see with horror that his text has been miskeyed and the final sentence now reads, "He doesn't have the necessary . . . biro."

*

When Mariana Biró was at school in Buenos Aires she had a desk with a hole cut in the top for a china inkwell, which would be filled every day with a fresh supply of ink. "I had long braids. And the boys sitting behind me dipped my braids in the ink for fun. I would go home crying, asking my parents to cut off this blue hair, and my father would patiently say, 'Soon you will be writing with something where you won't need blue ink in a well in your desk.' " Next door to her office, in one of the classrooms in the Escuela del Sol, are twenty or so desks retrieved from the grammar school she attended, which were passed on to her for use by the children—the inkwell holes are still there, although the need for both well and ink are long gone, as Mariana's father had promised her.

László Biró first took out a patent on his pen in Hungary in 1938, but he needed another six years of intense production work before he was able to resolve the technical issues that confronted him. Before leaving for Argentina he had worked in a Paris laboratory using parts of pens, metal nibs and inks sent from Budapest by his brother Georg. One of the critical factors was finding the right ink to work with different dimensions of the point—and Georg's background as a chemist proved extremely useful, as he concentrated on testing and combining different blends of inks.

The delivery of the ink to the point was a separate area of

concern. Initially László tried a screw-cum-piston arrangement to force the ink onto the point, but this pressure often forced the ball against the opening of the pen, stemming the flow of the ink, so he developed slots within the socket in which the ball was rotating to allow ink to continue flowing. All of these adjustments required the design and construction of specialist machinery. He later settled for an open-topped tube that would allow gravity to do the work and relied on the phenomenon of capillary action—in which the surface of a liquid changes its elevation when it comes into contact with a solid—to help keep the ball moistened and rotating. The company paid Mariana 50 cents an hour to test their pens. She would sit drawing incessantly on sheets of paper, which she still has at home and which she now uses for covering shelves. László later invented, naturally, a mechanical arm to do the job.

A series of patents were taken out in Europe and Argentina as the biro evolved and its writing performance continued to improve: during the Second World War the RAF took a consignment for pilots to write in midflight. Perhaps the most significant patent was the American one, logged in 1944. That year László sold the rights in North America to the Eversharp-Faber company for a cool two million dollars, and at the end of the decade the Argentinian company was bought by Parker Pens.

It took a while for the biro to be accepted. When the first pens came out, banks in Argentina would not accept ballpoint pen signatures on checks or official documents, and for a long time schoolchildren were not allowed to use biros in classes—except in the school Mariana attended.

In the mid-1940s an American businessman, Milton Reynolds, saw an early biro while he was visiting Buenos Aires, and he developed his own model and sold it round the world in a cheaper version. László's originals, the ones on display in the CAI, were, in comparison, luxury items retailing at $40. But there were still ongoing problems with the ink, and the cheaper versions leaked, and for a while the biro faded from fashion. Only in the late 1950s did the ballpoints produced by Parker Pens and by Baron Marcel Bich, who had acquired the rights from László Biró for Europe— and whose own name lives on in the brand name Bic—offer a truly reliable and disposable edition that revived the ballpoint's fortunes.

So much so that the biro became omnipresent—I have seen a sales figure quoted for the Bic Crystal alone of 14 million units a day. In *The Hitchhiker's Guide to the Galaxy* Douglas Adams riffs on this explosion. He describes the experiences of Veet Voojagig, an unassuming student at the University of Maximegalon, who, after a night out with Zaphod Beeblebrox bingeing on Pan Galactic Gargle Blasters, starts fixating on exactly what happened to all the biros he had ever bought. Veet visits the main locations of biro loss and develops a theory that there was once in the cosmos "a planet entirely given over to biro life forms" where biros could relax by "generally leading the biro equivalent of the good life." Veet eventually claims to have located the planet, where he says he had been chauffeuring a family of "cheap green retractables"— and is promptly locked away. When a team of explorers reach the planet he talked about, they find an old man who says it was all a lie, but there is never a satisfactory explanation for Zaphod Beeblebrox's "highly profitable second-hand biro business."

*

Buenos Aires is also the territory of another great writer, Jorge Luis Borges, Argentina's most prominent literary figure and for many people the finest 20th-century author never to win a Nobel Prize for Literature. Borges was an exact contemporary of László Biró. They were born a month apart in 1899—Borges on August 24, Biró on September 29. They died just over seven months apart: Biró on October 24, 1985, Borges the following June 14.

Alongside my journey to learn about László Biró, I traced a

parallel, phantom path in the footsteps of Borges, walking underneath the plane and fig trees lining Buenos Aires's broad streets to
catch a flicker, a distorted mirror glimpse, of the novelist and
short story writer whose work I had read as a student. I paid an
obligatory visit to two of Borges's haunts, sitting back in a half-
moon leather armchair at the Richmond Café and stopping off at
the bustling Café Tortoni (just up the road from the London City
Café where another talented Argentinian writer, Julio Cortázar,
wrote his novel *Los Premios*).

I visited a tiny room above the municipal library in the *barrio*
of Boedo where he was inspired to write his short story "La
Biblioteca De Babel" ("I have always imagined that paradise will
be a kind of library," Borges wrote) and had a lunch of some
seriously succulent lamb and a glass of Quilmes beer in an
arcade across the road from his final apartment on Maipú, next
to the bookstore called La Ciudad, where he spent many
afternoons.

I had wondered what kind of pen Borges would have used—
something rather elegant, I imagined—but at the Fundación
Borges, where they are raising funds for a permanent museum,
the small side-room of exhibits did not contain a Borges pen,
although there were some manuscript pages from "El Aleph,"
written in minuscule longhand script—surprisingly tiny given
Borges's deteriorating eyesight. As I suspected, it looked like the
work of a fountain pen. Somehow Borges would, I felt, have been
bypassed by the biro revolution.

★

After selling the rights to his invention and having made a substantial fortune in the process, László Biró did not indulge in
much laurel-resting. He continued inventing. As Mariana told
me, "If you ask an inventor which is his best invention, he will
always say 'the next one.'"

His ideas ranged far and wide. From 1943 onward László worked variously on a new kind of curtain hook, a roll-on deodorant (a natural extension of the ballpoint principle), a machine to extract energy from the motion of the waves and a one-stroke internal combustion engine. He developed a process for the production of phenolic resins, a system increasing the mechanical resistance of iron bars set in concrete, a foolproof door lock and a clinical thermograph. Shortly before his death he was investigating uranium enrichment.

Companies paid László to come and advise them on their products. "He would look at something first," said Mariana. "He didn't want to be told what it was. And then he would try and simplify it. Inventors like to simplify things."

"He was a very unpretentious man. The fact that he invented the ballpoint pen was simply one of the millions of things that he did. He didn't think it was terribly important. And there were many things he did that he valued just as much. He had no airs about him. He was a very simple man, which is a good thing because he had lots of time for other things, and he didn't like formalities. Honors didn't appeal to him at all."

The success of the biro meant that the family name could become a burden. When Mariana was at school in her teens she called herself Gómez for a while because she was fed up with the constant questions and comments about her family name.

I wondered, given that her father was a man who didn't like stasis and who tried to avoid the predictable, whether he found it frustrating to be trapped to some degree within his own success. She said he often complained that people confused him with his invention. And like the Elephant Man, he would wail, "I am *not* the ballpoint pen. I am László Biró."

The spirit of László lives on in the Escuela del Sol. "He liked to talk to young people because he said that young people have ideas that are much more useful than older people's. Young people are so passionate, and passion takes up so much space. When you get older, there is more space for the things you decide you really want time for, and that's wisdom also."

Mariana's educational philosophy is one she learned from her father as a child. "He wouldn't explain how something existed. He would say, 'If you want to know that, read it in a book.' But he would then say something that would really make us think, adding, 'Try to understand. Once you understand something, you cannot be against it.'" He would come down to the school to talk to the children about the ants he loved to study, and he would say to his daughter, "I'm so glad you set up this school. It's so nice. But don't ruin the children by teaching them. It is one thing to teach and another to allow them to learn." And then he would tell the children, "Don't let life go by. Be conscious of the greatest pleasure that exists. Life itself."

László Biró lived well into his eighties, despite a hefty smoking habit. "Since he was sixteen until he was sixty he smoked a hundred cigarettes a day at least," recalled Mariana. "When he was sixty my mother and I were bugging him so much that finally he said, 'OK, because of you I'm going to cut down to sixty cigarettes a day.'" He also drank a lot of coffee. "People would ask him, 'How come when you smoke so many cigarettes, you're not ill?' He'd say, 'Well, I drink a lot of coffee.' Others would say, 'Biró, you're drinking a lot of coffee. How come it's not bad for you?' 'That's because I smoke a lot.'"

When death came he treated it in the same way he approached life. He understood it. At the end of our conversation, Mariana Biró talked about his final days. "He wasn't afraid of death at all. He was afraid of pain. My mother was the other way around: she was afraid of death, but was able to withstand a lot of pain. My father used to say it doesn't make any difference when you die. Maybe to the people around, because it's a loss, but it doesn't make any difference to the person who dies. He was only in the hospital one day, and he told the doctors, 'If something hurts me,

I can't think and a person who can't think is not living. You know what you have to do.' "

"Just before he died, he woke up. My mother was there, and he said, 'I have a pain.' She said she'd call for the doctors. 'No. Don't call the doctor,' he said, and he held her hand. 'Allow me to die, permit me to die.' "

*

Every September 29—László Biró's birthday—is now el Día del Inventor in Argentina, National Inventor's Day. Mariana introduced me to Eduardo Fernández, the director of the Argentine School of Inventors. Both László's native and adoptive countries are able to claim him—and the biro—as their own. "My father is considered Argentine," said Mariana Biró, "because we all took Argentine nationality, but the invention was first patented in Hungary in 1938. Buenos Aires, of course, was the first place where the pen was actually manufactured. So the Argentines can say it's an Argentine invention, the Hungarians say it's Hungarian." "It's a universal invention," interjected Eduardo Fernández.

Eduardo was ten years old when he first saw László Biró on Argentine television promoting a product. He was already interested in inventing, making his own models and mock-ups and prototypes, and the sight of László Biró inspired him to continue along the path. When he was in his twenties Eduardo contacted László, who invited him to the family house. László was famously welcoming—"No was not a word for him," in Mariana's words—and he would receive a stream of aspiring inventors, each of whom he would listen to with the same tolerant attention, no matter how far-fetched, impracticable or downright incomprehensible their ideas. "All these crazy inventors, he would listen to every single one of them, extremely patient. I would have killed half of them," said Mariana.

Eduardo did not take his inventions to show László; he wanted to work with him. And so he became a research assistant in the laboratory in the Biró house. For Eduardo this was the perfect apprenticeship, a learning experience he compares to an inventing equivalent of the garden of Academe, where students would trail Plato as he discoursed. "He was a thinker, a fine mind, a first-class mind. A calm, long-term thinker, the opposite of a 21st-century attention span." László would think through his problems and then delegate the technical solutions: he was the imagineer, his assistants the testers and questers, who tried to provide the data to prove or disprove a theory. And always László would provide—for Eduardo's own projects—some extra thought, some additional insight, a little *yapa* of the mind.

The apprentice learned well. He set up a company called Inventchising, which researches inventions—anything from champagne cork openers to agricultural equipment—and then seeks investment to allow the product to be marketed. Eduardo also runs the Argentine Inventors' Forum and a Saturday morning Inventors' School at Mariana Biró's Escuela del Sol. He organizes inventing olympiads and has set up a Centre for Professional Inventors, offering advice for creative thinkers who may be unfamiliar with a business plan and seminars on how to present ideas to potential, but non-technically-minded, investors.

Argentina, I learned, has a tradition of celebrating inventors. Eduardo flicked through a PowerPoint presentation of some of them. The first animated cartoons, the first valve-inflatable football (created for the inaugural football World Cup in Uruguay in 1930), the fingerprint identification system, the heart bypass technique. All Argentinian: the country, Eduardo told me, ranks number fourteen for its invention rate per capita, outranking Italy, Spain, Australia and Canada. And Hungary, of course, has its own tradition of commercially successful inventions: I'm thinking in particular of another Budapest inventor, Ernö Rubik.

Just before we parted company Eduardo remembered to tell me a story he had heard that he wanted to pass on. Mariana had already told me that when her father was born he was tiny, so tiny that the doctors advised his mother that he would not live and she should let him pass away. His mother refused. She found a shoebox, lined it with cotton wool and shone a light over it for heat ("the original incubator"), and with special care and love he survived—and as we know, survived for eighty-some years. Eduardo told me that when László was five he was given a present by his uncle: a red scarf. "Why is it red?" asked the boy. "That's because it's been made with dragon's blood," said his uncle. "And if you wear it you will be invulnerable."

I still hadn't resolved my question about Jorge Luis Borges and the pen he would have used, and I mentioned this in passing to Eduardo. "Ah, but I met him. He was like Biró. You could ring him up and visit him at his flat on Maipú, just near the Plaza San Martín." Eduardo had worked for a local newspaper and had gone to interview Borges a couple of times. "He was very gentle and patient, just like Biró." Borges, because of his blindness, normally dictated to a coterie of volunteer secretaries, but he signed his own autographs, and Eduardo had asked him for one. And the pen? "Borges had the spirit of a nineteenth-century gentleman. He used a fountain pen."

CHAPTER 5

The Magnetic Appeal of Anton Mesmer

"An actor is at his best a kind of unfrocked priest who, for an hour or two, can call on heaven and hell to mesmerize a group of innocents."
Sir Alec Guinness

There is a moment toward the end of the first act of Mozart's opera *Così fan tutte* when Despina, the maid of Fiordiligi and Dorabella, connives with their aspirant lovers Ferrando and Guglielmo, who are pretending to be poisoned. Despina arrives disguised as a doctor and waves a magnet over their prostrate bodies to bring them "back" to life. And as she does so, she sings, *"Questo è quel pezzo di calamita, pietra mesmerica"*—"This is a piece of magnet, a Mesmerian stone."

The relevance of this line probably passes most contemporary audiences by, but for the first-nighters watching the opera's premiere at Vienna's Burgtheater in January 1790, the reference would have been readily understood. It is a deft little dig by Wolfgang Amadeus and his librettist Lorenzo da Ponte at the one-time Vienna resident Franz Anton Mesmer, the creator of mesmerism and the theory of animal magnetism, whose name is now deeply embedded in the language as the verb "to mesmerize" and the adjective "mesmeric."

At the time of the opening night, Mesmer's once ascendant star was well on the wane. The accusations of charlatanism and quackery that had pursued him since he first proclaimed his theories had driven him away from Vienna to Paris and from there into self-imposed exile. The Viennese operagoers would have turned to each other and raised an eyebrow or nudged each other in shared schadenfreude, as if to say, Mesmer, that poor old sap, that phoney, he certainly got his come-uppance.

However, the passing mention in *Così fan tutte* is more than a contemporary jest proving that the composer and his wordsmith had a topical touch. There was a direct connection: Mozart and his family had been friends of Anton Mesmer and his wife when Wolfgang was in his early teens; indeed they had stayed at the Mesmers' rather grand house in Vienna, and at a critical point in Mozart's career Anton Mesmer had given it a timely boost.

Leopold Mozart arrived in Vienna in 1767 after touring his son Wolfgang and daughter Nannerl around Europe—poor Nannerl, an extremely talented musician in her own right, she was doomed to be "sister of the more famous Wolfgang." Now Leopold wanted to crack the city that attracted anyone who was ambitious in the world of music. But the rapturous welcome he was expecting was somewhat muted. The family trotted along to perform for the Habsburg empress and her court, but although the concert went well, there was little follow-up. The composers of Vienna were certainly not likely to go out of their way to help promote this diminutive but clearly talented rival who was likely to eat into, if not devour, their livelihoods. And as Wolfgang entered his teens the original charm and novelty value of a five-year-old Wolfgang clambering onto a stool to dazzle with his undoubted skills was wearing thin.

Anton Mesmer was a music lover with a good tenor voice who performed creditably on the cello, piano and glass armonica (the instrument invented by Benjamin Franklin that mechanically produced wispy sounds from the rims of glass bowls). He stepped in and commissioned Mozart to write a one-act opera, *Bastien und Bastienne*—appropriately the tale of a magician reuniting a shepherdess and her beloved—that was almost certainly first performed in a small music pavilion on the grounds of the Mesmers' house in the autumn of 1768.

Franz Anton Mesmer was a successful doctor at the time. He had not yet started out on the path of controversial healing that would make his name and prove his downfall.

★

Anton—he generally styled himself as such—was not Viennese by origin: he was born on 23 May 1734 in Iznang, on the western shore of Lake Constance, then in the province of Swabia, part of the Holy Roman Empire (and now, just, in Germany). His father was a gamekeeper of some prestige as his employer was the bishop of Constance. The family were conscientious Catholics, and at least one of Anton's brothers became a priest.

Initially, that was also the plan for Anton. The family had some access to the episcopal residence—through which the boy acquired a veneer of social ease that came in handy later on—and hence to the patronage of the bishop, who funded his education. He was dispatched, aged nine, to a school run by monks, and in his late teens to two Jesuit universities in Bavaria, where he studied philosophy and theology. However, Anton decided relatively quickly that a life in the priesthood was not appealing.

Instead he switched to law, but again, after a year or so, that proved to be a dead end. His final choice of subject was medicine; at last he felt an affinity with what he was studying. He transferred to the faculty of medicine in Vienna, at a time when a mix of Dutch and local professors and lecturers was creating an atmosphere of enlightened progress and providing what was deemed one of the better educations in medicine around. Mesmer put in the necessary years of study, earning his degree and then working on a doctorate.

He produced a dissertation, which he titled *On the Influence of the Planets on the Human Body*. This was not some kind of occult cosmic fantasy, but to Mesmer a natural outgrowth of the interest in gravitation prompted by Isaac Newton's explanation of gravity in the 1680s. The hypothesis Anton evolved was essentially that we all exist within an unseen "universal fluid," within which electricity, magnetism, heat and light all flow and on which gravity and the planets exert a force, just as they affect the tides. Any disharmony in this fluid, Mesmer conjectured, was the primary cause of illness.

The paper was not in the least alarming to his tutors—who all merrily signed off on it—partly because of its "scientific" basis, partly because he had lifted most of the case histories in the dissertation from the respected English physician Richard Mead. Although Anton may well have continued mulling over his theories, he set them to one side after graduating and concentrated, now aged 32, on becoming a doctor.

He did the job pretty well, acquiring the trappings of the successful physician. He made the good choice of marrying Maria Anna von Posch, the widowed daughter of a high-up army doctor, who provided an aristocratic background, some significant wealth, useful connections, property and a teenage son—the couple never had other children. Their wedding in 1768 was one of the social highlights of the year, with the archbishop of Vienna doing the honors.

Their property in Vienna, or more accurately Maria Anna's property—her family, unhappy about her choice of husband, ring-fenced her money—was in the Landstrasse, next to the city's Prater Park. From a belvedere in its grounds Anton could admire the deer grazing beneath the Prater's chestnut trees. He had his own lab and dispensary, and there was a summer retreat at his disposal. Vienna was recovering from the end of a draining involvement in the Seven Years War and gearing itself up to become once more a glittering capital city. Anton could live the life of a socially acceptable professional man and—when he felt the urge—act as a patron of the arts to the likes of Wolfgang Amadeus Mozart.

A few years into his marriage there was a significant change in his career. One of his wife's cousins, Franziska Oesterlin, known as Franzl, came to stay. Franzl suffered from intermittent periods of hysterical fever, which were scary for all concerned. Anton tried to help her, using the tools of the trade he had learned at university, but electrotherapy and courses of drugs had no effect. He even resorted to some old-school tricks with a round of bleeding, blistering and purging. But having exhausted all other routes and noticing that her fever came and went, ebbed and flowed, just like the tides, he resurrected his theory of a universal fluid. He had heard that magnetism could be used to cure hysteria and ordered up some magnets from Maximilian Hell, the university's professor of astronomy. By getting Franzl to take a drink containing a solution of iron and then placing one magnet on her stomach and one on each foot, he was able to achieve some improvement in her condition. She felt, he reported, a painful current, but after six hours or so the fever broke.

Here he promptly fell out with Hell. The astronomy professor claimed it was the magnets that were curing her, but Mesmer said they were merely conduits. He used wooden and cloth "magnets" to make his point that (and here he took a huge leap of faith) they were only transmitting the "animal magnetism" contained within the body of . . . Franz Anton Mesmer. In other words, he, the man, was the magnet. He could effect the cure by moving his hands or an iron wand over the body. And so mesmerism was born.

Word about the cure spread. In 1775 Anton went to Rohow in Hungary to work with a Baron de Horka, who was suffering from throat problems. One of the baron's staff noted that Mesmer was already adding a sense of theater to proceedings, wearing a robe, sitting with one foot in a bucket of water, holding his wand and insisting on silence. The baron called off the treatment in the end—not because he didn't believe in it, but because the convulsions and spasms that the animal magnetism set off were too much. Mesmer accepted these convulsions as part of the treatment: they proved, to him, that it was working. But although the baron had had enough, every day the castle was besieged by people asking for Mesmer's help, and a room had to be set aside for him to receive his supplicants.

In 1777 he was introduced to a young concert pianist named Maria Theresa von Paradis, whose father was a secretary to the empress, also named Maria Theresa. The girl had suffered from blindness since the age of three, but a string of doctors had been unable to find any reason, since her optic nerve was undamaged, other than nervous hysteria. Her family turned to Anton Mesmer after trying all the treatments on offer in Vienna, including repeated and excruciating sessions of electrotherapy and in one case a tightly constricting plaster helmet, which had squeezed her eyes into unpleasantly distorted shapes.

Over a lengthy period, Anton employed his animal magnetism on her, and Maria Theresa even moved into the Mesmer home. Gradually her eyes settled and she managed to see some indistinct shapes. But just as things were going so well, events took an unfortunate turn. The doctors and physicians whose cures had previously failed with Maria Theresa started disputing what Mesmer was achieving. Then rumors started about what exactly he and this eighteen-year-old girl were getting up to while closeted in a darkened room.

Her parents turned out to be slightly nuts, definitely doolally— the father arrived one day angrily waving a sword—and took her away, ending any chance of improvement, and, sure enough, her blindness returned. It was something of a scandal, and the case of the blind pianist set the tone for the rest of Mesmer's career. Professionals and academics decried him, wrote him off as an impostor, an occult con merchant. But when ordinary people heard about his curing potential he was mobbed. He was trapped in a no-man's-land somewhere between the mystical and the rational, the scientific and the romantic, hovering between physics and metaphysics. The tagline for the 1994 film *Mesmer*, with a script by Dennis Potter and Alan Rickman in the title role, got it spot on: "Charlatan, fraud . . . or genius."

As a footnote, Maria Theresa—her eyes restored, thanks to Mesmer, to something more like their natural shape if not vision—resumed her piano career and was good enough for who else but Mozart to write his 1784 Piano Concerto No. 18 in B flat major, K456, for her. (He also wrote a couple of works for the glass armonica after hearing Mesmer playing his.)

As the cloud of controversy over Mesmer's techniques continued to mass, he and his wife decided to separate. They had become estranged as Maria Mesmer grew tired of her husband's obsession with animal magnetism. Apparently his social skills had deserted him, and he could barely talk about anything else, or if he did, he bored listeners with a raft of paranoid conspiracy theories about those out to do him down. He decided to relocate to Paris and never, as far as we know, saw his wife again.

In 1778 Mesmer arrived in Paris and set up in rooms on the Place Vendôme. He said he wanted to concentrate on securing scientific approval for his theories and practice. If a heavyweight body, like the Académie des Sciences or the newly created Royal Commission of Medicine, would come on board he would be justified, and prove to the doubters back in Vienna that he was for real. It was, as it happened, a good time to be in Paris. Science was in vogue, with amateurs dabbling in experiments, although the flip side was that fake scientists and pseudo faith healers were preying on that interest.

Anton Mesmer had hoped to make a fresh start, but tendrils of the gossip grapevine had already curled out from Vienna to Paris. There was a certain amount of skepticism waiting for him—and although he said he would not practice, but focus solely on science, word of mouth again ensured that those in search of comfort or cure came knocking at his door, a hundred or more each day. He moved to larger premises in Créteil, then a separate town outside Paris. And to serve the demands of his patients he designed a tub of iron filings, which allowed several people to experience animal magnetism at the same time—a tub known in French as *un baquet*.

*

There is a *baquet*, believed to be the only remaining example of a Mesmerian *baquet*, in the Museum of the History of Medicine and Pharmacy in Lyons. The museum is in a set of rooms on the ground floor of a busy university medical faculty, students hanging out on the steps of the courtyard outside, hospital hues of paint covering the walls. Off a corridor and through an unprepossessing door the museum has collected together phrenological head shapes and the extraordinary and eye-watering instruments of the medical profession alongside the molds of guillotined heads and waxworks showing the effects of some of the more repellent diseases ever visited on humankind.

A pair of retired faculty professors were on hand to help, and they jovially guided me to the *baquet*, which was perched in a corner of one of the side-bays. It is not technically a Mesmer *baquet* but one bought by one of his followers, a local master apothecary named Jean-Baptiste Lanois, and subsequently acquired and used by a former furrier named Christophe Beckensteiner through to the 1880s.

The oval *baquet* was much smaller than I had imagined. It would have made an unusual but stunning coffee table: a base made of deal, the main body walnut, the top inlaid with mahogany and maple, with a marquetry design of vaguely masonic symbols and stars.

I realized that when I had first heard that Mesmer's *baquet* was a tub, I had immediately thought of it as a precursor of the Jacuzzi, into which sufferers would immerse themselves in a swirl of universal fluid. In fact, users sat around the outside of the tub; its lid remained closed. From the top dangled eight jointed iron stalks, like lethargic antennae, which they could lift and hold to whichever part of their body was in pain. Two of the stalks ended in a double handle so that in total ten people could feel the force. There were knotted cords they could tie around themselves to hold them tight as and when any convulsions kicked in.

The museum curators kindly provided me with plans of what had been found when the *baquet* was opened. The iron stalks ran down to touch magnets inside the tub. The tub itself was lined with bottles of water in a mix of iron filings, ground glass and vegetal matter. In the middle a pewter-covered Leyden jar acted as an electric converter, with only one external pole, a handsome nodule on the top of the tub, which—as the museum's notes made clear—meant it was completely useless. The whole point was that it didn't matter. The *baquet* was not meant to provide magnetic or electric power. The iron rods, the magnets, the Leyden jar were purely cosmetic. The *baquet* was only there to focus the real energy, Anton Mesmer's personal animal magnetism.

The *baquet* was also Mesmer's way of dealing with the increasing number of patients demanding his attention, and he doubtless saw some commercial benefits from bashing through batches of ten patients in each session. From descriptions of his Paris rooms, he later had two or three *baquets* on the go, and I came across a contemporary account that pointedly described the ladies and men who were happy to go and get "convulsions for ten louis a month."

The museum in Lyons was equally suspicious. The *baquet* "shows how dangerous it can be to apply insufficiently developed science to clinical medicine." Mesmer "lacked knowledge of physics," but, the curators conceded, "he was a man of sincerity."

★

I wanted to get a 21st-century perspective on Mesmer and mesmerism from someone who was directly involved in the paranormal and who might understand something of the flak that had been hurled Anton Mesmer's way. Paul McKenna volunteered for the task. As one of the best-known hypnotists in the UK, he would, I felt, have some pertinent points to make.

We met at his office off a quiet mews in a villagey part of Kensington. A gigantic dog bounded up and greeted me at the open door. Paul McKenna emerged from the dog's far side. A neat, controlled man, he suggested that we move to the adjoining flat, a predominately monotone living space with modern art on the walls and a Buddha's head on a plinth, a friendlier and more elegant version of an upscale doctor's waiting room.

Paul's garb was relaxed, open-necked shirt and black jeans, but his schedule was tight, and he was clearly a man who knew how to focus. There was, I have to say, something oddly disconcerting about sitting there looking into the eyes of somebody who had made a career out of the power of suggestion and hypnotism. Luckily, the reflection in the lenses of his black-framed glasses obscured too piercing a gaze.

It was clear that Paul McKenna was a man who knew his subject. He had become interested in hypnotism relatively late—he had already had a career as a radio broadcaster—but had taken the time to study its history in detail. He was already well informed about Anton Mesmer and disappeared to his bookshelves from time to time, offering to lend me what he considered the best biography of Mesmer—*The Wizard from Vienna* by Vincent Buranelli—and showing me a maroon-bound volume from the 1920s called *Instantaneous Personal Magnetism*.

I told him about my trip to Lyons to see the *baquet*. Like me, Paul had wondered if people had sat in the tub or not, and, like the museum, he thought Mesmer had been sincere. "Oh, absolutely he believed in it." Remembering that at the museum one of the curators had mentioned how attitudes change, how wearing a copper bracelet and believing in its benefits is perfectly normal

these days, I said I felt that Mesmer had been before his time in the
1770s.

"The thing about Mesmer," Paul said, "is that the kind of
energy healing he was carrying out is now in vogue. It's a shame,
because I suppose that by today's standards he would have been
partly a hypnotist, but also a faith healer. In the way that the
martial arts community all talk about the 'chi,' the life force, the
energy, and how they control their chi to break bricks, he was
talking about an electromagnetic force running through us. He
would feel very much at home today."

That slightly tainted term "new age" came to mind. "Acu-
puncture is now a totally acceptable form of treatment: electrical
forces moving around the body, the placement of each needle
interrupting or redirecting the flow." Times change. "Yes, in
Mesmer's day there was a great interest in phrenology. Now no
one is interested in it.

"Just because something can't be analyzed under a microscope
or doesn't conform to the null set hypothesis doesn't mean it isn't
true. While there is no proof, there is certainly good evidence for
energy or faith healing working." Paul McKenna cited the work
carried out by Randolph Bird in America in the 1970s: double-blind
studies in which people who had had heart operations were prayed
for. Bird found that their postoperative recovery time was
significantly reduced and they had significantly fewer complica-
tions. "I keep an open mind about energy healing or faith healing."

As far as hypnotism is concerned, there are two principal
schools of thought, "state" and "non-state": the first believes
hypnosis is a special state of consciousness, the second that
hypnotism works because of an element of social compliance: in
other words somebody feels they can jump up and do a pole-
dance routine because everyone in the room is allowing them to.
Paul McKenna doesn't feel the need to subscribe to either school.
"I don't think it really matters, as long as it works. Hypnotism is a
focused and efficient way of achieving what you can also achieve

in waking consciousness. You don't *need* to fill a tub full of iron filings to achieve it." He thinks one of the keys would have been Anton Mesmer's force of personality. "He would have needed a strong personality to survive the attacks on him, but he also clearly possessed a great sense of theater."

We discussed the importance of Mesmer's mise-en-scène. In his Paris clinic he had developed it to a high degree. The atmosphere was deliberately muted, the room bathed in a half light with windows shuttered and doors draped. The air was heavily perfumed. The sound of a piano, or better still a glass armonica, would supply some suitably ethereal mood music. Mesmer wandered around the *baquets* in a pair of golden slippers, wearing a lilac silk dressing gown and holding his wand of wrought iron. Assistants, known as *valets toucheurs*, spoke in low whispers. When necessary Mesmer would intervene, especially when any of his clients' convulsions became too stressful or disturbing, and he would help remove the patient to a private, padded "crisis room."

Paul McKenna believes in the sense of drama needed for the best results in his own work, although he eschews the need for props and costumes—"that would make me look like a magician." His is more the drama of occasion. We talked about how this could help bring both practitioner and subject to readiness—and images flicked through my mind of preparations for rituals, the anticipation of walking on hot coals, the formalities before the rite-of-passage moments of baptism, marriage or funerals, or even, in a contemporary version of mass mesmerism, the ritual buildup to the arrival of a headline act at a rock 'n' roll show.

It was important to understand Mesmer as part of a tradition rather than as an isolated aberration. All the elements of mesmerism had been around long before he was. Bacchic followers went into trances; the Delphic oracle, sitting amid cold vapors, clad in robes, intoned prognoses that the attendant priests would interpret for the supplicants. Magnets had been recommended for

use in cases of hysteria in the 16th century by Paracelsus, aka the
wonderfully named Philippus Theophrastus Aureolus Bombastus
von Hohenheim ("Just call me Bombastus"), who straddled the
medieval and the new worlds on the cusp of alchemy and
chemistry.

There had always been healers who used the power of touch.
In Ireland a 17th-century country squire called Valentine
Greatrakes discovered that he had the power to heal and was
known as the Stroking Doctor. The tradition of the Royal Touch,
in which the kings and queens of France and England laid their
hands on sufferers from the King's Evil—scrofula—continued, in
France, into the 19th century. The infant Samuel Johnson
received the touch from Queen Anne in 1712.

Anton Mesmer pulled all these elements together under the
umbrella of mesmerism. And mesmerism, although it dropped
out of favor, never really went away. A 19th-century French
mesmerist, Charles Poyen, imported it to America, and via
Phineas Parkhurst Quimby the practice found its way to Mary
Baker Eddy, whose repudiation of it led to her creation of
Christian Science. Both spiritism and its near cousin spiritualism
extended Mesmer's influence. In Manchester, in the 1840s, the
Scottish-born neurosurgeon James Braid replaced the word
"mesmerism" with "hypnotism"—his own neologism (for some
reason one imagines it is an age-old word). Stage hypnotists kept
the practice alive and became a link in the chain running from
Mesmer to Braid and on to the French neurologist Jean-Martin
Charcot, whose students included Georges Gilles de la Tourette
and one Sigmund Freud. ("Freud didn't like hypnotism,"
mentioned Paul McKenna. "He wasn't very good at it.")

★

For seven or eight years after his arrival in Paris, Mesmer was a
success. He got extensive press coverage, and the turnover at the

baquets was swift, although he democratically allowed the poor to take the treatment gratis every other day, much to *l'horreur* of his aristocratic paying customers. However, he remained frustrated.

The intimate sessions in which Mesmer sat knee to knee with his often female patients continued to provoke ribald cartoons and jokes. But, says his biographer Vincent Buranelli, "no record exists of a jealous husband." Anton Mesmer was too focused on his grand obsession, on proving that mesmerism was a legitimate science, to have time for hanky-panky. Yet the one thing he could not do was convince any of the scientific and medical bodies in Paris to support his findings, even though he did pick up one significant disciple, Charles Deslon, then private physician to a brother of Louis XVI.

Mesmer became so annoyed with the lack of official recognition that he wrote a self-important letter to Marie Antoinette, an Austrian, asking for her help. This was not completely out of the blue: some said she had regularly and secretly visited Mesmer to use one of his *baquets*. However, she never replied. In umbrage, Mesmer flounced off to Spa for a little R&R and wrote a *Memoir on the Discovery of Animal Magnetism*. After a falling out with Charles Deslon, who had set up his own clinic, Mesmer forged a new alliance with Nicolas Bergasse, a lawyer from Lyons, who helped him establish a Mesmerian institution. The Société de l'Harmonie universelle sought subscribers who paid handsomely to be taught the secrets of mesmerism by the master himself. Founded in 1783, the society's HQ was the Hôtel de Coigny in Paris, but it soon had offshoots in Lyons, Strasbourg, Bordeaux and other provincial capitals.

Membership was secret, which gave rise to further speculation about Mesmer's activities, so much so that Louis XVI decided to set up two royal commissions to investigate mesmerism. One, under the aegis of the Academy of Sciences, was headed by no less a figure than Benjamin Franklin, the U.S. ambassador and inventor of Mesmer's beloved glass armonica, whose adventures in electricity would, one might have thought, have allowed him to keep an open mind about unseen forces. On Franklin's commission were eminent scientists, including the chemist Antoine Lavoisier and the astronomer Jean-Sylvain Bailly. The second commission, based on the Royal Society of Medicine, included the botanist Antoine-Laurent de Jussieu (a name I knew only as a Métro stop). What really riled Mesmer was that they chose not to examine his clinic, but that of Charles Deslon.

The reports, filed in 1784, were disastrously negative: animal magnetism, they declared, did not exist. Even if the patients' crises did, they were products of their imagination. Only Jussieu did not sign off on the report, saying they should suspend a final decision. A separate, secret report also raised the issue of the erotic side effects of mesmerism. The damage was done, and Benjamin Franklin's successor as ambassador, Thomas Jefferson, wrote that the doctrine of animal magnetism was "pretty well laid to rest," dismissing it as a "hocus pocus theory."

★

There was one member of Ben Franklin's commission I haven't mentioned: Joseph-Ignace Guillotin, whose name would strike terror into the hearts of his countrymen a few years later.

Guillotin was no blood-crazed vigilante, far from it. His background was similar to Anton Mesmer's. Four years younger, he had also experienced a Jesuit upbringing and then chosen medicine as a career, but his path was much more conservative. He had become a *docteur-régent* in the Paris University Faculty of Medicine and subsequently professor of anatomy, physiology and pathology—hence his inclusion on the commission investigating mesmerism. He enjoyed exactly the kind of prestige that Anton Mesmer coveted.

It was around the time of the commission that Guillotin started to dabble in the sphere of politics, and in 1789 he was appointed a deputy representing Paris in the National Assembly. I have the impression that he was earnest and probably rather annoying. Thomas Carlyle, in his history of the French Revolution, called him "the judicious Guillotin"; a contemporary called him "a busybody." His big day came on October 10, 1789, when, during a debate on the penal code, he proposed that a mechanism be created to put criminals to death swiftly and cleanly.

For Guillotin, the physician, this was a humane solution to the question of how to impose a death penalty in what would be the brave new postrevolutionary France. Previously death had been meted out by fire (for heretics or magicians), crushing on a wheel (for assassins and highwaymen), quartering (for treason) or decapitation by a sword for the posh and hanging for everyone else. There were legendary horror stories, not least that of the execution of Robert-François Damiens, a crazed individual who had failed in an assassination attempt on Louis XV. For this near-regicide, Damiens was tortured with red-hot pincers, his hand burned off and a cocktail of molten oil, lead and wax poured into his wounds. He was then torn apart by horses pulling his limbs in different directions, and when that didn't quite finish him off, the executioner gave a little help with a knife.

Guillotin—who had been born prematurely after his mother took fright at the sight of a criminal being tortured on the wheel—saw the machine he had in mind, a supersized cigar cutter, as a much more dignified end. The Assembly, and the press, applauded his suggestion. By early 1792 the prototype, constructed by a German harpsichord manufacturer, Tobias Schmidt, was in use. The following year Louis XVI and Marie Antoinette had breathed their last beneath it.

The guillotine was not a new invention: an earlier version had been sketched out by another Paris doctor, Antoine Louis, and the machine was known as the *louisette* for a while. But even before that similar machines existed. I went to see the Scottish version, the Maiden, in Edinburgh one raw St. Andrew's Day when a plangent skirl of bagpipes filtered down toward the Museum of Scotland. The Maiden, on display in a room containing witch's bridles, iron gags and thumbscrews, was first used in 1565. Tall, black, menacing, it was indisputably what a guillotine should be. A rope pulled a lead-weighted iron blade up the frame; the blade fell once a trigger was released, shooting down copper-lined grooves to dispatch its victim's head.

Guillotin, who had perhaps unwittingly reintroduced the idea, was, given his originally humane instincts, understandably disturbed as the guillotine became the symbol of the Reign of Terror. Miniature guillotines became a desirable adult toy: miniature effigies of the hate figure of the moment could be decapitated, emitting a blast of red liquid—actually perfume—to amuse dinner party guests. I have read, but never seen proved, that Guillotin first tried to get the name of the machine changed, and when that failed, had changed his own family name.

He managed to avoid the irony of losing his own head by the guillotine, the fate of many fellow deputies. Of the commissions into mesmerism, two members, Lavoisier and Bailly, were not so lucky. Anton Mesmer, who might well have been a prime candidate, had—fortuitously—already pulled a disappearing act.

*

In 1811 a group at the Berlin Academy of Sciences were discussing mesmerism. Somebody had a bright idea: why don't we go and talk to Anton Mesmer? Most people assumed he was long gone, a ghost from the previous century. But the Academy's Karl Wolfert found him in a house near Lake Constance, his home territory, working on a book, playing his glass armonica, keeping a pet canary.

When the reports from the royal commissions had appeared in 1784, Mesmer had gone through a particularly bad patch. On Good Friday 1784 he, probably unwisely, attended a piano recital by Maria Theresa von Paradis. Everyone found his presence embarrassing, and he was deeply humiliated. That autumn two satirical plays on the Paris stage mocked mesmerism mercilessly.

Mesmer had also found disharmony within his own Société de l'Harmonie universelle, which refracted into factions and schisms. He upped and returned, via the French provinces—where he was still well regarded by branches of the Society—to the land of his birth. There he kept a low profile, occasionally practicing treatments in a low-key way, receiving visitors from time to time, working on a new memoir and delving into more occult fields. In March 1815, aged eighty, he knew his days were numbered. He asked a local priest to come and play the armonica as a send-off, but by the time the priest arrived he had already died.

At the end of my conversation with Paul McKenna, he discussed the lack of understanding that had dogged Mesmer's life. "When I started out twenty years ago, people were very skeptical. They said hypnotism was dangerous, and it didn't work. That's what piqued my interest: this is dangerous *and* it doesn't work? . . . There is less skepticism now. Theories evolve constantly. Some of Niels Bohr's theory of quantum mechanics was wrong, but that didn't mean that all the plastic in the world suddenly disappeared. Maybe Mesmer was not quite there, but we may find he was ahead of his time. I have a sneaking suspicion that future historians will treat him more kindly."

CHAPTER 6

Jules Léotard, the Sultan of Swing

"Do you want to be adored by the ladies? Don't drape
yourself in those unflattering outfits created by women.
Wear something more natural that doesn't hide what you
should be showing off."
Jules Léotard

At the headquarters of Wham-O, the manufacturers of the original 1950s Frisbee flying disc, I sat and watched one of the company's earliest TV ads for their new product. It was straight out of baby boom America: a freckle-faced kid, his sister and grinning parents lobbing their Frisbee back and forth in a sun-drenched backyard where the hedges, as well as any Cold War angst, had been neatly trimmed. There was a flurry of flying saucer analogies in the sales pitch, and then out of nowhere there came a snatch of Victorian London. "It flies through the air," said the voice-over, "with the greatest of ease," the very words that George Leybourne, the music-hall performer whose dandified stage character was the original "Champagne Charlie," had written as a tribute to the original Daring Young Man on the Flying Trapeze, Jules Léotard.

The song celebrated Jules Léotard's fame as the dashing, daredevil aerialist who had brought his act across from France to wow audiences at the Alhambra Theatre, Leicester Square, and other London venues in the early 1860s. But oddly it was not Léotard's gymnastic bravado or his leaps into the unknown that lingered in the consciousness of history. I'm not certain how many people either in 1957 or today would be able to name the daring young man in the title of the song. Instead, his name lives on through the snug-fitting, one-piece outfit he designed and wore for his performances. Somehow it seems it would have been more appropriate for "leotard" to be the name of the act, not the costume.

Steve Gossard, an American circus historian who gave me some lowdown on Jules Léotard, has a good phrase to describe the feeling of going on a flying trapeze for the first time. It is, he says, like eating an oyster if you have never tried one before: "A great sensation, but you can't help wondering what possessed the first person to do such a thing." Well, that man was Jules Léotard, who made his public debut on the apparatus in November 1859, the first man to leap from one trapeze to another and the first to turn a somersault in midair between trapezes.

Jules could not only do this but, like Buzz Lightyear, he could do it with style. He was also a natural narcissist. His body was trim and taut, and to display his physique to its best advantage Jules turned fashion designer, devising a natty and body-hugging all-in-one outfit that gave him freedom of movement but, more importantly, showed off all his muscles. He knew exactly the impact it would have on the ladies in his audience. He was a born showman.

*

In 1860, when he was twenty-two, Jules Léotard published his *Mémoires*, a tiny leather-bound book. He said he had decided to set down his own autobiography when an acquaintance of his, "a man of letters called Nougaret," was digging about looking for a cigar in Léotard's writing desk. He uncovered a multicolored blizzard of fan letters, all from female admirers, which had been prompted, according to Jules, by his first appearance in his new one-piece costume. *"Mais, c'est charmant, mon cher,"* observed

Nougaret. *"Il faut publier ça."* Jules wondered whether this idea was his friend's devious way of getting his own back for an incident that had happened some time earlier when, trying out a trapeze exercise, Nougaret had completely missed the bar and landed flat on his back, leaving his body and ego both bruised. Perhaps, mused Léotard, suggesting he write a book was his friend's way of getting revenge, to see if Jules would stumble on Nougaret's own terrain.

I was intrigued to find that the instant celebrity autobiography is no newfangled phenomenon. In the introduction to his little book Jules spends quite some time slagging off an autobiography published in the same year by Marguerite Badel, who was a singer and cancan dancer appearing at the Délassements-Comiques Theatre and at the Gloria, a hip Parisian cabaret. She performed under the stage name la Rigolboche, a diminutive nickname she had made up from the word *"rigolo,"* meaning both amusingly funny and curiously funny. Her fame flared briefly, during which time her own nickname became a verb in its own right, *rigolbocher*, meaning, in Parisian argot, to dance, gossip or generally have a good time.

I have seen la Rigolboche's memoirs described as *rosse* (mean and nasty). They certainly got right under Léotard's skin, although he doesn't reveal why. He rather sanctimoniously complains that she was only interested in getting published because she wanted to become a *célébrité quelconque*—a C-list celebrity in contemporary lingo—and says that his own book will be a far more modest publication, and that he has decided to refrain from including a photograph of himself as originally planned. Commendable humility, rather undermined by his assertion a few paragraphs further on that "barely had I appeared on the Parisian horizon than the good old public, those arbiters of good taste, named me King of the Trapeze!"

The memoir is quite light on detailed biographical information, but it does provide some glimpse of his early life. He was born, on

August 1, 1838, in the noble city of Toulouse, *la ville rose*, where he was raised within the family business: his father ran a gymnasium in the city.

For some reason, and this had seemed strange given the family's very French surname, a number of articles and scholarly descriptions of Jules Léotard said that his father was Austrian. Jules's own book sets that misconception straight. His father, Jean, came from a small village in the Ariège department in the middle of the Pyrenees, so he was a true child of the Midi, but he sported a severe haircut, short sideburns and an "Austrian-style"—*Kaiserlich* or imperial—mustache, hence the confusion. Throughout his memoirs, Jules has a neat line in laconic maxims. At this point he pauses to illuminate us all: "Never," he proposes, "judge a man by his mustache."

Jules's father had trained at a gymnasium, spent five years working in Paris and then returned to the south of France to launch his own system of gymnastics in Toulouse. However, setting up in business there was not easy. Jules observes that "in Toulouse, it is not absolutely essential to be an artist to succeed. The only requirement is to be from Toulouse." His father, as an outsider, found that the local authorities went out of their way to put spokes in various wheels. Despite their best efforts, he managed to establish a pair of elegant, purpose-built gyms, where as well as pandering to the well-off children of the local middle-class families he opened up its facilities to poorer children, whose health might benefit from a dose of PE.

And so his son Jules was familiar from the outset with all the sounds and sights and smells of the gymnasium. We can evoke them easily for ourselves: a puff of chalk sending shards of white fluffing up into light pouring through high louvered windows, the squeak of shoes on overpolished wooden floors, that strange creak of a rope taking a body's full weight. Léotard family lore had it that when Jules opened his eyes the first object his eyes saw was a trapeze swinging in front of him, and that from then on whenever he was out of sorts, his tears would be gently rocked away be sending him to sleep on the gymnastic equipment. Retrospective storytelling, I'm sure, but I enjoyed his comment that *"le trapèze devint mon berceau naturel"* (the trapeze became my natural cradle).

Under his father's tutelage, Jules proved a ready pupil, to the point where, one day, he proposed to his father a move that was so difficult and so dangerous that his father refused to release the trapeze to his son. Jules clung on instead to his idea and bided his time until he found himself back in the gymnasium with only a few of the other pupils, less experienced and unlikely to tell the principal's son not to attempt what he had in mind.

According to Jules, he leapt high and managed, just about, to grab the swinging bar coming the other way. When he regained solid ground, he felt pale and shaken, but surging up through his body was an uncontrollable feeling of euphoria: he had experienced his personal eureka moment. Although he does not describe the jump in any detail, I am sure that this was the move that created his fame, leaping from either a fixed platform or a swinging bar toward another swinging bar—the flying trapeze routine.

Word spread of Léotard's expertise. A group of traveling performers from the Déjean troupe, a touring circus based in Paris, passed through Toulouse, saw him in action and spread the word about what they had seen. Their tales of the twenty-year-old's exploits sounded so unlikely to the circus owner, Louis Déjean, that he dispatched a trusty aide to Toulouse to double-check. This envoy came back equally effusive. Déjean still did not believe what he heard and went down to Toulouse himself to confirm if it was true. Jules was promptly signed to Déjean's Cirque de l'Impératrice and started packing his bags to head to Paris, with his father in tow, in July 1859.

However, like all good showbiz tales, there had to be a setback before the glory. Arriving in Paris, Jules got a bad case of nerves when he realized he was going to be performing in front of such a large and critical audience. Setting up his equipment in the arena, he felt, he says, that he was preparing his own funeral catafalque. Then, before he could overcome this stage fright, he was laid low by a bout of typhoid fever, which confined him to bed for a month, forcing his debut to be postponed, and during this time all of his muscles lost their tone. He returned to Toulouse to recuperate and lift his spirits and made a full recovery. Time for another handy—though this time generally less applicable—Léotard homily: "Make sure you never catch typhoid fever if you have something else to do."

His premiere in front of a Paris audience finally took place that November, at one of Déjean's other venues, the Cirque Napoléon, later renamed the Cirque d'Hiver, which still stands in the 11ème arrondissement. A plaque there records that on 12 November 1859 *"Ici Léotard créa l'art du trapèze volant."* The claim in his memoirs that he became King of the Trapeze at his first fell swoop was, in fact, true. He took the place by storm. No one had seen anything like this before.

Contraptions of various kinds from which athletes could dangle had been around for centuries. Stationary bars—the forerunners of the parallel bars in men's gymnastics—existed in Roman times and had been revived in the 1810s by Friedrich Jahn, a Prussian gym owner. There are also illustrations in calisthenics manuals from the 1820s of boys spinning from bars at the end of single ropes splaying out from the top of a kind of rotating maypole, and modestly clad maidens doing stretching exercises while holding a bar supported by two ropes coming from a single point on the ceiling (known from its shape as a triangle). There were also all manner of high wires, slack wires, rings and ropes on which acrobats could perform. The trapeze already existed: it was called the swing. When Jean-Honoré Fragonard captured its joy in his painting *The Happy Accidents of the Swing* in 1767 it was hardly a new idea.

Two German brothers, François and Auguste Siegrist, who performed in Paris and New York in the 1850s, were in the vanguard of the artists who turned the trapeze into an entertainment act and who constantly tried to outdo each other by increasing the danger quotient of their acts. Trapezes were suspended from hot air balloons. Performers teetered on top of chairs or ladders balanced on the bar of the trapeze. They supported the weight of half a dozen men hanging beneath them. All of this was performed without a net, genuinely death-defying stuff—for the balloon performers in particular it was a death that all too frequently could not be defied for long. What none of these artists did was to swing and jump from the trapeze. They climbed up to it by a rope or ladder and then performed their act on the trapeze. A Mancunian named Thomas Hanlon performed a routine called *"L'Echelle Périlleuse"* in which he jumped from a swinging bar to catch a rope or land in a net, but that was essentially a fancy dismount. What nobody ever disputed was that Jules was the first aerialist to jump and catch a swinging trapeze, and then to leap from one swinging trapeze to another, a piece of three-dimensional spatial awareness that required split-second timing and an iron nerve.

*

When Jules first performed the feat in Paris in November 1859 he very quickly made headlines and attracted a loyal coterie of female admirers—so much so that *Le Figaro* ran a long skit about *"Les Amoureuses de Léotard."* The tone of his abs, pecs and quads guaranteed that the seats at the Cirque Napoléon closest to his platform were filled by ardent fans. Once, when he was on the point of launching himself into a complex maneuver, he caught, out of the corner of his eye, a mêlée involving a blonde and a brunette, both going at each other hammer and tongs, either to get a better view or simply claiming precedence to his favors. The brunette, he noticed as he landed, delivered a punch to her rival that would have done justice to a champion boxer.

Later that night, as he often did after a show, Léotard nipped to a nearby boulevard café to wind down. The waiter approached him and told him that a lady wanted to speak to him. Jules was surprised: the only lady he knew in Paris, he said, was his laundress. Two women approached, one old and "wrinkled like a quince," the other hiding her face under a hood. It turned out she was the brawling brunette. Jules could only see her eyes, shining like a cat's. They asked if he would visit them at home. He apologized, saying he was "terribly busy." The women asked him just to promise he would visit them one day soon, but he turned them down again, perhaps a trifle too mockingly, because the old woman started grinding her teeth and the brunette flashed "tiger's eyes."

It marked the start of an onslaught from a prowling herd of horny Parisiennes. The cartoonist Durandeau depicted Jules swinging out high over the city's skyline while his fans, their tongues hanging out like bitches in heat, swung in pursuit or flew heart-shaped kites from the rooftops. Admirers dispatched their dandified gentlemen friends to sing their praises—Jules was disgusted by such pimping—and sent hundreds of letters that he derided in his book, the bulk of which is taken up with tales of his offhand treatment of their approaches and not, disappointingly, with descriptions either of his act or his costume. Coyly he never admits to any liaisons with any of his admirers, only allowing that he prefers blondes with brown eyes and brunettes with blue eyes: "I like eating melon in January, because it is more difficult to get hold of."

Though dismissive of his admirers—a disdain that, of course, merely propelled them to new and desperate attempts to attract his attention—Jules Léotard was extremely aware of the dynamics of showmanship and its effects on an audience. He wrote that he learned one very good lesson on one trip to London when he saw a poster put up by that consummate showman and huckster, P. T. Barnum. In capital letters, the poster announced that Barnum was "honored to inform his English brothers that in a public lecture he would tell them an honest and natural way of making a large amount of income by profiting from the stupidity of their peers."

The lecture was at Cheapside, admission one shilling; the place was packed. Barnum arrived on stage dressed in black suit and white tie, looking for all the world like an academic. He stared out at the audience, eager to learn how they could make a fast buck or at least a sprightly guinea or two. "Gentlemen," he told them, "there are 3,000 of you here. You have each paid a shilling to be here. If I give ten more lectures, you can work out the sums yourselves. I have nothing left to teach you . . ." His next words were drowned out by the uproar of 3,000 righteously indignant and highly embarrassed punters.

Léotard appreciated Barnum's sales and PR skills and quickly turned his own physical charms into a saleable item. Hence we find him developing the leotard, what Jules called his *"maillot,"* the French word for an undershirt or sports shirt, or—as in *maillot de bain*—a swimsuit.

There is no record of an original leotard on display in any theater museum collections, and there are hardly any photos of Jules wearing his leotard. Most show him in a variety of pseudo-classical loincloths or, in one instance, in a faintly Shakespearean doublet and hose. However, Charlie Holland—who runs the Circus Space, a circus school and training center in London—has collected what photos of Jules Léotard he has been able to find, and one of those does show what seems to be *the* leotard.

Jules, his hair on the long side and slicked back, is leaning nonchalantly against a balustrade in a photographer's studio, his feet—in leather booties—casually crossed. It looks as though he has a white one-piece body suit on underneath, covering his arms and legs. On top is a black belted leotard, with an extremely deep

V-neck, made of a material so fine it could be Lycra. This could have been a very fine wool, which circus strongmen of the time used for their outfits. The legs of the leotard are like shorts coming halfway down his thighs, and the ensemble immediately reminded me of a modern-day male sprinter's all-in-one. As Charlie Holland said to me as he showed me the photo, "He's quite the package."

For a contemporary description, there is a note by Arthur Munby, a British diarist, about one of Jules's London shows at the Alhambra in 1861. "Some thousands of people had gathered to see a man fling himself, in a highly dangerous & thrilling manner, from one swing to another across the building. The man himself, Léotard, was beautiful to look upon; being admirably made & proportioned; muscular arms shoulders & thighs; and calf, ankle and foot as elegantly turned as a lady's."

Georges Strehly, the French author of a 1904 book called *L'Acrobatie et les acrobates*, a work highly rated by circus professionals, also saw Jules Léotard perform. "It was my first time in Paris," Strehly says, "I knew nothing about the art of acrobatics, other than from the second-rate artists who toured the provinces." Jules was "a good-looking man, and much of his success was due to his physique: he had dark, curly hair, a pointed mustache, and was tall, slim, broad-shouldered and very muscular. He had something, a 'je ne sais quoi,' which in even the simplest of exercises picks out an artist of the highest class." Strehly also describes Jules's costume that night: the flesh-colored leggings and the all-in-one leotard, which was made, he thought, from black silk, "its deep V-neck showing off his bulging chest."

There was at the time much discussion about whether the physical charms Jules had on display were real or not. He reports that during one show he found his calves being tickled by two women. A satirical newspaper, *Le Tintamarre*, reported that a Léotard groupie, by virtue of dreaming about him, had given birth to a padded *maillot*. Jules complains sniffily about the journalists who have cast doubt on the *"sincérité de mon maillot."*

His looks spawned a mini merchandising operation. There were Léotard cravats, Léotard walking sticks, hairstyles and brooches. A Paris patisserie named one of its creations after him. And he was famous enough for Jules Verne in *Around the World in Eighty Days* to have Passepartout declare: "I've been an itinerant singer, a circus-rider, when I used to vault like Leotard, and dance on a rope like Blondin."

Following his London appearances—for which he got paid on one occasion £180 a week, half a year's pay for normal terrestrial beings—Dean & Son of Ludgate Hill published a movable book of famous acts. Card tabs made a paper Léotard swing in a half-thigh red leotard, as families of top-hatted gents, bonneted ladies and their children gazed from an arcaded gallery. The book also features Charles Blondin, who was appearing in Crystal Palace around the same time and who crossed Niagara Falls by tightrope a few months before Jules's flying trapeze debut. 1859 was a good year for aerialistic innovation.

A century and a half later, the Léotard family was preparing to celebrate the anniversary of Jules's leap that year. I had not come across any written account of any Léotard descendants, but Pauline Palacy, the trapeze instructor at the Circus Space, put me in touch with Michèle Pachany, who I was told was one of his relatives. When I called her at her summer home in Nice, she shocked me by revealing that she was in fact a direct descendant, his great-great-granddaughter: her maiden name was Léotard. She said that Jules had in fact been married and that he had had two children—one out of wedlock; facts that were rarely mentioned and certainly were not part of the general knowledge about his life. Her family had never, surprisingly, talked much about Jules, and she was going back through the notes in his memoirs, trying to check the facts they contained.

Michèle told me one story she had come across about Jules

visiting St. Petersburg in 1861. He had been invited to perform at the court of the tsar, but as he prepared to put on his leotard, the Russian general in charge of protocol intervened, explaining that it would not be appropriate for him to appear before the tsarina in such a revealing outfit. Instead, Jules would have to wear a formal black suit, complete with white gloves—he did somehow manage to complete his act, but tore the suit to pieces in the process. It highlighted the difference between the traditional, formal nature of a gentleman's attire of the day and Jules's free-form approach to dress. "He was really ahead of his time," Michèle said. "He appreciated the body as something of beauty."

Despite his international success, Jules's time at the top was limited. Within weeks of his appearance at the Alhambra in London other artists were copying his act and improving it. I only found out later on that he performed not far off the ground, and that he also had a padded platform underneath. Danger was not his selling point; it was the lateral midair flight using three and sometimes more trapezes (and of course that hunky body) that attracted the crowds. Richard Beri and James Leach, appearing at the Alhambra shortly after Jules, added an extra somersault to the flight between trapezes. Niblo the Flying Man added two. The Hanlon Brothers from Manchester traveled to see Léotard's show and devised their own version, the "Zampillaerostation," to rival his act. One of the first female copyists, Azella, dubbed herself "the Female Leotard" in 1868, the year Jules went to America.

By the time he arrived there, to perform at the Academy of Music in New York City in 1868, he was already old hat. His once innovative techniques had been superseded, though few if any matched his grace or ease of movement. Even the reviewer from the *New York Clipper*, who called his act "mediocre," described how he landed "as lightly as a bird" back on his platform after flying across the auditorium. But times were moving on. Steve Gossard, the circus historian, calls the back end of the 19th century the era of Reckless Invention. Soon any trapeze act worth seeing would need to incorporate multiple back somersaults or at least an element of freakery. In the 1870s there were performances by a one-legged trapeze artist, Frank Melrose, and by William W. Quillins, who had lost both legs.

By then Jules Léotard was dead, felled by an epidemic of small-pox in 1870, aged thirty-two, guaranteed an image untainted by raddled, arthritic old age and spared the fate of Thomas Hanlon, one of the Hanlon Brothers, who had fallen in a bad accident in 1865 and was unable to perform again. Sitting on the sidelines watching the aerial innovations he could not take part in, he sank into a deep depression and committed suicide in 1868. As Georges Strehly wrote in *L'Acrobatie et les acrobates*: "The life of an acrobat is a dream, sometimes brilliant, but always fleeting."

*

The leotard lived on. It found its way into the ballet world (Nijinsky apparently caused the tsarina of Russia to have a faint-ing fit when he appeared onstage in a leotard without the pair of shorts male dancers used to wear over them), and there the leotard remained, until a flourish of activity brought it into the mainstream in the late 1970s and early 1980s.

The music business started things rolling. The classic 1970s leotard was a Danskin, whose creative director, Bonnie August, used Lycra spandex in the fabric for extra snugness. On the cover of Fleetwood Mac's *Rumors*, Stevie Nicks appeared in black leotard, ballet shoes and a Margi Kent dress. Kate Bush single-bodiedly brought the leotard to the attention of a generation of sweaty late-1970s adolescents, to the point where Pamela Stephenson, in her *Not the Nine o'Clock News* days, parodied her in a song that pastiched "Them Heavy People" and "Oh, England, My Lionheart" as "Oh, England, My Leotard": "People bought my latest hits/'Cos they liked my latex tits/Everyone trying hard/To get inside my leotard, leotard, leotard . . ."

Linda *"Exorcist"* Blair wore one in the movie of *Roller Boogie*. And then Jane Fonda's workout videos took things to a whole new level, her headband-leotard-and-leggings look dominating exercise studios for the rest of the decade. Olivia Newton-John followed suit for the video of "Physical," and Jennifer Beals splashed out in *Flashdance*. Flo-Jo moved the leotard outdoors onto the athletics track, and Donna Karan even came up with a version that could be worn in the boardroom. And, in the spirit of Jules, the males in the entertainment industry reclaimed the leotard for their gender. Freddie Mercury pranced around at Live Aid in white, and even heavy metal rockers like David Lee Roth found them perfectly macho.

The leotard was now set in the cyclical pattern of fashion, a cycle that began again in 2006 when Madonna tapped into a seam of 1970s nostalgia and wore a leotard for that year's Grammy Awards. However, one of the enduring images for viewers of Britain's *Celebrity Big Brother* in 2006—and one that may have finished the leotard as a fashion item for some time to come—was of the dissident, if not downright maverick, MP George Galloway clad in a gut-clenchingly tight red leotard, attempting to perform a robotic dance illustrating "the slight feeling of bewilderment when a small puppy won't come to you when called." Ah, the dignity of public office.

If George Galloway has not terminally ended its career, the leotard will continue to hang in the wardrobe of eponymous clothing, up there alongside Amelia Jenks Bloomer's baggy panties and the Earl of Cardigan's woolly jacket. The earl would, I suspect, hate to have ended up preserved not as the blusterous military leader of the Crimean War but as an item of middle-of-the-road leisurewear (another Crimean commander lent his name to the raglan sleeve and overcoat).

*

I once tried my hand at the flying trapeze. It was part of a Christmas present, a thoughtful and original one: an afternoon's course at Charlie Holland's Circus Space. From time to time the school offers the chance for the less than genuinely daring to shake off some lethargy and try out a number of disciplines. On the day I went along, just after the New Year, they were offering acrobatic balancing, juggling (with bowler hats, almost impossible), a fixed trapeze and, the highlight for everybody there, the chance to swing on a flying trapeze. After working round the other activities and coming to regret the excesses of the holiday period—dangling from the fixed trapeze I felt very much like a Victorian plum pudding suspended from the ceiling—it was time to climb up to the flying trapeze. Clambering up an awkward ladder I stood on the platform, which was only 15 feet or so off the ground, but wobbled, and there was nothing much to hang on to. Although there was a net below, and mats below that, it was still alarming and unnatural.

With a final deep breath, I launched myself into the void, quitting all earthly bounds. As I swung, imagining myself in flight, I caught the sound of somebody shouting from below, an encouraging "Bravo!" I thought. They shouted again. This time I listened. It was the instructor yelling at me, "Breathe!!!" Something that in the excitement and tension of the moment I'd completely forgotten to do. For the short time it lasted, before the muscles on my arms and in my hands gripping the trapeze could take no more, it was extraordinarily exhilarating. I clambered back up the apparatus and had another go—only this time I remembered not only to breathe, but also a line from Burt Lancaster in his 1956 movie *Trapeze*: "When circus was real, flying was a religion." Amen to that.

CHAPTER 7

When Oscar Met Tony

"When the Academy called I panicked. I thought they
might want their Oscars back, and the pawnshop has been
out of business awhile."
Woody Allen at the 2002 Academy Awards

There are two Oscar photos I love. In one, Helen Mirren, freshly
crowned as the Queen of Hollywood in 2007, is chowing down on
a burger, sleeves rolled up, defiantly nonestablishment, while her
Oscar, like a prim Jeeves, looks on with an arched eyebrow. The
other is authentic Hollywood: Terry O'Neill's photograph of his
future wife Faye Dunaway on the morning after she picked up the
1976 Best Actress award for her role in *Network*. She is reclining on
a chair next to the swimming pool at the Beverly Hills Hotel, in
vertiginously high-heeled evening shoes and a silk gown of . . . I
want to say ecru and not beige. In the background the poolside
loungers are neatly aligned under yellow and white awnings. The
morning papers proclaiming her success have been artlessly flung
around her feet and on a table by her side. Faye is staring in
admiration or puzzlement or fatigue—it's hard to tell—at the
Oscar that stands by her breakfast tray. The shot may have been
staged (in fact I'm sure it was), but it's still glorious. Despite its
size, the Oscar dominates the photo.

The statuette, designed by MGM's art director Cedric
Gibbons, sculpted by George Stanley and first awarded in 1929,
is instantly recognizable throughout the world, I would hazard.
MGM scriptwriter Frances Marion (an Academy Award winner
in 1932, for Best Story with *The Champ*) came up with one of
the best descriptions of its looks: "A powerful athletic body

clutching a gleaming sword with half of his head, that part which held his brains, completely sliced off."

The award's very lack of personality—its expression inscrutable, even its masculine muscularity oddly androgynous—allows it to merge, Zelig-like, with any winner. And, of course, the statuette's shape is so handy for carrying in the limo to all those post-Oscar parties, a convenient-size chum to chat to: you're never alone with an Oscar. Clutched nonchalantly in the beefy grasp of overexcited producers or acting as chaperone for fragrant Best Actresses, Oscar is always the center of attention.

Yet although the statuette is eminently identifiable, the Oscar who provided its name is, well . . . no one is too sure. In fact, the origins of the Oscar's name are swathed in uncertainty. My interest was particularly piqued when I read one lexicographical source which stated that the mystery surrounding the naming of the Oscar was worthy in itself of a Hollywood screenplay.

There are three theories about who Oscar was. At some point Bette Davis, a double Oscar winner (for *Dangerous* and *Jezebel*), who was for a while the president of AMPAS, the Academy of Motion Picture Arts and Sciences, which bestows and administers the awards, claimed she had named the award. The middle name of her first husband, the singer and band leader Harmon Nelson Jr., was Oscar, and she said that the statuette reminded her of his physique. Her tongue-in-cheek claim, though highly unlikely, at least has a refreshing lack of pomposity.

Another theory and one that on the face of it has more plausibility comes from the late Hollywood journalist Sidney Skolsky. He claimed, vociferously and on numerous occasions, that he had been responsible for inventing the nickname Oscar. Skolsky was a New York refugee, a smart, gossipy, wisecracking entertainment journalist, who had cut his showbiz teeth as the Broadway columnist for the *New York Daily News* before heading west in the wake of all those Tinseltown hopefuls.

He reckoned that after one particularly lengthy awards

ceremony in 1934 he had headed back to his office to write up the event, and—unable to spell the word "statuette," and with the local sub-editor equally stumped—he had come up with the term Oscar, both to personalize the event and to annoy the people at the awards dinner, who in his view had been "acting high and mighty." Why Oscar? Well, he referred to an old vaudeville routine in which a pair of comics would teasingly pretend to offer the pit orchestra conductor a cigar with the words "Will you have a cigar, Oscar?" only to snatch it back before the conductor could take it. Hardly side-splitting stuff. Still, that was Sidney's story, and he stuck to it doggedly, repeating it forty years later in an entertaining mid-1970s memoir, *Don't Get Me Wrong—I Love Hollywood*. "I gave the gold statuette a name," he wrote. "I wanted to make it human." (He also took the opportunity to pooh-pooh Bette Davis's claim.)

The flaw in Sidney Skolsky's version is that he very specifically referred to first mentioning the Oscar in an article in March 1934, which I was able to track down. In the middle of one of his typical insider's columns is a coyly knowing mention that "although Katharine Hepburn wasn't present to receive her Oscar, her constant companion and the gal she resides with in Hollywood, Laura Harding, was there to hear Hepburn get a round of applause for a change." The use of Oscar, without qualification or explanation, suggested to me that the name was in fact already in common parlance, otherwise why use the word? And this was the article on which Skolsky based his claim. Case dismissed.

The third theory, and the one that the Academy of Motion Picture Arts and Sciences itself has allowed to persist since at least the mid-1940s, is that the name derived from the uncle of one of its employees, Margaret Herrick.

In essence, this particular story goes as follows: joining the AMPAS staff in the 1930s and being "introduced" on her first day at work to the statuette, Margaret Herrick declared: "It looks just like my Uncle Oscar." And thenceforth, so it is said, the name stuck. So far, so good. But there is much more to this than such a flippant story suggests.

Margaret Herrick is a central character, not just in this story, but also in the history of the Academy of Motion Picture Arts and Sciences. The "Oscar" remark was the throwaway line of a woman who became a genuine player in Hollywood politics. Although she joined AMPAS as a relatively junior librarian, she became the organization's executive secretary—effectively its CEO—for nearly thirty years, from the mid-1940s to the early 1970s. She was an unsung woman pioneer in a male enclave. And, pertinently for this story, she not only presided over the consolidation of the Academy's activities and finances, but she personally negotiated a deal with NBC in 1951 to televise the presentation of the awards, a deal that rescued the ceremony from the near-extinction it had often been threatened with in the previous decade. It is a wonderful happenstance that Margaret Herrick should be the woman at the heart of the Oscar mystery, and her story deserves further explanation.

★

To learn more about Margaret Herrick, the place to start, fittingly, was the Academy's Margaret Herrick Library, housed in the Douglas Fairbanks Center on South La Cienega Boulevard in Beverly Hills, a striking mission-style building that looks as if it might once have been a church but in fact turns out to have been the sometime waterworks building for the city of Beverly Hills. Heading down there, I remembered a line from Raymond Chandler: "Who was Beverly, and why was everything in this town named after her?" (In fact, the name was chosen by the area's property developers in the 1900s, a direct lift from Beverly Farms in Massachusetts, President W. H. Taft's vacation spot.)

From the lobby of the old waterworks building one doorway heads off to the Roddy McDowall photo archive, while the

Herrick Library and its Katharine Hepburn and Cecil B. DeMille reading rooms are reached via the sweep of the Kirk Douglas stairway. In the main reading room, where a warm December afternoon light suffused the shelves, I started to piece together a few shreds of evidence in the hope of gaining some understanding of who Margaret Herrick was and who Oscar might have been.

I was helped enormously by *Femme Boss*, a masters thesis written by Anne Coco, one of the library staff, which examined Margaret Herrick's life and career in the context of her particular generation of Hollywood career women.

Margaret's path to the Academy was via librarianship. Born in Spokane, Washington, she had taken a library degree at the University of Washington, after which she worked at the Yakima Public Library, but she contracted a disease, possibly meningitis or typhoid, and took some time out to recuperate in San Francisco. There she met and married Donald Gledhill, who, in 1929, was hired as press officer for the fledgling Academy of Motion Picture Arts and Sciences. The Academy had been founded in 1927 as, ostensibly, a cross-industry body bringing together studio bosses with directors, writers, actors and technicians, although it was frequently perceived as a studio-led organization with only a cursory nod in the direction of the other branches.

By the time Donald Gledhill and his wife moved to Los Angeles, the Academy was already preparing to hand out its new awards. Somewhere in the small print of its constitution had been buried a commitment to create awards honoring excellence in the film business, and the statuettes were first presented at a dinner in the Blossom Room of the Hollywood Roosevelt Hotel on Hollywood Boulevard in May 1929.

Margaret started helping out at the Academy in an informal way. Using her library experience, she gave some order to a collection of trade magazines and movie books that AMPAS had amassed. Her famous remark about "Uncle Oscar" is attributed to her in 1931, but she was not formally logged as an employee in the Academy's records until 1936. By then Donald Gledhill had lost his job as press officer but had been rehired as executive secretary. Four years later Margaret was recognized as the Academy's official, though still unpaid, librarian, with two assistants to help her out—and by this time the word "Oscar" was already being used officially by the Academy. Later I came across a reply she had sent in the 1950s to the editors at Merriam-Webster saying that she regretted what she described as a "thoughtless quip": "The Academy loses something in dignity every time the statuette is referred to as Oscar."

War intervened. In 1943 Donald Gledhill was drafted as a captain in the Army Signal Corps and sent to Washington, D.C. Two significant events occurred. In her husband's absence, the Academy—recognizing her administrative skills—appointed Margaret Herrick as his temporary replacement. (The title of Anne Coco's thesis was drawn from a *Variety* newspaper headline reporting this: "Academy Gets Femme Boss as Gledhill Joins Army.") When the war ended AMPAS, remarkably, did not give Donald his old job back but kept her in place. And while Donald was in Washington, D.C., he had become involved with another woman. The Gledhills divorced, and in 1946 Margaret remarried, her new husband a salesman named Philip Herrick.

From here on the Academy was her life. In his official history of the Oscars, Robert Osborne quotes Frank Capra as saying "she was the Academy's alter ego," and she relinquished her grasp on the organization only in 1971 when ill health forced her to. The job gave her a high profile in the movie business. It provided her with a significant salary: in 1950 she was being paid $21,000 a year, at a time when the average salary, male or female, was just over $3,300. And it meant her private life was public fodder. When she and Philip Herrick divorced the papers ran the story in detail (including her salary). Anne Coco wonders how many male executives of the time would have undergone the same kind of scrutiny.

Although she worked in the right location, had the correct credentials and access to material that the general public, including me, could not reach, Anne Coco told me she had experienced great problems trying to glean much personal information about Margaret Herrick. She found it extraordinary that so little was available on such a significant figure.

Two of Margaret Herrick's former colleagues were still alive at the time Anne Coco wrote her thesis in the mid-1990s: Margaret's longtime assistant Lois Hanby and Jim Roberts, her successor as chief executive. Both declined to talk. In fact Anne could not even get Jim Roberts on the phone. "His wife put the kibosh on any chance of an interview. That made me cross. I wasn't trying to dig up any skeletons. I just wanted to know what she was like. It was like trying to penetrate a ring of steel, but I didn't get a sense it was to spite me. They were old school, from a time when employees did nothing but protect their bosses and colleagues."

Lois Hanby told Anne that in any case there was no hope of finding any personal material, admitting that after Margaret Herrick's death in 1976 "she and a neighbor had gone through her belongings and trashed everything."

Any personal glimpses that did survive came from some lecture notes Margaret had written in 1952 for a speech she gave to the students of the women-only Stephens College in Missouri and from Richard Dunlap, the producer of thirteen of the Academy Awards. He was prepared to share his memories and spoke warmly of Margaret Herrick, although he made it clear that he knew her as an executive first and foremost. Tantalizingly, the lecture notes included a remark from Margaret that she would have liked to write an autobiography called *From Where I Sit*; any evidence of whether she ever got to start the book in her retirement disappeared in the trash.

This lack of real information is frustrating because it is clear that although Margaret Herrick was fiercely proud and protective of the Academy—"a tough-as-nails gal, and had to be," as Anne

Coco put it—she was no corporate apparatchik. A college yearbook photo of the then Miss Margaret Buck showed a girl with dark curly hair and a natural smile, which was evident in later photos. In 1941 Hollywood's *Citizen News* called her a "pretty, flashing-eyed young woman."

She might have been a *femme boss* but she was also a feminine boss. In her notes for her college audience she had written that she did not like the "aggressive, bristling Amazonian type of woman who devotes herself to proving that she can be tougher and more masculine than any man in the place." She enjoyed music and clothes, and her great passion was gardening. The writer Daniel Taradash, who delivered the eulogy at her funeral in 1976 (she died in the Motion Picture Country Home in Woodland Hills), said she tended her garden, of camellias, roses and cymbidiums in the same way she had tended the Academy— in total control.

Taradash, the Oscar-winning scriptwriter of *From Here to Eternity*, also told the congregation, "The news reports said 'there are no immediate survivors.' That is a factual error. We are all symbolic relatives." But the basic fact was correct; there were no children of either of Margaret Herrick's marriages. Given the silence of her ex-colleagues and the unrealized autobiography, there was not much left to go on.

If Margaret Herrick was a cipher, then so too was Uncle Oscar. I amassed what clues I could to his identity by filleting the Academy's clippings. I suspected that no one had spent time approaching the clippings from the point of view of the name, and I hoped I could tease out a few fresh angles. One source was a written reply from John LeRoy Johnston, director of press relations for Walter Wanger Productions, to a query about the naming of the Oscar from the *Spokane Daily Chronicle* in 1941. He suggested that a journalist had overheard Margaret and Donald Gledhill talking about an Uncle Oscar and had assumed they were talking about the statuette.

A clipping from the *Motion Picture Almanac* of 1947–8 went into greater detail. The article repeated the story of Margaret Herrick's first day at work and her introduction to the statuette as the "foremost member of the organization." But the writer had gone on to conduct some broader research and revealed that Oscar was not her uncle, but a second cousin, the first cousin of Margaret Herrick's mother Adda Buck, née Morie. He was named Oscar Pierce, "of a wealthy western pioneer family," formerly living in Texas, where he had "done well" in wheat and fruit and retired to California.

There was a stop press addendum: "Last reports from the Almanac's Find Oscar Expedition, received at press time, indicated that Mr. Oscar Pierce was, if extant, living in or near Oakland, California, and somewhere in the region of eighty years of age. Mrs. Herrick disclaims any marked resemblance between Oscar and Uncle Oscar, and admits now her history-making words were voiced in utter whimsy. Lots of history is made this way."

Since then authors and commentators had fleshed out Oscar based on these tidbits. Oscar was "a Texas wheat farmer of dignity, austerity and commanding authority," wrote one. Philip Howard, in *The Times*, expanded that to "a Texan pioneer who made a fortune from wheat and fruit, and retired to California to bask in sun and eponymous glory." But no one had checked out the genealogy.

Among the Academy's clippings I found one piece that threw a little more light on the matter. It was a copy of *The Canyon Crier*, a kind of broadsheet newsletter for residents of the Hollywood Hills. In March 1949 their reporter had headed out—"paddled out" he said—to Margaret and Philip Herrick's house at 3466 La Sombra Drive, on "a raw night when we whipped up the brick steps of the Herricks and into their tall stately home, pleasantly furnished with some antiques, lots of camellias, which are Mrs. Herrick's hobby, and wirehaired terriers," the latter called Charles and Cee Cee.

Over a scotch and soda, "we sat down beside the fire, where Mrs. Herrick, pumps tucked under her, and brown eyes level and candid, told us with an incisive air all about the Academy and 'Oscar.'" The story about that first day at work was repeated, but the article continued: " 'Although,' says Mrs. Herrick in mortification, "while I had an Uncle Oscar, I'd never seen him.' "

If that was true, what a bizarre remark to have made when she was first shown the statuette. It seemed strange that this name, which has acquired such immortality and such patina, was totally random. But here she was fifteen years later, six years into her tenancy as boss of the Academy, repeating the story and adding more details. She confirmed that Oscar lived in Texas, and went on: "The one time I did meet him was at a funeral in Long Beach some time later, when a distinguished, white-haired Texan presented himself and said with a faintly aggrieved air, "*I am your Uncle Oscar.*' "

Apart from this there were no other sightings of Oscar. In his memoir Sidney Skolsky had dismissed the claims of both Bette Davis and Margaret Herrick. "I don't like to argue with women, especially when they're talented and friends . . . I have yet to see a photograph of Uncle Oscar Pierce." Maybe he had a point.

I decided to try and find Oscar Pierce. If we could prove he ever existed, then one uncertainty would be removed. I enlisted the help of Connie Lenzen, a hugely experienced genealogist based in Portland, Oregon, and presented her with the fragments, shards, gleanings and rumors that I had uncovered, including Margaret Herrick's biographical information; her mother Adda (with two ds) Buck's birth and death dates and burial plot in Lewiston, Idaho; her father, Nathan Buck's, too. I told her that Margaret had been adopted by Nathan and Adda in 1902, and that her mother had also been an alumna of the University of Washington. I threw in what little was known of "Uncle Oscar." And I moved onto other things, specifically looking for the origins of the Tony Awards.

Naming awards after people has become a common activity. Perhaps humanizing a trophy makes it seem more personal and less portentous. The Society of West End Theatre's awards were known by the unfortunate, though probably quite accurate, nickname of the SWET awards until 1984, when they were rebranded in tribute to the then still extant Larry Olivier. France's national cinema awards are called the Césars, after the sculptor César Baldaccini, who designed a somewhat baroque, scrapyard-style, crushed metal trophy. The Mystery Writers of America, perhaps more predictably, offer the Edgar Allan Poe awards, the Edgars for short.

However, unexpectedly, the Emmys, which "recognize excellence" in U.S. TV production, are not named after anybody but after a thing, "Emmy" being a deliberate humanization—specifically a feminization—of the term "immy," which was the nickname given to image orthicons, the tubes central to television cameras throughout the 1950s and 1960s.

Then there are the Darwins, internet-driven awards for people who have died in unbelievably dumb ways, or as the founders of the Darwins put it so well, "honoring those who improve the species . . . by accidentally removing themselves from it!" The winners in 2006—all of whom had wholeheartedly and fatally embraced the organizers' mantra that "the tree of life is self-pruning"—included the Brazilian who tried to destroy a self-propelled grenade by repeatedly driving over it in a car, possibly to salvage the scrap metal it contained, and, when that failed, attacked the grenade with a sledgehammer, which did work, blasting himself and several cars to kingdom come.

And there are, of course, the Tony Awards, America's premier theatrical awards. Just as with Oscar, I wanted to find out who this particular Tony was.

*

My quest for Tony began with a dead end. But it was a good dead end to start with: Woodlawn, the northern terminus of New York's number 4 subway, the line that snakes its way up from the heart of Manhattan toward the Bronx. I caught a train at Lexington and 57th and watched the street numbers tick up through the double figures and into the hundreds.

The terminus at Woodlawn was quaint. The track entered the station between russet ironwork pillars holding up the eaves of a pitched roof. It reminded me of stations on miniature railways, like the Romney, Hythe & Dymchurch that still putters along the Kent coast. An exuberant sun, unshrouded in a brilliant blue sky, added to what felt like a festive mood.

I had come to Woodlawn to find the grave of Antoinette Perry, Tony Perry, the woman after whom the Tonys are named. Since there seemed to be very few relics of her life left other than the existence of the awards, I wanted to start with one fixed point, her tombstone.

I do like a good cemetery. As my wife can confirm, I will go a long way for a good grave. On holidays our itinerary often includes a rather large deviation to take in a particular tomb. So over the years I have stood in front of John Belushi's memorial, a powerful, squat slab of stone on the gently rolling slope of Martha's Vineyard's southern shore, a single word chiseled into its face: "BELUSHI." I have found tranquillity at Westwood Cemetery in the heart of Los Angeles, where Marilyn Monroe's final resting place was marked—on the day I went there—by a single red rose. I have taken the waterbus to Venice's Isola di San Michele, where the graves of Diaghilev and Stravinsky glitter. I can appreciate the ornateness of their tombs as much as the restrained formality of François Mitterrand's family sepulchre in Jarnac, or the simple headstones of Dylan and Caitlin Thomas, side by side in some final peace on the hilltop in Laugharne.

Woodlawn is one of New York's great cemeteries, a serious cemetery. Vast, rolling landscapes. Broad avenues and clusters of hillsides, each area named after a shrub or a tree. Woodlawn is quiet, calm, majestic, a distant hum from the streets outside; somewhere a love song sang from a passing car window. It is the end of the line for thousands of its inhabitants, incomers and immigrants, the merchants, entrepreneurs, artisans and laborers who supplied the energy that gave the city its backbone. Scattered across its acres were the kind of memorials designed to last: obelisks Cleopatra would have been flattered by, mausoleums that proclaimed wealth, prosperity and endurance.

Antoinette Perry was buried on Hickory Knoll. A handy chart provided by a warden at the entrance gates marked the graves of the great, the good, the filthy rich and the glamorous. I gently spiraled toward Hickory Knoll, taking in, out of personal interest, some of the writers, musicians and composers who inhabit Woodlawn: Damon Runyon, Irving Berlin, W. C. Handy, "the father of the blues," Coleman Hawkins—a particular favorite, whose sax duets with Ben Webster had been one of my first introductions to jazz as a teenager. Miles Davis, "Sir Miles," has a snazzy, gleaming black block just across the way from a very modest plaque for Duke Ellington. (At the time I thought, "Cool. Duke didn't want any fuss," but I later learned that the stone was only temporary while a family wrangle over funding for the real thing rumbled on.)

I pottered further. Antoinette Perry did not feature on the chart of celebrated graves. I wandered around Hickory Knoll without success, and it crossed my mind that I might never find her tomb. I looped back over one last crest—and there it was. A small, plain, oblong slab lying flat in the grass. Her name and dates, 1888–1946, in an unfussy serif typeface. And by its side a small Stars and Stripes.

*

I heard Antoinette Perry's name again, unexpectedly, only a couple of days later. I had gone to see *Infamous*, the "other"

Truman Capote movie, which came out a year after Philip Seymour Hoffman's Oscar-winning performance in *Capote*. Toby Jones's impish Truman was regaling his New York coterie—the women he dubbed his "swans," Diana Vreeland, Babe Paley, Slim Keith—with details of the Kansas killings that triggered *In Cold Blood* and recounting his encounters with the two murderers, Dick Hickock and Perry Smith. Marella Agnelli interrupts, "Tell us about Dick and Terry." "No," says Truman, slightly piqued. "It's *Perry*. Like Antoinette."

I wondered just how many people in that cinema on Broadway had picked up on the reference. Not many, I imagine. And I was sure it would have been missed by virtually everyone in a non-American audience watching the movie—a month earlier it would have gone over my head too—and by a hefty slice of U.S. moviegoers.

Very few people know anything much about Antoinette Perry. A rare exception is a Broadway observer and journalist named Ellis Nassour. I met up with Ellis on his home turf one Saturday night; he suggested that I join him to see a new play that had been drafted in from London to a residency at the Biltmore Theatre. It was grim. The laughs that must have been razor-smart in North London fell flat in New York; the audience was edgy and bored. During the first act Ellis had tapped the shoulder of a chap chatting away in the row in front of us and asked him to be quiet. Come the intermission, the culprit, a silver-haired, raw-boned dude who looked like an ex-oilman and certainly looked like he wanted a fight, turned around and tried to pick one ("he's five martinis to the wind," another theatergoer confided). "At least," I said to Ellis as we escaped to the bar, "we finally got some drama."

Ellis told me how he had become an expert on Antoinette Perry. He had been asked to research an article for the program to accompany one of the Tony Awards ceremonies and to answer the perennial question about the origin of the name. "If people thought anything, it was that the awards were called the Tonys because Broadway was ritzy, it had tone, it was 'toney,'" he said.

Antoinette Perry was one of Broadway's great personalities, a distinguished Broadway director and producer, a pioneering woman in both fields at a time when work for women behind the scenes in theater was generally confined to set design or choreography. She had also been a reasonably successful ingénue, who had at the age of fifteen joined a touring theater company run by an uncle. She once wrote, "I wanted to be an actress as soon as I could lisp," and although no one ever claimed she had great talent she possessed a spark and a charm that served her well. As a young actress she caught the eye of the great theater impresario David Belasco, who, according to Ellis Nassour, "had the hots for her."

She was not a classic American beauty. Her skin, commented everyone, was like porcelain, as if she rarely stepped outside to confront the elements. A portrait of her in her twenties shows a delicate, though determined, blond-curled woman in a rather sumptuous Gainsborough-style velvet hat and coat.

As it happened, concern with appearance directly affected the naming of the awards. Antoinette had generally answered to the diminutive Toni. But toward the end of her life a range of home-perm hair products was launched under the brand name Toni and heavily promoted—the company ran ads with the tagline "Which twin has the Toni?" Toni Perry was upset by this—perhaps she thought it was dumbing down her identity—and changed her name to Tony.

Antoinette was from Denver. Her family was well ensconced in Colorado; her grandparents had a homestead in the state's high central grasslands, at South Park (yes, the original one), and the family had money. But in 1909 she married someone even wealthier, Frank Frueauff, a Denver gas and electricity tycoon. The couple spent months in Europe on honeymoon, and their home in New York was an elaborate apartment on Fifth Avenue. Her husband wanted Antoinette to be a housewife and hostess, and for a while she took time out from the theater, raising two daughters.

However, her passion for the theater—"I'm just a fool for theater" was one of her catchphrases—resurfaced in 1920 when she was persuaded by a former press agent named Brock Pemberton to become an angel for his production of the play *Miss Lulu Bett*. It marked the start of a personal and business relationship between her and Brock that lasted most of her life. Brock remained married, but the affair was no great secret within their circle. Shortly after they met, Antoinette was widowed when her husband died of a heart attack in 1922, leaving an estate worth $13 million, a gigantic sum, and making her one of the wealthiest independent women in the States. She proved a savvy investor, and the money helped fund her and Brock's theatrical ventures. Together they produced and directed plays from offices next to the Imperial Theater on Broadway.

She returned to acting. Brock produced her in a play called *The Ladder* in 1926, which ran for eighteen months—back then a run considered as lengthy as *Phantom* or *Cats*—but a stroke curtailed her acting career, and she turned to directing. In 1929 she and Brock demonstrated their eye for a hit with *Strictly Dishonorable*, an early success for Preston Sturges, who went on to screenwrite *The Power and the Glory* and *The Lady Eve* and pursue a directorial career. Movie rights in the play were sold, and Antoinette and Brock continued to survive the hard times of the 1930s with smashes like *Kiss the Boys Goodbye*, a Scarlett O'Hara–style quest to find a leading actress.

One of the last plays Antoinette directed was 1944's *Harvey*. The writer, her friend Mary Coyle Chase, another Denver native, won a Pulitzer Prize for her script, beating off Tennessee Williams's *The Glass Menagerie*. The movie version with James Stewart as Elwood P. Dowd was directed by Henry Koster, who—according to those who saw both the stage version and the movie—directed it exactly as Antoinette had done on stage.

Alongside the directing, Antoinette produced. Although she might have appeared delicate, she was a tough, no-nonsense gal, and she had to be. She was "very loud, a yeller, not at all prim and proper," says Ellis Nassour, who believes she has never received sufficient credit for her pioneering work as a woman producer, far more important in his view than her role as a director.

She was also a generous benefactor. During the Depression she helped out actors, actresses and writers in financial hardship. In the Second World War she cofounded the Theater Wing of Allied Relief, later the American Theater Wing. Sondra Gilman, its current chair—and herself a Tony-nominated producer—told me that she was "a real Santa Claus, giving money to playwrights, paying actors' rent. The American Theater Wing started up the Stage Door Canteen, where movie stars would wait on tables, or cook in the kitchen, and service men and women could come and eat for free." And when actors who had been away on active service returned, the Theater Wing set up scholarships to support them.

Antoinette's largesse extended to herself: she had a ferocious gambling habit. During board meetings of the American Theater Wing, her secretary would come up and whisper the races to her, and she would place a bet in the middle of the agenda.

Her relationship with Brock Pemberton eventually cooled, but they continued working together and remained confidants. Ellis Nassour had tracked down one of Antoinette's daughters, Margaret, a former actress in her mother's plays, who had fled from the world of theater to return to the wilds of Colorado, back in South Park. To contact her Ellis had to leave a message at the general supply store. Margaret would head out to the store at an appointed time, sit next to the stove, pick up the store phone and reminisce about her mother.

"What touched me," said Ellis, "is that Margaret remembered Brock would call Tony every night. The girls would be doing their homework, the phone would ring. "Oh, it's Uncle Brock for you." Brock and Tony would talk, Tony would hang up and then go to bed. It was a beautiful, beautiful relationship and partnership." Margaret also recalled her mother's appetite for the theater, at one point running three productions simultaneously and directing rehearsals in their Fifth Avenue apartment "while peeling peaches for preserves." Margaret died in April 2007, and in an obituary posted by *Playbill* I noticed that one of her own four children was called Antoinette, known as Toni with an i.

Antoinette suffered heart problems, but she was a committed Christian Scientist and refused medical intervention, continuing to plow on with her work as a producer and director and running the American Theater Wing. She died the day after her 58th birthday in June 1946, apparently deeply in debt and subsisting on the royalties from *Harvey*—perhaps her gambling had taken its toll.

After her death, Brock, Jacob Wilk, a story editor at Warner Bros., and the theatrical producer John Golden—who shared a regular table at Sardi's, Broadway's famed restaurant—talked about honoring Antoinette with an evening of awards. They took the idea to the American Theater Wing, and they thought it was a wonderful idea. The first awards ceremony was held at the Waldorf Astoria in 1947, a low-scale, elegant event, with awards in the form of scrolls, along with small gifts of engraved cigarette cases, lighters, money clips and compacts. Brock, whose appraisal of his former lover was as "an individualist who met life head on, who dramatized life, and gave of a generous nature," presented an award, and described it as "a Tony."

Two years later a contest to design a permanent award was won by the Dutch-born theater and film designer Herman Rosse. His proposal was the medallion, featuring the masks of comedy and tragedy on one face, and a profile of Antoinette Perry on the other, which is still presented, now mounted on a crescent-shaped stand. On the medallion, Sondra Gilman, the American Theater Wing chair, told me, Antoinette's full name is inscribed.

In the sixty years since then the Tonys have become one of theater's highest accolades. And a tribute to a woman, who, like Margaret Herrick at the Academy of Motion Picture Arts and Sciences—was battling against the prejudices of the time.

To reinforce the point, Sondra told me a story from her own experience in the theater business. "In the early 1980s I was trying to produce a show. I would walk into an office looking to raise the money, all men. They would have coffee sent in, and wait for me to pour it for them . . ."

★

One night, months later, returning home at 2 A.M. after a delayed flight, I flipped through my stash of e-mails. There was one from Connie Lenzen, the genealogist I had asked to investigate whether Oscar Pierce ever existed. She had news. She had scored a direct hit. Margaret's grandmother, she wrote, had a sister named Louisa Berry, who had married one Nathan Pierce. They had had a son named Oscar, who was Adda Buck's first cousin and, consequently, Margaret's second cousin, exactly as the *Motion Picture Almanac* had said.

This was Oscar Clarence Pierce, born in Oregon on April 29, 1873, died in San Joaquin, California, on 14 June 1967. He also had a sister named Ada, who had died in Long Beach in 1942, reinforcing the story about Oscar accosting Margaret Herrick at a Long Beach funeral. He had been married twice and had one son, Nathan, from the first marriage—but Nathan had no children.

However, Nathan's niece, Beverly Payne, was listed in one of the records as living in El Sobrante, California, north of Oakland. The phone number was still current, and Beverly came on the line to tell me what she remembered of Oscar. "He was very much a gentleman," she said, "kind, gentle and considerate." When she knew him he had a business sharpening scissors and knives, driving a small truck around the Oakland neighborhoods.

According to census records he had previously been a mechanic, a machinist working in the U.S. navy yards—no hint of any Texan wheat farming, as far as she knew.

Unfortunately there were, Beverly said, no photos left of him. Physically, she thought of him as tall, slender and bespectacled in later life—but nothing like the statuette. In fact, my news about the Oscar link was a complete, luckily pleasant surprise. She had never known there was any kind of family link.

I was glad that we had been able to make that connection. Although there was no immediate explanation as to why Margaret Herrick would have compared the award to her cousin—and I don't think we will ever know that—there was definitely an Oscar Pierce. He was real. He did exist. At least one part of the mystery of Oscar was resolved. Cue credits. Dolly back. Fade to black.

CHAPTER 8

Messrs. Bougainville, Dahl, Freese, Fuchs and Magnol: A Floral Tribute

"What's in a name? That which we call a rose
By any other name would smell as sweet."
William Shakespeare, Romeo and Juliet

Let me make one thing clear from the start. I am not a gardener by instinct. My thumb has not as yet shown even a hint of green. But I am a great lover of gardens. I like to admire their visual effects and savor the calm of their space. Beneath the tower where Vita Sackville-West wrote I can wander for hours through the alleyways and controlled wilderness of the Sissinghurst Garden she created. In the grounds of the Four Seasons Hotel at Chinzan-so in Tokyo I discovered a garden of exquisite restfulness. And out on the bowsprit of the Getty Museum overlooking the spread of Los Angeles I found the arid minimalism of its cactus garden strangely and spikily alluring.

The plants and flowers in private gardens, on display at flower shows in the local garden center, often contain within their names a subtext of botanical exploration and endeavor. There are dozens of genera and species that pay homage to a generous patron or a celebrated botanist, and among the rose community alone, thousands of cultivars, cultivated varieties, have been named by their propagators after friends or celebrities. I chose five plants to bind up in a virtual bouquet on no other basis than the fact they are all among my favorites. So *pace* the begonia, the buddleia and the camellia—named after Michel Bégon, Adam Buddle and Georg Kamel, late 17th-century botanists all, French, English and Moravian respectively—and with sincere apologies to Claude Aubriet, Nicholaus Host, Joel Roberts Poinsett and Caspar Wistar, I present this eponymous anthology.

To saunter past their borders and beds I turned to Thomas Hoblyn, a garden designer based at Bardwell, north of Bury St. Edmunds in my home county of Suffolk. After working as a head gardener for a small estate in his home county of Devon and studying agriculture and commercial horticulture, Thomas trained at the Royal Botanic Gardens, Kew. "I wanted to expand my plant knowledge," he told me, "and to learn about plants from around the world rather than just in Britain." As a garden designer, he works from the plants outward, allowing them to create an overall mood, rather than establishing a design and finding the plants and flowers to fit. "All my gardens," he said, "are a vessel for the plants." He was the ideal guide.

*

We began with the dahlia. Thomas is leading a one-man crusade to reassess the dahlia and promote its beauty. It's one of the flowers he enjoys using most. At the 2006 Hampton Court Palace Flower Show he had picked up a gold medal for a garden that strongly featured *Dahlia* "David Howard," named after the nurseryman who had cultivated it and who had personally grown the flowers for Thomas to use in his show garden.

Why reassess the dahlia? Because it has suffered from being seen, along with the chrysanthemum, as slightly tacky: a staple of the suburban "gardens, lovingly tended by silver-haired grandmas. It was all very competitive. There were people who were dahlia mad, hugely obsessive. They would prune out the side buds to create one huge head that might win them a medal. To keep earwigs away from the flower, they would go through petal by petal removing the insects with tweezers." Thomas wants to move the dahlia away from the artificial, sometimes grotesquely overbred, versions, back toward a flower that retains something of the plant's original character. "The dahlia was really mucked around with. If you look at pictures of wild dahlias they are beautiful in themselves."

The dahlia is a native of the high plains and mountains of Mexico (it is the country's national flower) and Guatemala. The Aztecs used what they called *acocotli* both for nourishment and as a ceremonial decoration, and the stems of the larger species as small pipes. The plant was noted by the Spanish conquistadors in 1615 and "rediscovered" in 1787, when a box containing some seeds was sent to the Botanical Gardens in Madrid, where the Abbé Antonio José Cavanilles named the plant after a fellow botanist, the Swede Anders Dahl.

Initially, the plant was thought of as a source of food, as the Aztecs had used it, but soon its inherent qualities as a garden flower came to the fore. It is a natural hybrid and responds quickly to crossbreeding. "When the dahlia was first discovered in the wild," thinks Thomas Hoblyn, "it was probably obvious then how they would have hybridized. In the nursery world, you can see the impact and the results of breeding very quickly, within one generation." Of all the dahlia cultivars now available—ranging from those that look like waterlilies, anemones or orchids to semi-cactus forms—he is fondest of the pompom type, a "wonderfully symmetrical shape, with perfectly proportioned petals, like something designed on a Spirograph." The reason for the thousands of cultivars that exist is that the dahlia is what is known as an octaploid, which essentially means—and I don't pretend to understand the detail of this—it has eight sets of chromosomes, whereas the majority of plants have only two.

As well as its range of shapes and sizes, the dahlia is available in every conceivable hue, apart from, to date, a genuine blue—the end of the rainbow for dahlia growers (James Ellroy having already immortalized *The Black Dahlia*). *Dahlia* "David Howard" used by Thomas Hoblyn is "an orange ocher, very warm, very sunny."

By the 1830s the dahlia had become extraordinarily popular, the quest for new shapes and colors intense. In 1872 a batch of dahlia tubers was dispatched from Mexico to the Netherlands. Only one tuber survived the trip, but its flower was so striking—a brilliant red, with pointed petals—that from that one *Dahlia juarezii*, as it was known, a whole new species spread across Europe.

Anders Dahl never knew any of this. He had died in May 1789 at the age of thirty-eight, but in that time he had gained a reputation in the botanical arena fine enough to guarantee that not only Abbé Cavanilles in Madrid chose to name the plant from Mexico after Dahl, but a Swedish friend, Carl Peter Thunberg, tried to name another plant after him. Alas for Thunberg, he waited too long before publishing his proposal and found that Cavanilles had nipped in there first.

Dahl was a lifelong lover of the natural world. He grew up in Varnhem and Lidköping in western Sweden, the son of a preacher. Drawn to the natural sciences at school, he set up a branch of the Swedish Topographical Society in his teens and then headed off to Uppsala to study under the renowned Carl Linnaeus, the creator of the binomial system of classification of the natural world (Latin genus name, Latin species name) that we use to this day.

Dahl's father died shortly afterward and, deprived of funding for his botanical studies, Anders changed to medicine. However, Linnaeus recommended him to Claes Alströmer, a naturalist who owned a private botanical garden and an estate on which Anders could work, allowing him to continue his research. Following Linnaeus's death in 1778, Dahl inherited some duplicates from the great man's own herbarium. He took these with him to Finland when, in 1787, only two years before his own death, he was appointed an associate professor at the University at Turku.

The Dahl of his surname is pronounced "darl," as in Roald or Sophie, and although that is the pronunciation used today in the States, in British English the flower is pronounced "day-lee-a." "Technically," said Thomas Hoblyn, "under the international rules of nomenclature, it should be pronounced the Swedish way, but in day-to-day use that would just sound pretentious"—one of those quirks of the way the English language has evolved into two distinct linguistic cultivars either side of the Atlantic.

*

I am a huge fan of the freesia. I have always found its odd, angular, waxy stems pleasingly asymmetrical, the beauty of the flowers achingly fragile. And its heady perfume takes me right back to one long-gone February afternoon as a student, when a vaseful of yellow and white freesias bought from the nearby market permeated my rooms as I listened to my just-acquired copy of a Keith Jarrett album, *My Song*. To this day, if I smell freesias, I instantly hear the music of Jarrett and his Scandinavian quartet of Jan Garbarek, Palle Danielsson and Jon Christensen. If I listen to the album, it's as if the vase was still standing right beside me.

The freesia hails from South Africa, particularly Cape Province: the genus is part of the Iridaceae family of irises (the name iris coined by Linnaeus), which also includes the crocus and the gladiolus. Like all of them, the freesia is grown from a corm. It was named, in South Africa, by Christian Ecklon, a Danish botanist, who spent much time there collecting samples and who cowrote a definitive catalogue of South African plants published in the 1830s.

Ecklon named the best part of 2,000 genera and species, and his own surname endures in relative obscurity as *Ecklonia*, the genus name of a particular kind of sea kelp. It was a student of his, Friedrich Heinrich Theodor Freese, a German physician who had helped him in his work, who landed the more widespread immortality. That's the way it goes.

There was some confusion over the freesia. Before Ecklon named it after Freese, the plant had already been cultivated under different genus names—as a gladiolus and as an ixia—and it was only in 1866 that one G. L. Meyer described the freesia as a distinct genus. After one yellow type of freesia was discovered in 1874, growing in the Botanic Gardens of Padua by Max Leichtlin, a Baden-Baden–based horticulturalist, the flower rapidly established itself as a favorite with the nursery trade. It was, in one phrase I came across, "the caviar of flowers."

Thomas Hoblyn remembered, when he was growing up in south Devon, that the freesia was grown there commercially as a cut flower. "There were greenhouses full of them, but now they are flown in from abroad." I was trying to find a word to describe their scent, and he supplied an intriguing term for it, "peppery." I have read that some people are unable to detect the scent of the freesia, a sad omission in their sensory world.

*

It is clear that there has long been an interconnected community of botanists, who traveled together, worked alongside each other, compared notes, exchanged specimens and shared a common interest and passion. They would recognize and honor their fellow enthusiasts by naming a new genus or a recently dis-covered species after each other. And as with Ecklon and Freese, no one knew who in the long term would find the greatest glory—I think I might have asked not to have the sea kelp named after me, frankly, but each to his own.

Louis-Antoine de Bougainville, on the other hand, was not part of that botanical community, although he did love growing roses. He was a multitalented, swashbuckling 18th-century adventurer, "a Renaissance man in the Enlightenment," as one of his biographers described him. His tomb is in the Panthéon in Paris.

Born in Paris in 1729, Bougainville was helped up the social ladder by one of his uncles, who had a few useful contacts. He rose to the opportunity, showing prodigious mathematical talent—he presented a treatise on calculus to the Académie des Sciences when he was in his early twenties—but left academia behind to join the Marquis de Montcalm's Mousquetaires Noirs as the general's aide-de-camp in Canada, where he confronted the British General Wolfe.

Surviving the dangers of the military campaign, unlike Montcalm, who was mortally wounded at the Battle of the Plains of Abraham, Bougainville continued his quest for extreme challenges by undertaking a circumnavigation of the globe in 1760. He left his name behind him in various ways—an island in the northern Solomons (he also founded the first settlement on what are now the Falkland Islands) and a mountain on Alofi, part of the French overseas territory of Wallis and Futuna in the southwestern Pacific. But the plant that bears his name was not found by him. It was collected, not far from Rio de Janeiro, by a colleague on his ship *La Boudeuse*, the expedition's naturalist Philibert Commerson, who unselfishly named it after the commander of the vessel (wisely too, if he wanted to hitch a ride back to Europe). Commerson had smuggled on board his assistant Jeanne Baré, disguised as his "valet." As a result Baré became the first woman to circumnavigate the world; Commerson was not so fortunate: he died in Mauritius on the return voyage.

Thomas Hoblyn, during his time at the Royal Botanic Gardens at Kew, undertook a journey, not in the wake of Bougainville and Commerson, but of James Cook and his botanist Joseph Banks, who collected specimens of a woody shrub native to Australia, which was named in his honor, *Banksia*. Banks's diaries contained plenty of references to the Bougainville voyage a few years earlier, and Thomas provided me with one factoid he had come across: that Bougainville's crew had been responsible for introducing syphilis to Tahiti . . .

When I think of bougainvillea I envisage Mediterranean hotels or Caribbean walls, great swathes of magenta, orange, red and yellow flowers: the late fashionista Isabella Blow created a stunning red lipstick inspired by a bougainvillea she'd seen on St. Barts.

"The colorful part is not the flower," Thomas told me. "It's actually a bract, a modified leaf, that contains the color. The flower is the tiny whitish center." Close up, he thought, the plant was "not that exciting, a dry-looking, papery thing," and he pointed out that its appearance belied the fact that it was surprisingly thorny, which helps it scramble up those walls and over other plants: it is really a woody vine.

In later life Louis-Antoine de Bougainville was asked for which of his exploits and explorations he thought he would be best remembered. Presciently, he replied, "Well, I am also placing hope for my reputation in a flower."

*

For Thomas Hoblyn the fuchsia is "a bit like the dahlia, not in looks, but because it also reminds me of the pipe-smoking gardener with leather patches on his gardening jacket." He recalled a fuchsia specialist in Porlock in Somerset, with "a little greenhouse crammed full of fuchsias. To me, they are the epitome of the 1970s and hanging basket displays. The one I hated most as a gardener in Devon was the cultivar called 'Mrs. Popple,' no offense to the lady in question." She and Mr. Popple had a house in Stevenage, in Hertfordshire, between the wars. On a bank alongside the tennis court at the bottom of their garden grew a hardy scarlet and purple fuchsia, which a local nurseryman named Clarence Elliott admired, cultivated and named after her. Elliott himself is remembered by an Alpine saxifrage.

There are still plenty of small local associations dedicated to growing the fuchsia, and its popularity continues to ride high. The fuchsia is a member of the pomegranate family, Onagraceae, and its structure, with sepals not petals, is particularly fascinating for Thomas, suggesting to him that it must have "an interesting pollinator." In South America, the fuchsia's principal home territory, it is pollinated by the hummingbird. In Ireland and the West Country and on the Isle of Man, where a hardy species is used as a hedging plant, it is pollinated by insects.

The fuchsia arrived in Europe courtesy of Charles Plumier, who undertook three botanical expeditions to the French Antilles on behalf of Louis XIV in the late 17th century. He first spotted the fuchsia on the island of Hispaniola. For its genus, he decided to honor one of the great fathers of botany, Leonhart Fuchs (the fuchsia should correctly be pronounced "fook-sia," rather than the common "few-sia").

Fuchs is one of the "big three" of 16th-century botany, along with Hieronymous Bock and Otto Brunfels. He was a Bavarian and a medical doctor by training, but since plants and herbs were a central part of Renaissance medicine, a knowledge of botany was vital for any medical man. Fuchs, who became professor of medicine and chancellor of the University at Tübingen, a few miles south of Stuttgart, found that many of the plants he used were incorrectly identified in existing herbals. So he created his own, *De Historia Stirpium* (*On the History of Plants*), which was published in Basel in 1542.

One of the most stunning features of this book was the quality of the woodcut illustrations it contained; Fuchs himself acknowledged this by, unusually, including in its front matter portraits of those responsible, the artists Heinrich Füllmaurer and Albrecht Mayer, and the cutter Veit Rudolph Speckle. *De Historia Stirpium* was a massively important book. Three and a half centuries later William Morris owned a copy, and the influence on his work is clear. Fuchs was a worthy eponym.

★

Charles Plumier also discovered and named the magnolia, which he came across on a trip to Martinique. Its name was a tribute to Pierre Magnol, who, like Fuchs, was a major figure in the history of botany.

Based in his hometown of Montpellier, close to the Mediterranean coast of France, Magnol (born 1638, died 1715) had eventually become professor of botany at the university there. I say eventually because he was a Protestant at a time when, in Catholic France, that was a definite drawback, and he was passed over for promotion several times—in the end Magnol converted to Catholicism, and his career picked up.

Magnol's contribution to botany was an improved classification of plants. Previously, a kind of Book of Genesis mentality had applied, which followed the line that all species emerged during one seven-day period of divine work. Along with his contemporary, the Englishman John Ray, Magnol was one of the first botanists to group plants into families (he used the term *familia*) in his 1689 book *Prodromus Historiae Generalis Plantarum*— botanists are big on Latin. His work directly influenced Linnaeus, as the Swede acknowledged, in the following century.

Thanks to Plumier, the name Magnol rippled through botanical nomenclature. Not only was the plant magnolia named for him, but he also features in the subfamily *Magnolioideae*, the family *Magnoliaceae*, the order *Magnoliales*, the subclass *Magnoliidae* and, to top it all, an entire class of plants, *Magnoliopsida*, which includes virtually every flower and tree we know. If they hadn't stopped there, we'd have had to rename the planet after him.

The reason Pierre Magnol got such a big slice of the natural names on offer was because the magnolia is such an ancient plant, certainly one of the first flowering plants. Fossilized versions date from 20 million years ago, and it has been estimated that the plant has existed for up to 95 million years. It predated the existence of butterflies and bees, so its broad flowers were designed to encourage pollination by beetles or, as

Thomas Hoblyn put it, "by any old thing. It used to be thought that on the evolutionary scale it was very basic, very primitive, but using DNA sequencing, it's been discovered that it is simply not as specialized as, say, an orchid that can only be pollinated by one specific pollinator."

Given its antiquity, the magnolia is found on most continents, but the majority of species (many of which, a recent report revealed, are under threat of extinction) are in Asia, specifically southern China. *Magnolia grandiflora* is the species that has probably gained the most profile: it's the massive flowered tree, known as bull bay, that grows in the southern United States. Mississippi is called the Magnolia State, and the magnolia is both its state tree and flower.

I'm glad to say to say that Charles Plumier in his turn was honored. *Plumeria* is the genus name of the tropical shrub known as frangipani, itself a reference to an Italian perfumer, the Marquis de Frangipani.

*

Before we leave this corner of the natural world, I would like to doff my cap to Carl Linnaeus—or Carl von Linné, as he liked to style himself in later years—as his taxonomic efforts and his system of categorization affect us on a daily basis. He came up with the term *Homo sapiens*, when he moved on from plants to animals. The Swede was notoriously arrogant—he once claimed that "no man has ever transformed science in the way that I have"—but his energy for cataloguing was certainly a great legacy, even though his predecessors, like Leonhart Fuchs, Pierre Magnol and John Ray, had laid plenty of the groundwork.

Linnaeus, whose tercentenary was celebrated in 2007, came from the province Småland, toward the south of Sweden. He was born in Råshult, not a million miles from Agunnaryd, the birthplace of Ingvar Kamprad, Mr. IKEA, whose company name is an acronym for Ingvar Kamprad, Elmtaryd (the name of his family's farm), Agunnaryd.

He coined his own name too, since in his day Swedes generally did not have surnames as we do now but took their father's first name—Linnaeus's father was Nils Ingemarsson, son of Ingemar Bengtsson, and so on. To sign on at university Carl needed a formal surname, and he chose Linnaeus, a Latinate variation of *lind*, the lime tree.

It's good to know that Linnaeus was not above some personal niggle. Johann Georg Siegesbeck, a German botanist, once dared to criticize him, and Linnaeus got his own back for posterity, by naming in his honor *Sigesbeckia*, a smelly, mud-loving, creeping herb.

I like the fact that entwined with the nomenclature of plants are human beings, with all their frailties. The dahlia, the freesia, the bougainvillea, the fuchsia and the magnolia, plants that specialists can study for a lifetime, represent a chapter of botanical history, each a reminder of one person who left his mark, while the rest of us—like Voltaire's Candide—simply concentrate on trying to cultivate our own gardens.

CHAPTER 9

A Soft Spot for Dr. Gräfenberg

"For women the best aphrodisiacs are words. The G-spot is in
the ears, and anyone who goofs around looking for it any
farther down is wasting his time and ours."
Isabel Allende, Aphrodite

Of all the people featured in this book I imagine that the name of
Dr. Ernst Gräfenberg is by some distance the least familiar. All of
our other heroes and heroines have names that are instantly and
involuntarily recognizable, even if their own personal histories are
often far less widely known. But Dr. Gräfenberg? In the course of
writing this book I have come across only two or three friends and
acquaintances who were able, unprompted, to summon up even
the smallest detail about him. Who was he? Well, in brief, Ernst
Gräfenberg is the G in G-spot. I am not sure what the correct
philological term is for this kind of word. It's not quite an eponym,
nor really an acronym; perhaps we need to coin another term.

Ernst Gräfenberg was a highly respected obstetrician and
gynecologist who escaped from Nazi Germany to find refuge in
New York City, where he ran a private practice from the early
1940s to the mid-1950s. Since the term G-spot was created more
than twenty years later, in his honor, Ernst Gräfenberg never
knew that his name, albeit abbreviated to the sliver of its initial
letter, would find such international fame.

His full surname—umlaut and all—would never, I suspect,
have caught on in quite the same way, whereas the pared-down
version transcends linguistic borders: in French it's known as *le*

point G, in Spanish as *el punto* G, and in the doctor's native German as *G-Punkt*. Within a decade or so of being coined in the early 1980s, the phrase had become firmly rooted in the language not only of the rarefied vocabularies of sexological and anatomical research, but of popular culture.

Had Ernst Gräfenberg known this, he would, from what I have learned, have preferred the anonymity of the initial. He was a very modest man. One of his patients in New York, Sophia Gosselin, told me that after he had saved both her and her child during a life-threatening pregnancy in 1946, he visited the new family and asked what they were going to name this new baby, a boy. She and her husband had never discussed a name; they had, if anything, presumed that their son would automatically be named after his father. "I looked at my husband and said, 'Ernst,' " she said. "And Dr. Gräfenberg stepped back a little bit, with a mixture of annoyance and gratitude for the honor, but then he said, 'Have you thought about this? This child is not able to defend himself; you are here to protect him. Would you really lumber a child with the name of Ernst?' "

★

Whenever you start talking or writing about G-spots, you are heading into treacherous territory. This is the domain of innuendo, both deliberate and unintentional. So before we set out to trace the life of Dr. Gräfenberg, let me dispose of the humor right now. Any nudge-nudge elements from here on will be entirely accidental, although I will doubtless miss an entendre or three. The G-spot does lend itself to jokes, and before I start sounding too prim, let me share one that tweaked my fancy: "What is the difference between a G-spot and a golf ball?" it goes. Answer: "A guy will actually spend two hours looking for a golf ball." Boom boom.

Back to the serious stuff. That Ernst Gräfenberg was honored by having a part of the body named after him is far from uncommon. Like animal or plant names, there are many examples in the world of human anatomy and medicine. One list of medical eponyms I scrolled through, whonamedit.com, compiled by a Norwegian medical historian and journalist named Ole Daniel Enersen, catalogued at the last count 7,896 eponyms, a mind-boggling inventory of syndromes, ligaments, procedures, fissures, trachomas, techniques and the occasional ganglion or gland.

Most of these terms remain resolutely confined to the world of medicine and rarely appear outside textbooks and case studies, but a number of them have passed into more common usage. Sometimes news stories have pushed them into a wider consciousness. The bacteria *Salmonella*, for example, is a piece of 20th-century Latinate neology named after Daniel Elmer Salmon, an American veterinarian who was chief of the Bureau of Animal Industry from 1884 to 1906. A colleague of Salmon's, Theobald Smith, is generally considered to have discovered the genus, but Salmon applied his *droit de seigneur* to undertake the actual description, securing his place in history.

The increasing recognition of Alzheimer's disease has brought to the fore the name of Alois Alzheimer, the German neurologist who first published a paper on the condition in 1906, after spending five years studying the behavior and deterioration of one of his patients, Frau Auguste D., at the asylum in Frankfurt. Tourette's and Asperger's syndromes have likewise become more widely known. The French neurologist Georges Gilles de la Tourette identified what he originally called *la maladie des tics* in 1884; it was his mentor, Jean-Martin Charcot, who named it for him. Hans Asperger, an Austrian, who worked as a pediatrician in Leipzig through the 1930s, defined Asperger's syndrome toward the end of the Second World War. It was initially confused as a variant of autism, or generally ignored, until the 1990s, a decade or more after his death, when the specific nature of Asperger's was accepted and later brilliantly explored and explained through the narrative voice of Christopher, the protagonist of Mark Haddon's *The Curious Incident of the Dog in the Night-time*.

Parts of the body named after people that the average patient might recognize are far fewer in number. Gabriele Fallopio, a highly influential 16th-century physician, professor of anatomy and surgery at the University of Padua, wrote treatises on everything from the middle ear to rudimentary condoms and gave his name to various nooks and crannies of our bodies. The fallopian tube is the one that everyone has heard of, but he also lives on in the *acqueductus Fallopii*, a canal of the facial nerve. This reminds me of Schlemm's canal, part of the inner workings of the eye, which I heard was always used by one malingerer to blame for a day off work—a mention that he was suffering from "an infection of Schlemm's canal" usually discouraged any further questions.

Where the G-spot differs from all of these is that it is, generally, used in a positive and pleasurable environment. Words describing conditions or organs tend to enter the vernacular only because of disease, deterioration and trauma. The G-spot is absolutely the opposite.

I realize that I have assumed that everybody knows what the G-spot is (though not necessarily where). In case it is still a mystery, the best place to start is with the book that made it famous: *The G Spot and Other Discoveries about Human Sexuality*. When it was published in 1982 it created the kind of stir that scientific books have when—despite the sometimes quite technical nature of their content and the seriousness of their intent—they flip over to a much broader general readership, like *A Brief History of Time* or *The Blind Watchmaker*. Through some mix of zeitgeist and alchemy they tap into public consciousness at exactly the right moment. I was going to say they touch a nerve, but that would be almost too appropriate for the G-spot book.

★

The authors of *The G Spot and Other Discoveries about Human Sexuality* (in the title there is no hyphen in G-spot, although it has since acquired one) were Alice Kahn Ladas, a psychologist, the sexuality researcher and nursing educator Beverly Whipple and John D. Perry, an ordained minister who was a psychologist and sexologist. This was an amalgam of two research teams.

Beverly Whipple and John D. Perry had met through AASECT, the American Association of Sexuality Educators, Counselors and Therapists, and joined forces in their research into female sexuality. In examinations of hundreds of women, they reported, they had in all cases been able to locate an extremely sensitive area, which they proposed calling "the Gräfenberg spot." Through a reference in an article in the *Journal of Sex Research*, they had learned that in 1950 Ernst Gräfenberg had written and published a paper that identified both this "erogenic zone" and its location—although Gräfenberg did not use the word "spot."

Shortly after the pair had made their discoveries public, Alice Ladas was giving a presentation during an international meeting in Dallas of the SSSS, the Society for the Scientific Study of Sexuality, where John Perry and Beverly Whipple were also presenting. Alice Ladas set out the findings of a questionnaire she had sent out to a group of female therapists asking them about their professional and personal experience in the area of bio-energetic analysis, a questionnaire conducted anonymously so that the women could feel free to be as revealing as possible.

It emerged that there was some overlap between the work of the two research teams, and the Ladases, who were writing a book about the Whipple/Perry research, asked Beverly Whipple and John Perry if they would get involved. At that point the authorial team was becoming too large, and Harold Ladas gracefully stepped back—the book is dedicated to him, "our silent partner."

Although they had aimed the book at a general audience—their brief was to write it in the style of *Scientific American*—the sudden success of *The G Spot and Other Discoveries about Human Sexuality* was astounding. From the relative obscurity of published research on the Gräfenberg spot and female ejaculation, they were catapulted into national and international consciousness. In 2006, the year her latest book, *The Science of Orgasm*, was published, Beverly Whipple was named by *New Scientist* as one of the fifty most influential scientists in the world. I spoke to Dr. Whipple in a tiny gap in her hectic schedule, somewhere between talks in Mexico, conferences in Australia and lectures in Japan.

She told me that since all of her research had been "to validate the sexual experiences of women, the irony of the area being named after a man is not lost on me"; indeed, some hardline feminists have objected to that very point.

Before she and John Perry settled on the name, one of her colleagues suggested calling it "the Whipple tickle," her own brush with immortality. But in the research that they had conducted on female ejaculation, when they unearthed Ernst Gräfenberg's work in a back issue of *The International Journal of Sexology*, they felt that he was the first researcher of modern times to deal with it coherently and cogently (the Kama Sutra and Chinese and Japanese erotic manuals had already written about the topic). The term they wanted to be used was "the Gräfenberg spot," not least to convey the seriousness with which they took the subject. "I wanted it to be pure science," said Beverly Whipple.

The book they wrote with Alice Ladas covers much other ground, but it was the G-spot chapter and the book's title that got the most attention. A journalist or subeditor who wanted to add some extra hype to an article on the topic sexed it up by shortening the Gräfenberg to a G and using an "Oh gee!" headline. The book's publishers immediately saw the shorter name's sales potential. I asked Beverly Whipple whether she had now come to terms with the fact that, as a result, the tribute she intended to Ernst Gräfenberg had been diluted. She said she had, "Yes, just about."

Most people now use the G-spot abbreviation, bar a few specialists who have clung to the longer version, something Dr.

Whipple approves of, although I am less sure she would whole-heartedly approve of its appearance in the title of two porn movies ("porno classics" according to their blurbs), *The Grafenberg Spot*—starring some of the aristocracy of porn, including Traci Lords, Ginger Lynn and John Holmes—and its follow-up, *Grafenberg Girls Go Fishing*.

What was the reason for the book's success? What factors in the early 1980s provided Beverly Whipple and her coauthors with their particular zeitgeist moment? And how come—as the skeptics had asked when they gave their presentation to the SSSS—nobody had really talked about it before? One reason was that most research in sex studies prior to the 1970s had been overseen by men, for whom the existence of the G-spot might have been in some way a threat.

If, according to the introduction of *The G Spot*, the 20th century was when "human sexuality became a legitimate subject for scientific study for the very first time in Western history" it was primarily a male preserve (Virginia E. Johnson of the Masters and Johnson research team being a significant exception) until the 1970s, with the arrival of powerful writing and research on female sexuality by Shere Hite, Germaine Greer and Anne Koedt, among others. They ushered in the beginning of the end of an era in which, as Germaine Greer put it, "The woman was to be the violin, the man the virtuoso." (In the same article, however, she refers to "the myth of the G-spot"—not everyone was convinced.)

At a time when women were feeling more confident about asserting their sexuality, the "discovery" of the G-spot unleashed a wave of consciousness. One woman wrote to Beverly Whipple and her coauthors from Panama saying that she and her fellow countrywomen had always known of its existence and that locally it was called *la bella loca*. But not all readers were pleased. One "self-proclaimed Don Juan" wrote in complaining that "the discovery and its publication has cost me a well-kept and very valuable trade secret."

Not to feel left out, men have been given their own equivalent of the G-spot—theirs is known as the A-spot (I have also seen it referred to as the B-spot). Desmond Morris in *The Naked Woman* adds C- and U-spots. (This all suggests a potential run through the entire alphabet, after which the ZZZ-spot will presumably be that bit of the pillow where you can finally lay your head in peace.)

In 2000 Beverly Whipple was invited to prepare a talk about Ernst Gräfenberg to be given in Berlin to the Fifth Congress of the European Federation of Sexology. She knew that he had come from Berlin to New York but discovered that any information about his early life was scarce. She found a niece and nephew and learned that he had been married but that there were no children. Although she was honored to be asked to deliver the speech—"I felt we had done the right thing by naming the area after him"—she was drawing on thin resources.

She referred me to a short but thorough biographical article about Ernst Gräfenberg written by two doctors from the University of Kiel on the centenary of his birth. She also recommended that I contact Erwin Haeberle, a distinguished sexologist and professor, but he merely confirmed that there was precious little available on Dr. Gräfenberg and in particular on the first sixty years of his life in Germany. "It is unfortunate," he said, "that nobody cared about the sexological pioneers when there was still time to find out more, but when it counted, nobody gave a damn. I can sing a very sad song about that myself. I never received sufficient support for my work when some of these men or their relatives were still alive. I never met Dr. Gräfenberg myself, only a colleague of his, now also long dead. Under the circumstances, I have to be grateful for the little I did manage to find out."

★

These are the fragments that have survived. Ernst Gräfenberg was born on September 26, 1881. He came from Adelebsen, a small

town near Göttingen in Lower Saxony, in the northwest of
Germany (Hanover is the capital of the region and its best-known
city). He studied medicine in Göttingen and later in Munich,
receiving a doctorate in 1905. Then he pitched up in Bavaria,
practicing ophthalmology in Würzburg, and moved on to Kiel
University as a junior doctor in the department of gynecology and
obstetrics, hence the biography of him written on the anniversary
of his birth by the two Kiel doctors. There, the dozen or so papers
he published over three years showed an incisive and inventive
approach to the research he undertook. (At Kiel one of his tutors
was Hans Hermann Pfannenstiel, a physician and surgeon—
Pfannenstiel's incision, an abdominal cut, is still used in operating
rooms.)

By the time the First World War intervened Ernst Gräfenberg
was based in Berlin; he saw active service as a medical officer,
specifically as a sanitation officer, on the Russian front but
continued writing papers even when he was on battle stations,
adjusting to his immediate environment by concentrating on the
effects of gunshot wounds.

Returning to Berlin, he focused throughout the 1920s on female
physiology, which laid the foundation for his subsequent interest
in both sexology and birth control. The most significant outcome
of this was his pioneering work on IUDs, in particular an early
version made from silkworm gut and later a spiral ring of silver
wire, which became know as the Gräfenberg ring, a particularly
safe form that remained in use for over thirty years until plastic
IUDs were developed, although it was only in the late 1950s that
his ring was given due and long-lasting recognition. He was not
the first person to investigate IUDs as a method of contraception
(Dr. Richard Richter from Silesia, then part of Germany, now in
Poland, had developed a version in the 1900s), but Gräfenberg
applied the observations of a decade of research to its evolution.

At this point Dr. Gräfenberg's star was ascendant. He had
an office on Kurfürstendamm, one of the most fashionable

boulevards in Berlin, ran a private hospital with sixty beds and had a high-class, high-powered list of patients.

His private life remained private. He left no autobiographical notes. We know only that for a while he was married to a woman named Rosa Goldschmidt, who was later a correspondent for *Newsweek*, wrote a number of books and before or afterward was married to a member of the Ullstein publishing family and subsequently to a Count Waldeck.

But in the Germany of the 1930s practicing and researching birth control was an area fraught with difficulties. In order to survive all militarized states—and those gearing up—need a regular and plentiful supply of cannon fodder. Birth control runs counter to that requirement. Contraception itself and providing contraceptive advice was increasingly denounced and eventually made illegal in Germany. Ernst Gräfenberg's position was in jeopardy. Moreover, he was a Jew, and in 1933 he was squeezed out of his final job heading the Berlin gynecological and obstetrics department.

There is a theory that he was allowed to remain for some additional time because many of his patients were married to Nazi higher-ups (a theory Gräfenberg himself apparently subscribed to, since he did not leave straightaway), but by 1937 he was under scrutiny again, this time under arrest on some trumped-up charge of smuggling a valuable stamp out of Germany. He was fortunate. He was sent to a civilian jail near Frankfurt, not a concentration camp, and because of his work and travel giving lectures on birth control, a group of friends and colleagues overseas, particularly those involved in the International Society of Sexology, came to his aid. A ransom was raised and his release organized, although this was not at all usual. Circuitously and rather mysteriously—by way of Siberia and Shanghai—he traveled to California in 1940, where one of the people who helped him on arrival was Erich Maria Remarque, the author of *All Quiet on the Western Front*, who had also fled to the United States.

Dr. Gräfenberg headed east, via Chicago, to New York, where he set up a private practice in Manhattan, on Park Avenue. He continued working in the area of birth control, but he was a man of wide interests, and so in 1950 we find him publishing the article titled "The role of the urethra in female orgasm," which nearly thirty years later prompted Beverly Whipple and John Perry to pay tribute to his contribution to sexual research.

He retired from private practice in 1953, three years after his pioneering paper, as he had developed Parkinson's disease. (James Parkinson was a physician based in Hoxton Square at the turn of the 19th century, who published his paper on "shaking palsy" in 1817.) Ernst Gräfenberg spent the remainder of his life working with the Margaret Sanger Research Bureau, America's first legal birth control clinic. He died quite unrecognized: not one major obituary in either the mainstream press or scientific journals.

This was all good and interesting stuff, but I could not get a feel for the personality or soul of Ernst Gräfenberg. The handful of photographs of him as a younger man gave little away. One, from his Kiel days, shows him turning a level, unflinching stare at the camera through pince-nez glasses and sporting a neat mustache upturned at the ends. Since he had left no children, no memoirs and little in the way of a visual record, I was not sure if I could find anything to bring this man to life.

*

Then Beverly Whipple came up trumps. She put me in touch with one of Dr. Gräfenberg's patients from his time on Park Avenue, a woman—now in her eighties—who lived, it transpired, in Tunbridge Wells, that bastion of English conservatism. This was Sophia (not her real name), who first met him in 1946 when she was twenty and a recent bride.

Sophia proved to be bright as a button, an enthusiastic, petite lady, who, despite the onset of arthritis, kept a very firm grip on the current state of the world via the internet. She was highly informed and a wonderful talker about Ernst Gräfenberg. She believes he was a great man, "possibly the greatest I have ever known, even if always with a certain cold distance between us." She owed her own life and that of her son to his knowledge and experience, and she often broke into laughter or veered toward the edge of tears as she remembered the doctor.

In 1940, when she was a teenager, Sophia had arrived in America from Europe. "My mother had plenty of money saved and she put me in a school just outside Washington. I went overnight from little short socks, skirt and a blouse to high heels, makeup and furs. America was a shock." She traveled back to Paris after the end of the Second World War and met her future husband, a journalist. "We got married, found an apartment, bought a poodle and had a lovely life. But then I fell pregnant and I became dreadfully ill. I was constantly hurting from head to foot, never any of the nausea, just pain everywhere, and that's not what pregnancy's supposed to be, is it? We returned to America because I was frightened."

The couple went to stay with Sophia's mother in her apartment on Riverside Drive and consulted her MD. Initially he did not know whom to refer Sophia to, but when they came back a week later, he told them, "There is a doctor I can recommend. He is a German refugee, and he is the best obstetrician in New York, in America and in the world." As Sophia said, "You don't hear that very often." Her mother was working for a French press agency in New York. She had never heard of Ernst Gräfenberg but asked around, and was reassured that he came with suitable credentials.

Sophia and her husband went to Ernst Gräfenberg's office. "It was surprisingly stark. His own office had a desk and two chairs and a door that led to an examining room with beautiful bright windows—one looking out on Park Avenue, the other on East 77th—through which the sun poured in." She found him to be "extraordinarily reserved but friendly, not hail-fellow-well-met, a

proper European. His English was perfect but it wasn't American."
In the late 1920s Dr. Gräfenberg had been to meetings in London,
where others attending included Marie Stopes, Vera Brittain,
George Bernard Shaw and Bertrand Russell. "Now, *that's* how
you learn English."

By the time Sophia met Dr. Gräfenberg, he had been in America
for five years "so like me, his English had changed to mid-Atlantic
junk, but he switched as easily into German. In those days there
were several different forms of German. The one that the civilized,
upper classes spoke was High German, *Hochdeutsch*, only taught in
a few private schools." Sophia's schooling had been in just such an
institution. "The High German speakers understood each other. I
went back to Germany with my son and I came across a taxi driver
who spoke High German. It was such a shock to hear it again. It
just doesn't exist anymore. It's not clipped, but very soft, what the
Germans now call 'stage German.'"

She remembers particularly Ernst Gräfenberg's quiet self-
assurance, his voice lowish, almost a whisper much of the time, "a
voice that reminded me of my father." Sophia told him she did not
understand why she felt so unwell and asked him if it was normal.
Dr. Gräfenberg looked at her and said, "No, you're not normal."
She felt her stomach churn, but immediately he carried on: "I'm
not normal either, you know." "Obviously the man is crazy, it's
time to reach for your coat, get out of there. But he opens a drawer
and hands me this miniature barrel, beautifully made of wood
with staves and everything and a lid that came off. He kept
paperclips in it. He says, "That's a miniature, but I have a bigger
one in my office over there. It's human-sized, really, really big, and
it's filled with formaldehyde. And the first "normal" person I meet
I am going to grab them and shove them in there and nail the thing
down before they escape!" Why I didn't laugh I don't know; I was
too frightened. But I realized he was trying to teach me a lesson
and he never stopped trying to teach me from the day we met till
his last words to me." He advised her with sage, sensible,

pragmatic advice on diet, on child care ("He was one of the best pediatricians in the world"), on coping with her fears.

Ernst Gräfenberg's principal task was to monitor Sophia's pregnancy. He refused to carry out a Cesarean, already a fashionable option for New York women. "He wouldn't do it. A German reply. A woman should be free to do sports, to swim and play tennis." He became worried as the due date neared, "taking measurements in this lovely beautiful examining room." He thought there might have been error in the calculations. When labor did begin, her husband drove her to the hospital. He was waiting there for them. "Can you imagine a consultant doing that nowadays? You can tell how well respected a doctor is by the way fellow professionals treat him. I've been trying to think of a way to describe the respect that Dr. Gräfenberg inspired, and the only person I can really come up with is the queen and the archbishop of Canterbury. And not once did that man touch me without asking, 'May I have your permission to examine you?' When said in Hochdeutsch, it is even more flattering."

Sophia repeated often to me that Dr. Gräfenberg deserved to be seen in the context of his wide-ranging wisdom, knowledge and research, which included cancer, birth control, anatomy, pain and gender dysfunction (and remember that he had started life as an ophthalmologist).

She felt that the naming of the G-spot, although a fine tribute, had somewhat skewed his memory, since sex studies formed only a small aspect of his work. "He spoke to me at length on very many subjects and tried to educate me in matters scientific and medical. The word 'sex' was never uttered once. When speaking of sex, he used euphemisms. Female sexual satisfaction was not his primary field of medical research or interest. It is almost as if Albert Einstein were to go down in history as a man who helped little girls with their math homework." (This Sophia knew, since when she was a schoolgirl worried about her lack of math ability, she had met Einstein, who told her he was useless too!)

She was upset, personally affronted, by a newspaper article she had read about Ernst Gräfenberg that suggested he ran something akin to a massage parlor out of the Park Avenue office or practiced exclusively on lesbians, and is puzzled why—despite her requests for information on the net—no other patients of his have ever come forward to round out her view. She continually reminded me that hers is, indeed, only one person's view of him, but it has the ring of authenticity. "There's no one else to stand up for this man. He cared about humanity to a degree that I cannot express. He had a respect, an admiration for humanity, for nature's ability to create the variety of humankind. Nature in her infinite variety. He was in awe of it."

★

I'll leave the last laugh to Dr. G. I read a copy of his 1950 article in *The International Journal of Sexology*. Sophia had pointed me toward what she observed in it as a tone of voice quite different from anything else he had written professionally, "a tone of amused irony," she called it. The passage she had in mind is the closest I am sure that Ernst Gräfenberg came to including a gag in his published writings.

He referred to one of his patients, who had married a much older wealthy husband, and "pestered me persistently with questions as to why she could not experience an orgasm." Despite his patience, he became bored with endless discussions with her about this, and "finally asked her if she had tried sex relations with another male partner. 'No,' was the answer, and she reflectively left my office. The next day, in the middle of the night, I was awakened by a telephone call and a familiar voice who did not give her name asked: 'Doctor, are you there? You are right,' and hung up the receiver with a bang! I never," he notes wryly, "had to answer any further sexual questions from her."

CHAPTER 10

The Earl of Sandwich and a Small Slice of History

"Too few people understand a really good sandwich."
James Beard

Given the impeccable Englishness of the origins of the sandwich—and despite the fact that I like to think of myself as definitively *not* an Old World snob—I was, nonetheless, a little surprised and disconcerted to find myself sitting in the Downtown Disney Marketplace at Walt Disney World in Florida, chatting about the history of England's great and noble Montagu family with Ian Schneider, a fast-talking New Yorker, while a man dressed as a character from *Peter Pan* strolled across my line of sight.

I had arranged to meet Ian because he was in charge of franchise sales operations for the Earl of Sandwich restaurant chain, a company founded in 2001 by Orlando Montagu and his father, the current (and 11th) Earl of Sandwich, in partnership with Robert Earl, whose entrepreneurial energy drove forward both the Hard Rock Cafe and Planet Hollywood.

So we're in Orlando, Florida, and the founder of the Earl of Sandwich restaurant chain is named Orlando Montagu. His ancestor is the very Earl of Sandwich after whom the snack we know and love is named. His father is the current Earl of Sandwich, and his business partner is Robert Earl. That is weird, huh? "Yeah, those coincidences keep me awake at night," confided Ian, who sat down with me for lunch after showing me around the restaurant. This, the original link in the chain, opened in 2003, the first third-party restaurant ever allowed to launch on a Disney site.

One of the things that struck me most about the Earl of Sandwich restaurant was the attention to detail. The freshness of food preparation is impressive—the meat, slow-roasted each morning, is cut in front of you, the fresh-baked bread prepared while you wait, the whole process taking two to three minutes from order to delivery—but I also loved the way that, where the connection to the earls of Sandwich past and present could easily have been quite cursory, the decor and the spirit of the place have been methodically thought through.

There was a strong Sandwich presence within the restaurant; here was a family who had embraced the name and the way it had become part of the language rather than shying away from it. The walls featured magnified details from maps and documents kept in the archives at the Montagu family home, Mapperton House in Dorset. Underfoot, at the entrance to the main door, were the three lozenges of the family's coat of arms, a device repeated through the rest of the store. There was a library corner with comfy chairs and bookshelves of books you might actually want to read and a pantry corner with a high table like something out of *Gosford Park*.

The authenticity of the Sandwich-ness was driven home in the taglines hanging over the counter. "The original sandwich since 1762," "Original. Simple. Worthy." And the one I liked best: "The sandwich you'd make if your name was on it."

The menu's hot sandwich menu offered the Earl's Club Sandwich, the Full Montagu and one called Cannonballs!, complete with exclamation mark. For my lunch I settled on an "original 1762" sandwich, a no-nonsense combination of roast beef in two rustic slices of toasted bread, with cheese and a small dose of horseradish that appealed to the mustard, wasabi and harissa freak in me. As dessert I treated myself to an ice cream sandwich—clearly not a genuine 18th-century recipe, but sheer scrumptiousness easily quashed any inkling of historical pedantry.

Ian confined himself to a Cobb salad and sketched out the

restaurant company's aims: fast preparation, fresh ingredients and a desire to create a business where they could "build the finest sandwich, bar none." All the restaurants in the evolving chain were in the United States (two more outlets in Florida, plus one each in Texas, Indiana and California), but if they could cut it there, in the world's toughest and most sophisticated fast-food market, they would be ready to expand beyond the States.

British tourists were already arriving in large numbers, attracted no doubt by the comforting familiarity of the chain's image. In passing, Ian Schneider told me it was these visiting Brits who liked to come in and inform the staff—incorrectly—that they'd spelled the Montagu name wrong: "You've missed off the e." I could just imagine the know-all certainty and smug condescension with which they'd say it, too.

One thing Ian said really stayed with me. Talking about the care and attention and involvement of the family in the business, I asked him what his impression of the earl and his son had been. He said that "when you meet them, although they're British and very correct, you come away with the feeling you've been hugged!" When I got back to the UK it was time for me to experience a Montagu hug.

*

Orlando Montagu met me at a posh fish restaurant in Mayfair— "There's no decent sandwich places round here . . . yet," he said with a twinkle in his eye. He was in his midthirties, still boyish, tall, good-humored but focused. "If you are someone who finds concentration as difficult as I do, it doesn't matter in what area you find yourself restless, you are restless. I'm not very good at sitting still; my attention span is not very long."

I wondered if this constant energy was a family trait. Orlando thought that the fourth earl—the Sandwich who gave his name to the food—was both busy and restless and that he shared another characteristic, that of going out and doing things his own way. "I think I'm a typical Montagu in being relatively unimpressed by the beaten track. It's possibly a bit of a weakness that we instinctively head for the long grass, and therefore life is often much tougher than it need be. My problem is I find the people I meet and the things I see in the long grass more interesting."

Urgency and restlessness is also a sandwich (lower case s) characteristic: food delivered quickly for minimal impact on forward momentum, the perfect foodstuff for a 21st-century, high-pressure, high-tech lifestyle. As he talked, I noticed Orlando's eyes flick down to check a BlackBerry message that had just beamed in; it was from his cousin, mailing him from a Royal Navy ship heading to the Gulf. Point taken.

The Earl of Sandwich restaurant business was Orlando's idea, but this was not the wacky, last-ditch scheme of an energetic scion from some grand old family desperately trying to scrape up revenue to save the family estate and paper over the cracks in their nonexistent finances. Orlando had been traveling around Europe after leaving school. In Milan he came across a couple of sandwich stores called Panino Giusto—"The true sandwich"— which used the Montagu coat of arms on the menu and had the story of the sandwich up on the wall. "I met the owners, got on very well with them and made sure they didn't go too far down the route of using our name, without being too heavy-handed about it. I realized that here was a fast-growing sector of the fast-food business, but as yet there was no dominant global sandwich brand. I also realized that our family had an internationally recognized brand but no business. I said to my father, 'We have got to get into this business,' and he, as any concerned parent would, told me to go to university, go and get a proper job, which I duly did."

After working in private equity for a number of years, Orlando felt ready to draw up the business plan that might attract the necessary investment. "I don't think my father would have stopped me if I had wanted to go ahead earlier, but his advice was quite right." Orlando did his research and met a number of potential partners. "However, it was clear to me that, if he was interested, Robert Earl, given his track record at Hard Rock Cafe and Planet Hollywood, would be the perfect partner, but initially he did not respond to our advances." Only later did Robert Earl concede that he had instructed his secretary to shred all new business proposals while he turned around Planet Hollywood. "Then, maybe eighteen months after I had first contacted him, Robert called. It turned out that he had obviously not shredded the letters, but had thought carefully about the proposal and done his own research. He agreed to meet."

The initial response from Robert Earl was to tell Orlando "that the essential thing here was to build a world-class food operation that was worthy of our name and our brand. If we could get that right, there was the opportunity of a great business." The first outing for the partnership was a test run in 2001, supplying central London venues with freshly made sandwiches from a flotilla of delivery scooters. After two years, the Walt Disney Company came forward with a prime site for the fledgling Earl of Sandwich to open a store. The company was ready to slice its first sandwich.

I asked Orlando what his long-term goal for the chain was. "We do not want to be the biggest business by volume. Our brand is about quality. But in twenty-five year' time, we hope to be the leading brand in the premium fast-food sector. Although the Sandwich brand has been around for nearly 250 years, we are only at the beginning of this particular voyage."

*

Orlando Montagu had previously showed his entrepreneurial mettle as a teenager by attempting to salvage the *Royal James*, the flagship of the first Earl of Sandwich, Edward Montagu. He was an admiral of the fleet, who lost his life when the *Royal James*, the brand-new, year-old star of the British Navy, was sunk in action off the coast of Suffolk. This was during the Battle of Solebay of 1672, the opening engagement in what became known as the Third Anglo-Dutch War—one of the Dutch fireships landed a mortal blow on ship and commander alike.

Orlando met a North Sea diver who had located the wreck, and together they decided to try and raise the *Royal James* over the next couple of summers—the North Sea is too rough and unworkable the rest of the year. Although they retrieved a large bronze Spanish cannon, which might have been related to the battle, the ship itself remains where it foundered just off Southwold. "I can't give you the exact coordinates, otherwise you would go off and find it and run off with the treasure." I later learned that the Montagu family motto, rather pertinently, is "After many shipwrecks, harbor."

That first earl, Edward Montagu, was the only son of a courtier at the courts of James I and Charles I, and the family home was Hinchingbrooke House in Huntingdonshire. Edward had been ennobled by Charles II in gratitude for the support he had given the monarch during his Restoration, not least commanding the fleet that sailed to the Netherlands and returned Charles to his realm—this despite the fact that Edward and Oliver Cromwell were neighbors.

Edward initially wanted to become the Earl of Portsmouth, an appropriate choice given his naval skills. The trouble was, there already was a Lord Portsmouth, and there was a strongly worded exchange to determine who should have precedence: the lord whose family had borne the title for hundreds of years or this upstart Montagu. The existing Lord Portsmouth held sway, and so the earldom was named after one of the Cinque Ports, the Kent town of Sandwich, another of those quirks of fate that have directly affected the current shape of our language. As Orlando Montagu pointed out, "We were this close to the cheese and pickle portsmouth."

It was the fourth earl whose activities linked the name

Sandwich with the snack. He was John Montagu, born in 1718. He inherited the title at the age of eleven, his father, Viscount Hinchingbrooke, having died prematurely and without becoming earl when John was four. By the time the earldom came his way, his mother had remarried and John had been unceremoniously packed off to Eton, where he consoled himself by becoming an enthusiastic cricketer, a passion he pursued for the rest of his life.

He went up to Trinity College, Cambridge, but failed to collect a degree, and then, instead of undertaking the traditional Grand Tour with his contemporaries, created his own offbeat version, chartering a ship and heading off around the great sites of the Mediterranean, visiting the Nile, climbing Mount Vesuvius and admiring the highlights of the Ottoman Empire.

Back in England, the earl had to confront a major hurdle. He really didn't have the fortune he needed to cut it as a mid-18th-century peer of the realm. The previous earl, his grandfather, had spent most of what fortune the family did have, and his grandmother—who had managed to hang on to her own personal wealth—was alive and kicking in Paris and showing no signs of keeling over in the immediate future.

John Montagu went into politics instead, under the patronage of the Duke of Bedford, and when the duke became first lord of the admiralty in 1744 the young earl, then twenty-six, became his number two. By this time he had married his countess, Dorothy Fane, the daughter of an Irish viscount. The marriage was problematic, not least because Dorothy suffered from increasingly severe mental problems, which put an immense strain on the happy family façade. Our earl took over as first lord of the admiralty when the Duke of Bedford moved on to another government post, but two years later he fell foul of some anti-Bedford factional fighting, incurred the displeasure of King George II for some injudicious comments criticizing the Hanoverians and ended up being sidelined from his political career for a decade.

However, it was the earl's approach to work at the admiralty both before his fall from favor and following his return to high office that led directly to the naming of the sandwich. Even his political and personal opponents never denied that he was tireless in his work rate, a brisk and conscientious administrator, charged with that Montagu energy. The flip side might have been accusations of impatience or stubbornness, but for sheer industry and long hours he was unimpeachable. Getting in early and working through to the evening, in a period when dinner was traditionally eaten in the late afternoon, between 4 and 8 P.M., what more pragmatic solution for a man deep in his paperwork then to ask for a round of salt beef slapped between a couple of slices of bread? When Orlando Montagu and his father were developing the sandwich for their restaurant chain, one of the current earl's stipulations was that, like the original, you should be able to pick up the sandwich in one hand, leaving the other hand free to carry on writing.

This version of events seems far more likely than the one usually trotted out, which claims that the earl invented the sandwich as a way of fueling himself during round-the-clock gambling sessions. This theory seems to have wormed its way determinedly into legend via Pierre-Jean Grosley, a French lawyer and author, who wrote a travel memoir about his experience of visiting London in 1765. It's a wide-ranging look at life in the capital, including chapters on sculpture, music, Quakers, Moravians, suicide, madmen and lunatics, and antipathy to the French.

In a section on clubs, Grosley describes the vogue for gambling. The English, he says, "who carry all their passions to excess, are altogether extravagant in the article of gaming," and he illustrates his point with the story of a minister of state playing for "four and twenty hours" at a public gaming table, so absorbed that "during the whole time, he had no subsistence but a bit of beef, between two slices of toasted bread, which he eat [sic] without ever quitting the game. This new dish grew highly in vogue. It was called by the name of the minister, who invented it."

Although this is fine contemporary reportage, there is one flaw in it: the fourth earl was not, by most accounts, an inveterate gambler. He simply did not have enough money to be a high roller, especially living, as his biographer N. A. M. Rodger in *The Insatiable Earl* puts it, "as a public man on the income of a country squire." Although gambling was very much a part of life, particularly club-land life, and the earl was a member of a number of clubs, he preferred smaller scale wagers, especially on his beloved cricket.

The truth, Orlando Montagu says, is more straightforward: the earl was a busy man, not given to lingering over social chitchat, who wanted the best-quality food using his favorite ingredients (he was a big salt beef fan) brought to him quickly to be consumed at pace. "As a family we're not very good at ceremony. We don't play court well. We're not very social, in the sense that a lot of other older families might have a clubby set, a certain routine to the year that is socially focused. We're not a frivolous family." But even if Grosley's account is inaccurate, I noticed that he described a sandwich with toasted bread, just like the one I'd enjoyed in Florida.

The arrival of the sandwich into the English language was captured by no less an observer than Edward Gibbon in his *Journal.* In November 1762—the year the Montagu family have set as the year of its "invention"—he had spent a busy month reading the works of Tollius and Ubbo Emmius for hours on end, passed a few days as a houseguest at Uppark in Sussex, returned to his family home at Beriton in Hampshire and headed to London on the 20th. On the evening of November 24, he dined with his friend Holt at the Cocoa-tree in St. James's Street and went out to see *The Spanish Fryar,* a play by John Dryden, before returning to the Cocoa-tree. "That respectable body," he wrote, "of which I have the honor to be a member, affords every evening a sight truly English. Twenty or thirty, perhaps, of the first men in the kingdom, in point of fashion and fortune, supping at little tables covered with a napkin, in the middle of a coffee-room, upon a bit of cold meat, or a Sandwich, & drinking a glass of punch."

Bread-based snacks were nothing new, however. In the Middle Ages a slab of stale bread often served as a temporary plate for meat, handily absorbing any juices. This slab, called a trencher, could then be eaten or thrown to the dogs for them to devour. Bread and meat or bread and cheese were fairly obvious combinations: in Shakespeare's *The Merry Wives of Windsor* Corporal Nym declares, "I love not the humor of bread and cheese." Buttered toast as a snack in London was mentioned by 17th-century travel writers. But there was no single word for the concoction of bread and a filling until the term "sandwich" caught on—now there was a single entity to savor.

In Charles Dickens's *Martin Chuzzlewit* Mrs. Gamp describes her method of making cheese sandwiches. By the time the novel was written in the 1840s the sandwich had certainly been introduced to America: Eliza Leslie, from Philadelphia, who had spent time in England, published a recipe for a ham sandwich in her book *Directions for Cookery*. The proliferation of the sandwich in the States was swift. By the end of the century the club sandwich existed—most strongly claimed by the Saratoga Club in Saratoga Springs, New York. The Reuben followed in the 1910s, the peanut butter and jelly version during the Second World War (Elvis's favorite was fried peanut butter and banana), joining Denver sandwiches, BLTs, subs, heroes, the hamburger . . .

In its homeland the sandwich pursued its own evolution, the British fondness for square white bread giving rise to the doorstep jam butty, the dainty cucumber triangle and the "morning after" sausage sandwich. Just before the First World War a restaurant on the boulevard des Capucines in Paris created France's own take on the sandwich, the *croque monsieur*. The Earl of Sandwich's simple salt beef and toast has spawned a plethora of breads, fillings and techniques.

An alternative version of the sandwich story exists in a parallel
universe imagined by Woody Allen. It appears in the short story
"Yes, But Can the Steam Engine Do This?" from his *Getting Even*
collection (he also performed this as a sketch). In Woody's tale he
comes across the fact, reading a magazine in a Park Avenue
therapist's waiting room, that the sandwich was invented by the
Earl of Sandwich and is inspired to pen a biography of the earl,
while admitting his knowledge of history is vague and that he has
a propensity to embellish. In his version the young Earl of
Sandwich discovers, while still at school, an "unusual interest in
thinly sliced strips of roast beef and ham." At Cambridge he is sent
down after being caught as a bread thief. Such is the intensity of his
obsession that he loses family, fortune and friends, but, disowned
and disinherited, he plows on, researching cheeses and sardines,
desperately trying to make the elements work together. His first
attempt, two slices of bread topped by a slice of turkey, is a total
failure, as is a later version with only three slices of ham (no bread).

Despite all the rebuttals and the opprobrium, the earl never
falters in his task, until—"at 4.17 A.M. on April 27, 1758"—he
triumphantly places strips of ham between two pieces of rye
bread and as an inspired flourish adds a dash of mustard. The
success of the sandwich is instant. The earl is fêted throughout the
realm, granted the Order of the Garter and later invents the hamburger. Allen has the German poet Friedrich Hölderlin deliver
Sandwich's funeral oration: "He freed mankind from the hot
lunch. We owe him so much."

★

The 4th Earl of Sandwich was a tall man—as his descendants are
today: the 11th earl is six foot six—and ungainly, a word used of
him in at least two biographies. He possessed a pair of left feet so
pronounced that one dancing master is reputed to have asked the
earl never to reveal who had instructed him, as it would have

ruined his reputation as a teacher. However, despite his short-comings on the dance floor, John Montagu was a gallant, polite, affable fellow. In the 1750s, after separating from his wife (she was finally declared insane) and inheriting his grandmother's fortune, he received a stream of letters from women, most of whom he had never met, looking for financial help or offering themselves as the next countess of Sandwich. The soul of discretion, the earl certainly had liaisons both before and after his marriage broke up, but he was not the randy lecher that a connection with Francis Dashwood and the dubious goings-on at the Hellfire Club might have suggested, just as he was not the inveterate 24/7 gambler of legend.

The earl's longest emotional relationship was with a young woman named Martha Ray, whom he met in 1761, when she was sixteen going on seventeen, a staymaker's daughter, serving an apprenticeship with a Clerkenwell dressmaker. It is not known whether the pair encountered each other strolling around one of London's parks, or whether the earl saw Martha and she was procured for him in some way. But he became her protector and oversaw her education, making sure that she received schooling in France and providing her with music and singing lessons.

Martha had a good voice, and music was one of the earl's passions, especially the operas and oratorios of Handel. He used to host two mini-festivals a year at his Huntingdonshire house, Hinchingbrooke, in midwinter and summer, during which he would sing and play enthusiastic timpani. In other words, he was offering Martha the chance to acquire the attributes of a society wife, although it was a society into which he could not formally introduce her. She matured into an elegant and—within his circle—open consort, who bore him five children; they stayed together for nearly twenty years.

During that time, the earl ended his political hiatus, returning as first lord of the admiralty in 1771 as a member of Lord North's Tory administration. This was a period when the admiralty was at full stretch. James Cook and the *Endeavour* were traveling and acquiring new lands for Britain—including the Hawaiian islands, which Cook named the Sandwich Islands, the earl's other eponymous legacy—and confrontation and war with the American colonies were approaching fast.

Orlando Montagu was keen to make a point about the fourth earl's involvement in the American War of Independence (or the American Revolutionary War, depending which side of the Atlantic you are on). "Because of the war, the bias has been toward the idea of these incapable Brits, but historically the earl was much more interested in France. I think by then Britain had said that these colonies in America were much too big to manage, and that we had reached our colonial peak over there." Nonetheless, the earl's reputation was soured by his connection with the war, as it had been a few years earlier when he had helped prosecute John Wilkes, a sometime friend and a member of Parliament's awkward squad, who was unpopular in the House but had public support. This was the occasion of the widely repeated exchange between them, when the earl told John Wilkes he would die "either on the gallows, or of the pox." "That, sir," retorted Wilkes, "depends on whether I embrace your Lordship's principles or your Lordship's mistress."

In 1779 the Earl of Sandwich suffered a devastating sideswipe to his emotional life. Martha Ray was leaving a performance at the Opera House in Covent Garden, accompanied by two acquaintances, when she was shot and fatally injured by James Hackman. Hackman, a recently ordained priest and ex-soldier, had met Martha while on an army recruiting drive in Huntingdonshire and become infatuated with her, bombarding her with unwanted attentions. He was, in short, a stalker, and when Martha rejected a proposal of marriage, he meted out fatal retribution. After killing her, Hackman tried to commit suicide with the same pistol, but he failed and was hanged by the notorious executioner Jack Ketch. There was no sense of justice having been done, however. A cloud of sadness hung low over the remaining years of the earl's life.

★

I wondered what the fourth earl would have made of his multiple-great-grandson's restaurant chain, and whether he would have cheered the current generation's attempt to reclaim the sandwich for the family: Orlando Montagu's aim is to reestablish and differentiate "the sandwich with a capital S," to recapture its history. "It is time," as he put it, "for the people to fight back. It's a brand with a living family attached. I think that's part of its attraction. Each of us adds our own character to it."

The fourth earl would have approved, I am sure, of his descendant's enthusiasm for top-quality ingredients. Hinchingbrooke, the fourth earl's estate, had an extensive kitchen garden. "By the standards of any kitchen garden I've seen today it was enormous," Orlando told me. "The Montagus had been farmers for as long as they had been military and naval men or politicians. The concept of eating what you didn't grow would have been alien to them. They owned large estates in Cambridgeshire and Dorset." Those Dorset estates, acquired by the family via the marriage of the fourth earl's son to the heiress Mary Paulet, abut the Montagu family's current principal home, Mapperton.

This commitment to fresh ingredients was reinforced when I went, somewhat perversely, to get a French view on *"le sandwich."* I took the opportunity on finding myself in Lyons, on the trail of Anton Mesmer, to visit Paul Bocuse at his home base in Collonges au Mont d'Or, north of Lyons, on the banks of the River Saône. Paul Bocuse is one of the great French chefs, who hails from a long line of cooks dating back to the 17th century. I had read in a newspaper article somewhere that Bocuse had created a sandwich, and I wondered what he had wanted to achieve and what he had decided to put in it.

I was reminded of one of my favorite books, *Between Meals*, a sensational *tour d'horizon* of French gastronomy between the two world wars by the sublime *New Yorker* writer A. J. Liebling. Liebling quotes his friend Waverley Root, who said, "Lyons is a heavily bourgeois city. The cooking of Lyons fits the character of the city. Hearty rather than graceful, and apt to leave you with an overstuffed feeling."

Root had clearly not dined chez Bocuse. After lunch—exquisite: my head still reels as I see my notes on *Escalope de foie gras de canard poêlée au verjus* or the *fricassée de volaille de Bresse à la crème aux morilles*—the chef came to sit down, offering a glass of Bocuse cognac on the house, to talk sandwiches. In his eighties, he remained firmly at the helm of the ship, cheerfully issuing commands to deferential aides and sous-chefs, and still gallantly flirtatious to my lunch companion Agnès, an old friend from student days near Paris, whom he charmed with an elegant kiss. ("*Une bise de Bocuse!*" she reminisced afterward.)

He told me that he had wanted to create a version of the sandwich for his slightly faster food outlets in Lyons, the brasseries that cater to a scurrying postwork commuter clientele. He had researched the sandwich, gone through books of recipes and concluded that the key—just as Orlando Montagu had said—was always to use the best and the freshest ingredients available. The bread had to be perfect. Bocuse's bread came from the Poilâne bakery in Paris, which is now run by Apollonia Poilâne, after her father Lionel, maybe the first celebrity artisan baker, died in a helicopter crash off Brittany in 2002.

One of the Bocuse aides brought, at his boss's request, the recipe for the "Maine Sandwich de Bocuse." The instructions were precise, specifying how to cut the bread to the centimeter, the exact type of wheat flour, how slowly to knead the dough and how long (five hours) to allow for fermentation "*sur poolish*"—a mixture of water, flour and yeast. And that was just the bread.

The ingredients included lobster tails cooked in a court

bouillon, hard-boiled eggs, tomatoes, crème fraîche, herbs, mustard, seasoning and both ketchup and, perhaps in a nod to the sandwich's origins, *sauce anglaise*. The "dressage" instructions were as precise as those for the bread-making. Now I understood why the Bocuse menu quoted Vincent van Gogh. *"Comme il est difficile d'être simple."*

With this gourmet sandwich playing around my gastric synapses and gracefully accepting another glass of M. Bocuse's cognac, I mused on whether it would be possible to create an entire meal of eponymous foods.

The dessert course would not be a problem. The meal could be rounded off by crêpes suzette (legend has it that the dish was named after a dining companion of the future Edward VII) or a peach melba. That ice cream, peach and raspberry concoction was created by Auguste Escoffier in the 1890s and dedicated to Dame Nellie Melba, the grande dame of Australian opera. She had been born Helen Porter Mitchell in Melbourne in 1861 and took her stage name from her birthplace. She is also celebrated by melba toast—thin, crisp, lightly toasted slices of bread, which were part of a convalescent diet when she was languishing with illness and which had originally been prepared by Escoffier for the wife of César Ritz.

An alternative dessert trolley might offer a pavlova, the meringue, cream and fruit dish named for the ballerina Anna Pavlova, the Sacher-torte chocolate created by Franz Sacher in Vienna in 1832, or pralines, the sugar-coated nuts prepared for the 17th-century French marshal, minister and diplomat Comte du Plessis-Praslin by his military cook (the wonderfully titled *officier de bouche*).

For starters maybe eggs Benedict, a hair of the dog restorative run up by the Waldorf in New York, it is said, for a hungover stockbroker of that name. And for preprandial drinks a martini, perhaps, for which the most likely theory is that it was named after Martini di Armi di Taggia, chief bartender in the 1910s at the

Knickerbocker, another Manhattan hotel, on Broadway and 42nd Street. Or a margarita, maybe, for which there are various claims, including one that it was named for Rita Hayworth, real name Margarita Cansino. And after lunch, a nice cup of Earl Grey tea . . .

I was stuck on what the main course could be, until it came in a flash—what else but beef Wellington, that Iron Duke of a dish, tenderloin wrapped in pâté and coated in a duxelles of mushrooms (a seasoning itself named after a Marquis d'Uxelles), the whole enveloped in puff pastry before baking.

This brought me back in a culinary circle to my conversation with Orlando Montagu. We had been talking about his family traits and how the Montagu restlessness might be difficult to live with—his words, not mine. He said his wife complemented his nature. "She is methodical, prepared, ready for everything, whereas my family have always been slightly impulsive." Honor Montagu was born a Wellesley, and is the granddaughter of the current Duke of Wellington. It had been pointed out to both of them and by both of them many times, of course, but it was still very satisfying, that—almost uniquely—their union of the sandwich and the wellington was a true marriage of eponyms.

CHAPTER 11

Driving Miss Mercedes

"Thus the Mercedes comes, O she comes. This astonishing
device, this amazing Mercedes, with Speed."
William Ernest Henley, "A Song of Speed"

Stuttgart is a city shaped by horsepower. The very name of the
place explains its origins: *stutt* means mare (it's the root of the
English word "stud") and *gart*, garden. In the 950s Liudolf, Duke
of Swabia, the son of Emperor Otto the Great, set up a
Stutengarten on the banks of the River Neckar to breed and raise
his horses. A black horse still prances on the city's coat of arms.

How appropriate, then, that a different kind of horsepower
helped underpin the city's development throughout the last
century. The internal combustion engine was created in
Stuttgart, an invention whose influence headed outwards, up and
away from the Neckar Valley, and immutably changed the nature
of our daily life. Stuttgart is the home of one of the great
automotive manufacturers, a company that was among the
pioneers of the motorcar as we understand it. But the badge of
this company is not a prancing black horse—that was taken by
Ferrari. No, this is the home of Daimler. And because of Daimler,
it is also the home of one of the most evocative of all car marques:
Mercedes and its instantly recognizable symbol—the three-
pointed star.

As I approached the Untertürkheim district of Stuttgart, having
dropped from the high plains above the city, switchbacking down
along the tram tracks and then crossing the Neckar to the southwest of the city center—in a Mercedes taxi, naturally—I could see

a three-pointed star revolving slowly in the distance. I was heading for the epicenter of Mercedes, the Daimler Untertürkheim works, which have dominated this part of Stuttgart for a hundred years.

I was in town to look at the company's archives but also to visit the latest addition to the site: the gleamingly new Mercedes-Benz Museum, its freshness still palpable, which opened in May 2006. Positioned at the crossroads of two urban highways, down which commuters cruise every day of the week, it is a silvern, curvaceously modern building, its inside a double-helix version of the Guggenheim in New York, with gently sloping galleries that wind down and around each other to retell the story of Daimler and Benz and Mercedes.

I took a futuristic elevator to the top of the museum, perambulated slowly through the days of motorized travel, past the first tentative internal combustion engines, and stopped at a blue, open-topped, two-seater car, its front axle pockmarked from use, its spare tires apparently ready for fitting in case of a flat. Spotlit beneath concentric circles of glass teardrops, this was the oldest extant Mercedes car, an original 1902 Mercedes Simplex 40 PS, registration 508-M. And on screens nearby there flashed images of Emil Jellinek, the man whose energy and tenaciousness had pushed the Daimler company to produce the car for him, and of his oldest daughter, Mercédès Adrienne Manuela Ramona Jellinek.

★

Emil Jellinek was a wealthy Austrian businessman based in Nice. In the late 1890s he sported a prolific pair of muttonchop sideburns, and he had a penchant for the pith helmet, a habit retained from a youth spent in North Africa. He was also a top-notch salesman, with an acute sense of PR and plenty of blarney, a hustler, but a couth one—certainly not a crook—with classy contacts and bags of energy and charisma.

He came from a Jewish Austrian family of intellectuals: his two brothers both ended up as professors. Born in Leipzig in April 1853, Emil was something of a wild child and had been packed off to North Africa to keep him out of trouble. As a young man in Tangiers and Oran he fine-tuned his wheeling and dealing skills by trading in tobacco and local products. After moving into banking and insurance, he oscillated between Europe and Africa, seeking wealth first and foremost but also its accoutrements in the form of honors and material goods.

By the time he settled on the Riviera—he hated the cold, apparently—he was acquiring plenty of both. He had a posh villa on the Promenade des Anglais with a view over the harbor. He owned motorboats and yachts. He was asked to act as the consul for the Republic of Mexico and later for the Austro-Hungarian Empire, and he stood proudly for formal photographs in full Ruritanian regalia: cocked hat crowned with ostrich feathers, tasseled epaulettes, sash, crosses and medals liberally scattered across his chest. At a time when the Côte d'Azur was a favorite winter destination for the well-off and leisured, he rubbed shoulders and slapped backs with the likes of the Rothschilds, Astors and Vanderbilts.

Emil Jellinek was also into cars. He had arrived there via an interest in bicycles before motor vehicles became readily available, and in less stout days had used his own pedal power to make an ascent on two wheels of the La Turbie hill climb above Nice. But as soon as the motorcar came on the market he simply had to have one. He was a classic early adopter, flaunting his new acquisitions in the late 1890s: a De Dion-Bouton tricycle, a Léon Bollée Voiturette, a Benz. He would show them off to his circle of chums in Nice, often selling on a car to one of them so he could get another that was newer, more powerful and, above all, faster.

As a co-driver and navigator through the twists and turns of Mercedes history, I turned to Doug Nye, a vastly experienced, hugely prolific writer on automotive history. The great thing about Doug is that although his knowledge is genuinely encyclopedic and he can go head-to-head on technical matters with the most high-octane of gearheads, he can translate this vast reservoir of information into a highly intelligible version for those, like me, who have rarely lifted a hood except in extremis.

In the early days of motoring, driving was left to a chauffeur, a natural delegation of dirty work by those at the top end of the hierarchy. To maneuver the clunky primitive gearing and turn the wheels demanded the biceps of a docker, and one of the stable lads could be togged out in leather overcoat, hat and goggles. "You had to have a chauffeur," Doug Nye told me. "Early on, Emil Jellinek would certainly have done. Driving was so bloody difficult, and you'd look a right Charlie if you got it wrong. And someone of Jellinek's standing did not want to look a right Charlie."

But sitting alongside their chauffeurs, many of the owners were twitching and itching to have a go themselves. And so began the era of the "gentleman driver," who would take over the wheel or the steering handles and lurch onto the roads, frightening the horses, terrifying the populace and occasionally—given the lack of road handling—bagging a brace of them beneath his wheels. For the gentlemen drivers this was unfortunate collateral damage in the pursuit of automotive fun. If there was a fatality, a quiet word to the commissioner of police at the next social function or across the table at the casino would ensure that no more need be said.

After learning the basics of how to drive, a competitive spirit took over: motor racing was a natural evolution for these gentlemen of the road. Emil Jellinek was no exception, and he was constantly seeking improvements. Sometime during 1897, reading the papers in his villa in Nice, he saw an advertisement for a Daimler car, with rave reviews: the Daimler Motor Company was based, the ad said, in Cannstatt. "Where's Cannstatt?" he barked, expecting an answer from one of his family, a staff member, anybody. One of his children's nannies obliged. She knew where it was—a suburb of Stuttgart. With little further ado, Emil Jellinek made up his mind to go and see the people behind the company. He traveled to Cannstatt and had a meeting with Gottlieb Daimler, whose name the company bore, and Daimler's chief designer, Wilhelm Maybach.

When Jellinek arrived in Cannstatt he encountered a company that had already had a major impact on the development of the motorcar. Without going into that in any detail (libraries overflow on the subject), there had been two major break-throughs in the year of 1886. Both were by German designers and engineers. In Mannheim Karl Benz patented an innovative light three-wheeled gasoline engine–powered car and developed a trustworthy spark plug. In Stuttgart Gottlieb Daimler and Willy Maybach added their own internal combustion engine to what, effectively, was still a horseless carriage. Each marked a staging post on the way to the modern car. Subsequently, popular myth has combined these two machines, so that many people believe Daimler and Benz worked together on the invention. In fact, as Karl Benz later confirmed, he never met Gottlieb Daimler (the mid-1920s merger between their two companies to form Daimler-Benz merely heightened the confusion).

Daimler and Maybach started working together in a converted greenhouse on the grounds of a villa that Daimler had bought on Taubenheimstrasse in Cannstatt. The greenhouse is still standing, tucked away in wooded parkland behind the city's Kursaal spa rooms, and is preserved as a permanent museum and memorial. That it is still in one piece is a fluke. During the Second World War Stuttgart was pounded mercilessly by both the RAF and the USAF. In fact, Doug Nye told me the story of Dean Batchelor, the American editor of *Road and Track*, who visited the Mercedes factory in the mid-1950s and was asked if he had visited Stuttgart before. "Well," he replied, "I've been over it once, with a few friends"—he had been a pilot of a Liberator and left a calling card of destruction. As Doug pointed out, "Stuttgart lies in a deep valley around the Neckar, a very enclosed and compact target. If you were a bomb aimer you'd be ashamed to miss."

But the greenhouse did survive. It is small and rather elegant, and inside tools lie on a workshop bench begging to be picked up again. In one corner stands a tall, thin, wooden vat, like an over-sized stein, of gasoline. This is where the internal combustion engine was cultivated. It was still very much a cottage, or green-house, industry when Emil Jellinek visited and chatted with the Daimler bosses. He made his intentions very clear. He wanted to buy their cars—in fact, he had been so impressed with the phaeton that had picked him up from Stuttgart Station that he bought one immediately. In the Mercedes archives there's a photo of him perched atop one of his early purchases, looking like a camel driver in his pith helmet, heading across the Semmering Pass in 1899, a girl in a flower-decorated hat and her father looking on in wonder, or terror.

Jellinek's proposal was to acquire Daimler cars and sell them on to his moneyed pals back on the Riviera. "He was fearfully grand," said Doug Nye, "living down there on the Riviera, meeting other fearfully grand people. They were all having a topping time, larking about in their cars. If you look at the early photos there are grenadiers acting as crowd marshals, in pickelhaubes, medals and gold braid. So much scrambled egg, it was unbelievable. There was a 'look at me' mentality that was very characteristic of early motor racing."

The deal sounded promising—Gottlieb Daimler was as commerce-minded as Jellinek—and a business relationship was embarked upon, but the Cannstatt team had no idea what a ferocious terrier they had brought into their midst. The relation-ship would give them a very bumpy ride.

Emil Jellinek wanted new cars so he could run them at Nice Speed Week. This was a social highlight in the Riviera calendar.

As Doug Nye put it, "like the Goodwood Festival of Speed, Henley and Ascot all rolled into one." Two cars were duly delivered, but time had been short, and neither was as finely prepared or tuned as the company would have liked. They were driven for Emil Jellinek by two professional drivers using the pseudonyms Mercedes I and Mercedes II.

Pseudonyms for racing drivers were a common feature of the early days of racing. Scions of wealthy families, who had not yet inherited their fortunes, did not want to broadcast the fact that they were dicing with damage in unstable motorcars: a pseudonym would keep Papa in the dark and protect Mama from an attack of nerves. Baron Rothschild raced as "Dr. Pascal." There were Italian racers rejoicing in the names Pal Joe and Kipper. Even as late as the 1950s the Le Mans–winning pair of Beurlys and Eldé were pseudonyms for Jean Blaton, a Belgian industrialist, and his co-driver Leon Dernier. So for Emil Jellinek to name his drivers after his oldest daughter was far from remarkable.

Alas, the race was a tragedy. Willy Bauer, the driver known as Mercedes I, lost control, smacked his car into a cliff face and was killed. The Daimler Motor Company nearly lost its nerve about any further involvement in racing. The problem was that the design of the cars was not suitable for fast speeds on uneven surfaces. The cars of the time were square boxes, with a high center of gravity. Take a corner fractionally too fast, and the thing would topple over. Hit a pothole and the driver had no chance of correcting the line.

After talking the accident over with his friends and fellow drivers, Jellinek approached the Daimler company with a new proposal in April 1900: that they would produce another vehicle that could overcome the top-heaviness of the existing cars. With Jellinek pushing for speed and lightness and bombarding the plant with a fusillade of telegrams—"I don't want the car of today or the car of tomorrow, I want the car of the day after tomorrow," he wrote—designer Willy Maybach brought together a number of design and engineering innovations that he had already been working on.

He created a new radiator design that could control overheating more efficiently, allowing the engine to handle greater power. There was a new gearshift gate—no longer sequential, when the only option was to go up or down the gears in turn. There was an accelerator pedal to control engine speed. The engine was at the front, planted on a longer, lower and substantially lighter chassis for better stability. At the turn of a new century, the car was radically different from any and every motor vehicle previously produced.

Jellinek had also ordered enough of these cars—thirty-six in total, a huge order representing a massive outlay of cash—to give himself the clout to insist that this new car was not going to be a Daimler. This car was going to be a Mercedes.

Emil Jellinek had something of a fixation with the name Mercedes, I think it's fair to say, or Mercédès to give it the correct accents. The house in Nice he called the Villa Mercédès. He later acquired hotel property in Paris and named one building the Hotel Mercédès. He had a motorboat named Mercédès and a yacht named Mercédès-Mercédès, which seems a little over the top. (In 1903, when the cars had become a success, he even changed his own family name to Jellinek-Mercédès, "probably the first time a father has taken his daughter's name," he remarked.)

He had picked the soft Spanish name—literally meaning "mercies"—for his elder daughter. According to his son Guy in his book *My Father, M. Mercedes*, Spain was close to his heart and he spoke the language well. It was also the name he wanted to see on the front of the cars that Daimler was constructing for him. And in case you think this was merely the wish of a softhearted father's fondness for his oldest daughter, listen to what he told Daimler: "The name is both exotic and attractive. It can be easily pronounced and it sounds good. You can call these cars whatever you want, but the cars I sell will be called Mercédès." This was a man who understood the value of branding.

The Mercédès in question was then aged ten. She had been born in September 1889, Emil's third child from his first marriage (his first wife Rachel died in 1893, and he remarried and had four further children). According to her half-brother Guy, Mercédès was slim and highly strung and yearned to be involved, somehow, in the arts—she had a good soprano voice, he said. The pictures of her in the company archives show a slightly solemn girl—although that may have been her photograph face—with long, frizzy blond hair, puppy dog eyes and a hint of an overbite. A T-shirt on sale in the shop at the Mercedes-Benz Museum pays tribute to her as *ein hübsches, lebensfrohes Mädchen* (a vivacious, pretty young girl).

★

The first Mercedes car arrived in Nice in early 1901. Its debut outing, at a race at Pau in southwest France, was not a success. The new gearing failed, the 'clutch jammed, and the car was pulled from the race. Emil Jellinek dispatched another salvo of telegrams to the Daimler works. The cars, he demanded, had to be absolutely ready and right for Nice Speed Week, less than a month later.

Whatever it was that he did in the intervening weeks, Wilhelm Maybach worked marvels. In Nice the Mercedes cars simply ran away from all the other vehicles. The technical forward leap meant they were like space rockets taking on go-carts. Paul Meyan, the general secretary of the French Automobile Club, coined an epigram to sum up their impact: *"Nous sommes entrés dans l'ère Mercédès,"* he wrote ("We have entered the Mercedes era").

Needless to say, credit for this triumph was claimed by all parties, not least Emil Jellinek—the man who put the "Me, me, me" in Mercedes—who was quick to claim his share, and his son's book about his father certainly weighs in with support for him, suggesting that it was Jellinek who had proposed both the front-engined design and the lower chassis.

However, Willy Maybach's official biography, not unnaturally, disputes this. Emil Jellinek was many things, but he was not a technical man. He communicated what he observed and what he distilled from conversations with other drivers, added to a basic common sense and competitiveness. As his son Guy observed, "The Grande Corniche and his stopwatch were the means of disclosing weaknesses." Doug Nye tends to favor the theory that Maybach was the man behind the technical advances. "Emil Jellinek came up with objectives. He was a catalyst. He encouraged Maybach to make great strides. You would too, with a gadfly like that up your rear end. Maybach is the great unsung hero; he takes huge credit for the modern motorcar."

What Maybach, Daimler and Jellinek achieved together was remarkable. The radiator design alone is phenomenal. Previously, with few surfaces to cool the heat produced by the internal combustion, gallons of water would be used up in the course of a journey, much of it escaping as steam. Maybach created a honeycomb radiator—8,070 long, square-sectioned tubes, arranged in a grid, producing a much greater surface area while allowing air to run through and cool down the hot water—with a fan behind to increase the effectiveness of the device. And that's before you get on to the gearing, the chassis construction, the front-mounted engine, the low center of gravity . . . Look at the Mercedes Simplex in the Mercedes-Benz Museum and forget the *Chitty Chitty Bang Bang* styling, and you can see all the basics of the 20th-century car (and to date the 21st-century car, come to that).

The next few years were a period of improvement and adjustment. "Jellinek became Daimler's man on the front line," said Doug Nye. "They were pretty insulated and isolated in their environment, too busy to go out, relying on received knowledge."

This progress was despite a fire in June 1903 that completely razed the company's Cannstatt factory, the plant they had moved to once the greenhouse proved too small: one molten lump of bronze remains from the three cars they were in the course of preparing for the Gordon-Bennett Trophy in Ireland. (A private owner named Clarence Dinsmore kindly lent them his own Mercedes, and it won.) The company transferred to new premises in Untertürkheim, on the site where it still operates.

Despite the success of the Mercedes cars, both in competition and with potential owners, the relationship between Emil Jellinek and his Daimler partners lurched along, always on the edge of disaster. Gottlieb Daimler had died in March 1900, just as the first Mercedes cars were finished, and his son Paul had taken over the company. Paul Daimler realized that Emil Jellinek had played a huge part in the success of DMC—as Emil was always happy to remind him in any correspondence—but resented his ego and his bombast.

Willy Maybach also had a difficult relationship with his employers, the Daimler Motor Company. He left once, and they tempted him back, but he split with them finally in 1907, moving on to design airships. Emil Jellinek also parted company with Daimler, soon after, when they refused to give him any further free spare parts or repairs. ("This is the gratitude of the Daimler Motor Company, which I have built up from nothing to what it is now," he fumed.) Intriguingly, the name Mercedes remained part of the Daimler side of the bargain after they parted. There must have been some incredibly airtight contractual obligation, since it's hard to see Emil Jellinek gaily relinquishing his rights to a name he held so dear.

By the time of the First World War motoring had changed significantly. In the late 1910s there had been a severe economic recession, not as bad as the Great Crash of 1929, but severe enough. After 1908 the French Automobile Club did not organize any Grands Prix for six years. The sport of city-to-city racing had already come to an end following the disastrous 1903 Paris–Madrid race, which claimed eight lives. Racing drivers were increasingly professional, either test drivers or mechanics, and private owner-driver racers were thin on the ground. According to Doug Nye, one of them, Charles Jarrott, "said motor racing was no longer a sport for gentlemen, now that hoi polloi were racing, all these greasy-fingered oiks at the wheel."

During the war Emil Jellinek left Nice for Germany and then Switzerland. While he was away he learned he was being demonized back in France, accused of being a spy, the Villa Mercédès was taken over by the local prefect's office, his vehicles were sequestered, and his yacht was scuttled. The glory days of parading down the Promenade des Anglais were finished for good. He stuttered through the final years of the war, still hurling out orders and missives, but was dealt a serious sideswipe when his youngest son died of a perforated appendix in January 1917. A year later to the day Emil Jellinek took to his bed and died that same night.

*

The Mercedes brand carried on. The company had since 1909 used the three-pointed star device, said to symbolize motor travel on land, on water and in the air, since Daimler produced motorboats and airships as well as cars. They also registered a four-star design at the same time, which was, much later, used for an aerospace venture. The same year the name Mercedes was formally shorn of its accents. The marque maintained a reputation for engineering excellence, and in the one final Grand Prix that took place just before the outbreak of war in 1914 Mercedes had reinforced its racing pedigree by scooping first, second and third places.

To get a sense of the post-Jellinek heritage of Mercedes, I popped down to see Gordon Murray. He was in an industrial park in Shalford in Surrey, in the middle of overseeing the setup of his new car design company, where he would work on an eco-friendly car. Gordon Murray, to me, is a contemporary descendant in a lineage of great car designers that stretches directly from Willy Maybach onwards.

I once read somewhere, or somebody told me, that Gordon should have been a jazz drummer. It's true: he's tall, languid, mellow, thoughtful, though rock 'n' roll is more his taste in music. In the 1970s and 1980s he was chief designer for the Brabham Formula One team under Bernie Ecclestone. His cars won two World Championships for Nelson Piquet and, when Gordon moved on to McLaren in 1986, for both Ayrton Senna and Alain Prost. In the early 1990s he had total control over the design and engineering of the McLaren F1, at the time the world's fastest and most expensive production car—240.1 mph and one million dollars—which won the Le Mans 24 Hours on its first attempt.

Gordon is a student of car design and of cars in motion. I remember one Sunday during a recent Goodwood Festival of Speed, that cavalcade of all things wondrous and automotive, clambering up onto one of the public stands. Behind me, on the very highest benches sat Gordon, his eyes glued to each historic car as it took a right-hander to head past the front of Goodwood House and on up toward the hill climb at the end of the course. He was totally concentrated, watching, observing, learning. He told me he would still go down to the Goodwood paddock at seven each morning to peer inside the cockpits and under the chassis of the classic cars parked there, because he could always learn from how engineers of the past had solved problems.

Gordon's first exposure to Mercedes was as a young boy in South Africa in the 1950s. This was an era when the Stuttgart works were emerging from the shattering aftermath of the Second World War, gradually easing themselves back into motor racing. They had started again with bicycle manufacture before relaunching any kind of a car program. In any case, the French authorities prevented German car companies from taking part in any motor racing during the immediate postwar years. The return of Mercedes was dramatic. "The cars had engineering style and engineering foresight, but they also had aerodynamic style as well," remembered Gordon. "That period of Mercedes was brilliant."

The supreme example of this was the gullwing Mercedes 300 SLR, which allowed Stirling Moss to carry off the Mille Miglia, the Tourist Trophy at Goodwood and the Targa Florio of 1955 and scoop the World Sports Car Championship. That car was sumptuous, flowing, curvaceous, and fifty years later, in tribute, Gordon Murray worked with Mercedes to recreate a new road-going car, the Mercedes-Benz SLR McLaren.

"We were aiming to rekindle that era and the spirit of the original car, but bring it bang up to date. If you dig back into what made companies like BMW or Mercedes great, it almost invariably boils down to individuals." In the case of postwar Mercedes it was chief designer Rudolf Uhlenhaut. "That period of Mercedes was so individual and so engineering-led. The style came out of the aerodynamic studies they were doing. There was obviously a single hand guiding that style, because you can create an aerodynamic car that is a dog to look at. It was pretty unique even in the fifties in a largish company that could afford to do their own engine, their own gearbox, aerodynamics, chassis, suspension, brakes, body, the whole car, to find one individual who had enough clout. That has now faded away in virtually all those companies. I was able to do it with the McLaren F1, but that was different. We set up a new company, and nobody interfered with me."

Rudi Uhlenhaut had first joined Mercedes-Benz in the 1930s, when the company—along with Auto Union—was given the green light, and the funding, by the Nazi high-ups to undertake a no-holds-barred, no-expense-spared assault on the Grands Prix. As Doug Nye put it: "Motor racing was wielded as an instrument of state invincibility. The W125 of 1937 remained the most power-ful car ever built, through to 1982. It was 646 hp, supercharged, doing 190 mph in a straight line, and driven by men from Mars. Goebbels had wanted a projection of Teutonic power and stature and of the Führer's will—and he got it." The 1930s cars were completely the opposite of the elegant 1950s Mercedes. "They were huge out-of-control beasts on three-and-a-half-inch tires traveling at 200 mph," said Gordon Murray. "That was enough to capture anybody's imagination."

Alongside Stirling Moss's 1955 Mille Miglia–winning 300 SLR, Uhlenhaut and Mercedes created a car that carried the Argentine Juan Manuel Fangio to the Formula One title: a statue of both driver and car is parked outside the Mercedes-Benz Museum. However, stylistically it was less immediately attractive, its original wheel-covering streamlining removed because it made handling twisty circuits difficult and because Fangio insisted that he should be able to see the wheels of his car. As a result, the car lost a good deal of its charm. Doug Nye went so far as to call it "fat and flabby, like a good old Stuttgart hausfrau!" Doug deserves the freedom of many cities, but I suspect Stuttgart will not be on the list.

Gordon Murray once had the opportunity to drive Fangio's original Grand Prix car at the Untertürkheim test circuit in the middle of Stuttgart. "It was quite nerve-racking sitting in the car, bolt upright with no seat belt. It made me realize how brave those guys must have been. And the final thing that struck me was both how slow it was, and that it had absolutely no grip whatsoever. My little 700 cc Smart coupé has five times the grip."

"After eighteen months back in motor racing," added Doug Nye, "Mercedes wrapped up the two titles, Formula One and WSC, of 1955. Then they said, 'There you go, we *are* the champions,' and locked up their racing garage for the next three decades." The brand name continued to grow in stature—"They hung on to their reputation for engineering integrity," said

Gordon Murray—but there were few revolutionary moments, other than the remarkable CIII, which was designed to smash world speed records—and did so—in the 1970s. "The CIII popped up out of nowhere," Gordon told me. "I saw it and thought, 'Christ, *that*'s a motorcar, smallish, looks light, consideration of packaging, style, not overengineered. Where did that come from—I bet there's only one guy behind that.' " There was; it was Rudolf Uhlenhaut's swan song.

★

And what of Mercédès Jellinek? She never drove a car as far as we know. That she was not a driver was not unusual for the time, since women drivers were something of a rarity for many years, even if Bertha Benz, wife of Karl, was one of the first people to drive a motorcar over any kind of distance, traveling 60 miles to visit her mother in 1888.

Mercédès followed the pattern of the day. In 1909, aged twenty, she married into a family who knew the Jellineks well. Her husband was a former playmate of her brothers named Baron Karl von Schlosser. She bore him two children in the 1910s, a daughter, Elfriede, and a son, Hans-Peter, and the family relocated to Vienna. But according to her stepbrother Guy, she never lost the yearning to achieve something Bohemian. In the mid-1920s she abruptly threw over her lifestyle and ran off with another baron. Where Karl von Schlosser had been cultured, correct and conventional, this new baron, Rudolf Weigl, was an artist and sculptor, "conceited and unstable," according to Guy Jellinek-Mercedes.

She spiraled down into Rudolf's lifestyle and watched him drink himself to death shortly after they married. Mercédès died of consumption a few years later, in February 1929, in a small flat in Vienna. She was thirty-nine years old.

Her name lives on—a strange name, on reflection, for a

German car marque. BMW (Bayerische Motoren Werke), Volkswägen, those are better names surely, but the fey Hispanic flair of Mercedes seemed to suit the style of many of the cars that emerged under her name. As I walked from the Mercedes-Benz Museum in Stuttgart back to the company's archives on the next block, I looked up as I crossed the road—this was Mercedes-Jellinek-Strasse.

In her immortality she was luckier than some, and the fact that her name covered a whole range of vehicles, from trucks to buses, meant that her memory was untainted by the flop of any one particular model. Unlike, for instance, Edsel Ford, son of Henry and president of the Ford Motor Company from 1919 to his death in 1943. The company honored him posthumously with a new model in the late 1950s. The Edsel bombed, one of the least successful product launches in automotive history, and it was consigned to the scrapyard.

In one of the books on the Mercedes I found a poignant foot-note: an advertisement from 1908 for a new car. This was the Maya, named after Mercédès's half-sister Andrée Maja. The ad said: "The sister of Mercedes. Latest and crowning achievement of the Daimler works." That model too disappeared without a trace.

Mercédès was cremated in Vienna's Zentralfriedhof Cemetery, "that immense cemetery where the wind swept over the plain," as her brother Guy wrote later. The icy wind, he said, took the mourners' breath away. The Zentralfriedhof is also the last resting place of Gluck, Beethoven, Schubert, Brahms, Johann Strauss Sr. and Jr. A cenotaph honors Wolfgang Amadeus Mozart. Even if she had not achieved peace in her life, Mercédès left behind her own enduring legacy. *Kyrie eleison*. May the Lord have mercy upon her.

CHAPTER 12

The Shadowy Life of Étienne de Silhouette

"Study the silhouette of every object; clarity and outline
comes to the hand that is not weakened by a hesitant will."
Paul Gauguin

I was surprised to learn that the silhouette was named after a
flesh-and-blood human being, an 18th-century French minister of
finance named Étienne de Silhouette. The fact that I had never
thought about a M. de Silhouette proved to me how deeply
ensconced in the language the word has become, moving on from
its original meaning, referring to black profile portraits, to
describe any backlit outline, and from there transforming itself
into a verb: "She stood silhouetted against the skyline."

This story begins in the field of silhouette portraiture, which
had its heyday, approximately from the 1780s to the 1860s, when
the primary centers of activity (despite the French-ness of the
name) were Britain and, later, America. The art of the silhouettist
is by no means defunct, and I started my inquiries by talking to
two of the most highly regarded contemporary silhouette artists,
both British: Michael Pierce and Charles Burns. It was important
to speak to both of them because, as they explained to me, there
are two very distinct schools of silhouette art: those painted onto
card, or any other surface, and those cut out with scissors.

Michael Pierce comes from the painting school of silhouettes
and was tutored as a youngster in the 1950s by one of the last
practicing Victorian artists, Winifred Ellis. Michael told me that
she was then a very old woman and that she had been taught by

another profile painter, so he is able to claim a direct lineage back to the great silhouette artists of the 18th century, most of whom painted their profiles rather than cutting them out. In fact, in one of the definitive books on silhouette collecting, Desmond Coke's *The Art of Silhouette*, published in 1913, Coke makes exactly that point, going on to say—and suggesting that if only his publisher would agree, this phrase should be given an entire page all to itself—"The best silhouettists never touched a pair of scissors!"

Michael Pierce lives most of the year in Bloomington, Illinois, where he runs a studio with his daughter, a glassblower. We met up in a pub in Clapham on one of his sorties back to England. He had the precise diction, unhurried delivery and rounded vowels of a former actor, but it turned out he had been in the RAF. "As a boy I announced I wanted to be a pilot or an artist."

He had, as a youngster, come across some examples of silhouette art. "I saw these beautiful, contrasting black-and-white images, and I was smitten. What a wonderful way of portraying not only people but things." He described silhouette-making as giving "full range to the subconscious" and told a favorite story about a bunch of schoolchildren asked by their teacher what they had watched on TV the night before. "Nothing," pipes up one of them. "I listened to the radio instead." The teacher asks why. "I think the pictures are better." From Michael Pierce's perspective, "that's what silhouettes are all about."

And so, through his mid-teens, Michael spent school vacations and weekends studying the art of the silhouette with Winifred Ellis, "as much as a callow youth could absorb." After his time in the RAF, and with a mortgage and two kids to educate, he turned to retail design as his principal career, creating shop and store interiors. Silhouettes remained a hobby.

In 1983 he decided to pursue the hobby full-time, placing an ad in *Country Life* and hiring a PR adviser to help with his personal image-making. "I had grand visions of a studio in Harrods. My first job was six months in a holiday camp." It was a great training.

Before the first season was three-quarters finished he had completed a thousand profiles. Michael found a studio in a set of Georgian shops, "complete with boot scraper and tinkling bell," and started working on his painted silhouettes, primarily individual commissions, although he has also drawn on his RAF connections to create two limited edition books, *So Few*, a tribute to the survivors of the Battle of Britain, and *So Many*, to those of Bomber Command, both of which feature his delicately and painstakingly rendered silhouettes. One I saw, of a veteran, ramrod straight in long coat, bowler and umbrella clasped behind his back, his graying hair and row of medals picked out in silver highlights, astonished me. I had not expected—out of ignorance— to find such character and finesse.

★

Enter our second silhouettist, Charles Burns. Where Michael Pierce is a silhouette painter, Charles is a cutter. And whereas Michael will work for hours, days even, on the detail of a silhouette ("Precision is paramount"), Charles's approach is all about speed, though his line will be no less precise. At a pinch he can deliver a freehand head-and-shoulders silhouette in sixty seconds; certainly two or three minutes is ample.

After leaving art school Charles set up a stall in the street entertainer's mecca of Covent Garden. He had seen somebody cutting silhouettes and thought, as he puts it, that "here was a chance to earn cash while waiting for my glittering gallery career to take off." No one taught him how to cut. There was nobody around, no equivalent of Winifred Ellis still teaching at the Slade to pass on the knowledge of a previous century, so he learned by studying examples of cut silhouettes and by trial and error.

I asked Charles Burns what he thought of August Edouart, the 19th-century Frenchman who I had read had a high reputation as a cutter. Charles was not a huge fan. Although he could admire the man's technique, he thought the Frenchman was rather too vain and pompous, and indeed Edouart's book about his art, *A Treatise on Silhouette Likenesses*, parades on its title page a self-aggrandizing puff for himself as "silhouettist to the French royal family and patronized by HRH the late Duke of Gloucester and the principal nobility of England, Scotland and Ireland."

Charles Burns felt much more akin to a less grandiose school of cutters who worked on Brighton Pier in the early part of the 20th century, particularly Hubert Leslie, who worked there from the 1920s and who Charles thought had an even more elegant line than Edouart. That he had been able to study and compare both silhouettists' work was a legacy of their meticulous record-keeping, which ensured that their work, which could have been transitory, has survived.

August Edouart's technique was to take a single piece of paper, black on one side, white on the other, which he would fold in half, so that when he cut out the silhouette, he was left with two copies of the image. One was for the customer, the other for his own files. On the back of his reference copy he would carefully note the client's name and the date and venue of the portrait. Over the years his archive totalled over 100,000 profiles. He constructed a complex filing system, with notes on his duplicate silhouettes, with an index and further indexes to that index. In 1849, returning from ten years' touring the United States, he was shipwrecked in a storm off Guernsey, his files lost. Some were salvaged, and he left them in the care of the family who had given him shelter on the island.

His curatorial cataloguing was an approach that Hubert Leslie, in his booth on Brighton Pier, copied. He left his diligently compiled books of duplicate portraits to the National Portrait Gallery, where Charles Burns spent "many happy hours, poring through the books, working out exactly how the scissors are used," and he still uses a similar system for his own likenesses. Charles liked the fact that these archives of silhouettes provided "an alternative history of art," a completely different tradition from that of fine art, peopled by professional artists working at small studios, country fairs and seaside piers, recording the faces of people from all walks of life.

What are the skills a silhouette cutter needs? According to Charles Burns, the talent required is being able to "draw with a pair of scissors" (his own are German-made, surgical scissors with short blades and long handles for greater control). "One of the great benefits of the kind of work I do"—he often appears at social events and corporate functions—"is that I get immediate feedback from customers. The strange thing is that there are often artists in the audience who come up afterward and tell me, 'I can draw, but I couldn't do what you do.'"

*

When we met, Michael Pierce had given me a potted history of the silhouette. Something he cleared up immediately was that both the painted and cut outline portraits predated the use of the term "silhouette" to describe them. They had previously been known as "shades" or "profiles." The word "silhouette" was imported to Britain from France in the 1820s by none other than August Edouart.

When Edouart arrived on the scene silhouette portraiture was on the verge of fading out of style; he gave it a much needed boost. The fashion had first taken hold during the previous century. Copying and drawing shadows on walls was nothing new—some silhouette historians hark back to cave dwellers daubing the shape of shadows on their cavern walls and the outlines on Etruscan vases—but profile painting and cutting evolved as a coherent and popular art form only in the mid-1700s.

A number of factors came into play, Michael Pierce told me. There had been a breakthrough in paper technology. Rather than a highly prized commodity available to the few, the arrival of technology facilitating the bulk and economical production of paper meant that both paper and card were available for more frivolous purposes.

The lighting of the time was primarily from candlesticks and oil lamps set at tabletop height—"we lived in a world of shadows," in Michael's words. Using that light to cast the shadow of a sitter onto a piece of paper tacked to a wall, anyone could draw around the profile and cut it out. Profile drawing and cutting became a pastime ideal for whiling away interminable winter evenings.

This coincided with the publication of a bestselling book called *Essays on Physiognomy* by Johann Kaspar Lavater, a Swiss cleric whose theory (a tentative, though never proven, "science") was that a person's outward appearance gave direct insight to their inner character. To illustrate his theme, his hefty tome included profiles of many famous Europeans. With his friend Goethe—no mean cutter himself—Lavater also designed a chair specifically for profile-sitting. This piece of furniture kept the sitter's head and body rigid, with a light source sending a stable shadow onto a glass frame against which the profilist could capture the outline.

The fad took off, and entrepreneurs spotted the business opportunity. Professional profile artists offered to carry out the tracing or cutting and guarantee some level of accuracy. Every major town had its silhouette studio. Bath, a spa town, boasted up to twenty in an attempt to keep up with demand. An elite of talented profile painters—more sought after at the time than cutters—grew up. Mrs. Isabella Beetham opened her studio on Fleet Street. Mr. Charles of 130 The Strand worked in his bow window as passers-by looked in, not far from the studio at 111 The Strand where John Miers worked. Miers is considered by many, including Michael Pierce, to be one of the very finest of the period.

Miers controlled all aspects of his work, mixing his own pigments to achieve the depth of black he wanted, a cocktail of soot from beeswax candles and beer. Michael Pierce is dedicated to continuing the tradition of Miers, Beetham and co., but he now uses a set of high-tech pens and an illuminated magnifying glass, and he often works from photographs as an aid, something he freely admits might raise a sharp eyebrow from his predecessors, although it was not an option available to many of them. To maintain a connection with the past, he does draw on an antique rosewood drawing desk—and, of course, drawing ability is timeless.

The shade business mushroomed. Profiles were accurate, speedy and affordable. Not everyone could commission a Gainsborough or a Joshua Reynolds. A set of profiles of the family could be taken away on trips, duplicates sent to relatives or swapped with business acquaintances, the 18th-century equivalent of the concertina set of kiddie photos. They were cheap enough for most people to afford them, but fashionable enough for the great and the good to sit for them: Miers cut likenesses of Sarah Siddons and Elizabeth Fry; and Georges III and IV, Nelson and Napoleon all chose to be profiled.

The family of Jane Austen were typical enthusiasts. There are existing profiles of many members of the Austen clan. Her older sister Cassandra and her sister-in-law were both painted by Charles Miers, and Jane cut out her own self-portrait in profile.

Such was the power of the profile that it is said Goethe even managed to fall in love with a silhouette—of the Baroness Charlotte von Stein. He was entranced by her outline and effected a meeting with her, and she became his intimate friend and muse for over a decade.

The high tide of the shade was receding by the time August Edouart started cutting. The use of machines like the pantograph, which allowed full-size profiles to be reduced in size, copied and framed, had put the technique of making shades within reach of even the least talented. From 1800 or so onwards, in a bid to add some glamour into what was rapidly becoming a diluted art form,

John Miers and his assistant John Field developed the idea of "bronzing," highlighting images with flecks of gold paint to add a twinkle to a military gent's decorations or a lady's jewelry, a technique one of Michael Pierce's clients once described as "brushing with moonlight."

Ultimately the silhouette was superseded by the daguerreotype and the photographic camera. Also, according to the silhouette specialist Peggy Hickman, the arrival of overhead gas and, later, electric lighting made the use of tabletop lighting seem passé. Photography offered another bonus. Silhouettes required, not surprisingly, a strong profile, whereas, as the silhouette historian Desmond Coke observed, the camera was "the chinless mortal's refuge." Not everyone was happy with their profile, once it was painted or cut, simply because it was rare for anybody to see themselves from that angle (to a certain extent that is still true). "No one is acquainted with his own profile," said August Edouart. Most of his clients were surprised when they did see it, and quite a few asked for more hair, or to be thinner or taller, a silhouette version of Photoshop.

*

August Edouart introduced the word "silhouette" into the English language after traveling across the Channel to England in 1814—he had previously served in Napoleon's army—and looking for a way to earn a living and support his wife and five children.

His first artistic endeavor was creating wax portraits, using human hair embedded in the wax for extra authenticity, a technique he also used for favorite pets. However, at dinner one evening, after he had been in England for ten years or so, he was shown a mechanically produced profile by one of his hosts. He rashly declared he could do better. His fellow diners called his bluff and provided him with scissors and card. Cutting freehand, August proceeded to produce a profile that was so accurate that he decided to abandon his line in wax pictures and concentrate on what he now called his "silhouettes."

He became one of the premier cutters in Britain, noted particularly for his ability to capture children's likenesses—"In them I find nature in perfection," he wrote. "They have no pretension, not that amour propre to wish to appear what they are not"—and for a wide range of silhouette types. In addition to his human sitters, who included Paganini and Robert Burns, he cut animals, cityscapes, tableaux on themes like "jealousy," family groups, and even, on request, posthumous likenesses.

However, the art of shade-making had fallen in public estimation, so much so that in his *Treatise on Silhouette Likenesses*, Edouart complains about the low reputation of the craft in the 1830s. It was seen, he felt, as a vulgar art, and, in a neat turn of phrase, he said he was often "regarded with looks as black as the paper of which I made the likenesses."

Using the word "silhouette" was a way of differentiating what he was doing from the much-derided shades, and it added a little Gallic flourish to his activities. In his book Edouart plays up his Frenchness, and—although he writes quite fluently in English— he pokes fun at his own stumbles in the language. He had been told, he says, that it was rude to call someone "fat"; a more appropriate choice of word was "stout." At dinner one night, he was offered some beef by his hostess, to which August says he replied, "Yes, Madam, if you please, with a small piece of stout . . ." much to the hilarity of his dinner companions (collapse of stout party).

But how did the name of Étienne de Silhouette, finance minister of France, become associated with shades and profiles? This is the way Edouart tells it: "In the reign of Louis XIV, there was a prime minister, whose name was Silhouette: he was a man disposed to economy, even to sordidness; whose conduct was mean, and whose mind was narrow." That's a great final phrase, but I do need to interrupt and point out that Silhouette was actually the chancellor for Louis XV. Carry on, August.

"He was very much disliked, especially as he was not a pro-moter of the fine arts, and artists in general had a very great hatred to him on this account. It was at this time that likenesses produced by the shadow were invented. Their cheapness was a great encouragement to many persons to have them in this way: the artists perceiving at length, that it would end in their detriment, for the people taking a fancy to them, styled them, in derision, 'Portraits à la Silhouette,' signifying that they were paltry, and only suitable to persons like the Minister." Even though Edouart's English goes a little wonky toward the end there, we can get the gist.

The key here is that Étienne de Silhouette ended a brief career as minister of finance—it lasted only a few months—thoroughly loathed by pretty much everyone in the nation, and the reason for this opprobrium was . . . money. Silhouette, most people reckoned, had, in an attempt to sort out France's rocky financial situation, squeezed them dry.

In the mid-18th century France's finances were feeling the strain. Much of this came down to the demands of war. The country had spent decades either fighting against Prussia with the help of Austria or vice versa or alone against the old foe England. The country's resources, and its credit lines, were close to exhaustion. And short-term solutions for drumming up enough cash to pay the troops merely exacerbated the long-term problems.

A series of chancellors attempted to solve the problem. In 1749 Jean-Baptiste de Machault d'Arnouville tried applying a universal tax, but the clergy and the nobility ganged up with Louis XV and overrode him. His successors would, according to Étienne de Silhouette's 19th-century biographers, Pierre Clément and Alfred Lemoine, arrive on their first day in the job brimming with enthusiasm, which would promptly evaporate as they realized the enormity, if not impossibility, of the task confronting them, and as it dawned on them that the only way of returning the country to a sound financial basis was indeed to tax everybody and reduce the size and extravagant habits of the royal court. Neither solution was going to win them any popularity contests. As soon as they reached this realization, and at the first sniff of a cutback in court expenditure, Louis XV's hugely influential mistress, Madame de Pompadour, would make sure that the chancellor's job was the first cutback of all.

This was the job that Étienne de Silhouette took on in 1759. He was an unlikely candidate, as he came from a relatively humble background, born on July 25, 1709 in Limoges, where his father was a tax collector. He did not have the usual background for future treasury ministers. As with the higher echelons of the clergy, the law or the civil service, jobs were generally the precinct of the wealthy and already privileged.

What Étienne de Silhouette did possess was, reported his biographers, "a lively and brilliant imagination, a precocious sense of taste, reinforced by study, a certain aptitude for philosophical and literary questions, and"—probably the most essential characteristic—"unceasing ambition." He also practiced another very useful skill, which was remarked on by Jean-Baptiste Rousseau, an exiled French poet. Silhouette, he remembered, was an extremely good listener.

By his early twenties Silhouette was acquiring a growing reputation based on his academic writings; one of his typical titles was "The general idea of government and morals of the Chinese, and a response to three critiques on Confucius." He studied public law in Leiden and then headed off on a grand tour of Spain, Italy and Portugal through 1729 and 1730, rather pleased that his writings were causing a stir.

He made some occasionally pointed observations on the countries he visited and the people he met. Some would apply equally well today. Of the English abroad, he notes that "they travel mechanically, never mixing with the people of the country they are visiting. They are not very sociable, drunk and debauched." The inhabitants of Faliraki or Playa de Las Americas might applaud him. And the Spanish, he observes, "are a strange, unimaginable composite. They imagine that for something to be great, it must be Spanish."

He continued writing throughout the 1730s: treatises on mathematics and translations of Pope and covering a range of subjects, not primarily economic or financial. However, in 1739 he found himself in London researching the importance of the tobacco trade and in that year the Marquis d'Argenson, an often waspish diarist, called him a *garçon fort savant*, like a wily old politico spotting the latest rising star by describing him as "a very bright lad." Silhouette purchased a position as councillor at the parliament of Metz and caught another eye, that of the local governor Maréchal de Belle-Isle. Three years later he had become *maître de requêtes*, a roving judicial inspector reporting to the chancellor of France. He spent another period in London, investigating the finances, commerce and navigation of England and noting approvingly that in order to fund the navy, "parliament can impose taxes as heavy as they wish." Rather than hiding their wealth where the chancellor could not find it, as his French compatriots did, the English, he believed, were happy to display their wealth as it gave them increased standing in the community.

This memoir was circulated among members of the government in France, and Silhouette's—I almost hesitate to use the word—profile grew. He moved over to act as a chief secretary and then chancellor for the Duke of Orleans's family and took on a role as one of three commissioners dividing up French and British possessions in Louisiana. He also made a prudent marriage, in his mid-forties, to Anne-Jeanne-Antoinette Astruc. Her father was a doctor of medicine at the faculty in Paris and, significantly, one of the doctors who treated the king. Her uncle was president of the *cours des aides*, a sovereign court dealing with high-level financial disputes.

Silhouette's progress to date had certainly been ambitious, but steady, as yet not spectacular. That changed in 1758 when his mentor from Metz, the Maréchal de Belle-Isle, became minister of war, making a breach in the highest reaches of power that Silhouette and his "unceasing ambition" made the most of. He developed a working relationship with Madame de Pompadour. The diarist d'Argenson was less warm now: "This Silhouette seems wise, but isn't really. He gains his knowledge through flattery and finesse." He reaped the rewards. In March 1759 he replaced Jean-Baptiste de Boullongnes as *contrôleur-général* of France. De Boullongnes was generally agreed to be an able and sensible administrator, but that had not been enough to save him.

Silhouette arrived in the post with a reputation as a systems man and a mission to save money. "Prudence" was his byword, economy his mission. But so it had been for the string of *contrôleurs-généraux* who had come before him. Teetering on the brink of his much-longed-for success, savoring the recognition of his talents, he steeled his nerve for what he quickly understood would be an enormously challenging task. At his first meeting with Louis XV, the king's only line of questioning was whether the paneling in Silhouette's offices had been properly varnished. Silhouette was left speechless.

In his new role as *contrôleur-général* Étienne de Silhouette started out with seriously good intentions. He said he would cut all unnecessary expenditure and bring a sense of order to the public revenues. The manifesto was easy. Delivering that in practice was going to be an uphill battle. Only a couple of weeks after taking office, he was writing to an acquaintance that "it will require plenty of courage and more to get us out of the difficulties we are in," but he still retained confidence in the providence of God and a frankly misplaced belief that Madame de Pompadour—"an honest and much misunderstood woman"—would allow him to source the funds he needed from the fortunes of her relatives and friends. She had, of course, no intention of anything of the kind.

In April 1759, a month into his post, Silhouette set out his plans, which included taking away the immunity from tax of a whole stratum of officials and bourgeois citizens and canceling various pensions, sinecures and handouts. There was, predictably, general uproar, especially from the *fermiers généraux*, not a posse of militaristic agriculturalists, but a powerful body of financiers who underwrote the public revenues. He did have one supporter, though. Voltaire wrote, "God has sent M. de Silhouette to help us," but he warned that his drastic measures were like those of a doctor giving his patient an emetic far too early in a course of treatment.

Silhouette plowed on, hampered by the fact that France was not at peace, which might have given him some breathing space, but in the middle of the Seven Years War against Britain and the combined German forces (the battles of Bergen and Minden took place that spring and summer), as well as fighting to hold on to its Caribbean colonies. He remained positive, though, and somewhat belligerent—"The aroma of the flowers that have been thrown to me have not gone to my head. Fear of stones will not frighten me." In July he was named minister of finance—a title usually granted after years of service—but this only heightened the scrutiny he was under. His next move was going to be critical.

Alas for Silhouette, he made the wrong move. A new wave of edicts doubled the tax on luxury goods, on gold and silver plates and jewelry, on horses and carriages, and he imposed import taxes on silks, velvets and braids. There was a whole raft of measures, and he was still coming up short on the balance sheet. His new measures were modified but approved by parliament in September, when Silhouette again wrote about the need to stay firm, but by then the storm clouds were massing. In October Voltaire received a letter from a friend, the Marquise du Deffand, complaining that "they are not taxing the air we breathe, but apart from that, I can't think of anything that's escaped." Meanwhile word had got out that Silhouette was benefiting from a tidy annuity. Voltaire remarks, "Silhouette, who is trimming back everybody else's income, has found a nice little one for himself. Bravo!"

The end, when it came, was swift. In the previous century the finance ministry had been forced to call in gold and silver from the court and the church, losing thousands of masterpieces in the process. On 5 November Silhouette had to do the same. Less than three weeks later, not yet nine months after taking over the finances, he resigned. Voltaire again: "They thought he was an eagle, but the eagle turned out to be a goose."

As Silhouette's biographers wrote, "You can imagine the insults, jokes and satires that followed his fall from grace." There were songs and skits full of vicious ridicule. In particular the term *à la silhouette* was applied to anything deemed cheap and penny pinching, not only to profiles and shades, but to culottes—where the lack of a gusset indicated how far Silhouette had reduced people's finances—or to a coat made by a bespoke tailor but without either lining or pockets to keep the price down.

*

After his brief moment in the sun, Silhouette bought a château at Bry-sur-Marne, southeast of Paris (not far from the site of Disneyland Europe and its enchanted castles). He bunkered down there for the remainder of his life, dying in 1767 at the age of fifty-seven. According to some sources—John Woodiwiss in his book *British Silhouettes*, for example—Silhouette was "a clever amateur cutter" and, unable to show his face in public, spent his time pursuing his hobby of cutting silhouettes, although I have not come across any contemporary evidence that he ever did.

Sadly, there was nothing to see at Bry-sur-Marne. I had hoped, if the rumor *was* true, to find a museum in the château with examples of Silhouette's silhouettes. But when I talked to the president of the local historical society she told me that the château had been razed to the ground, nothing left at all, and that there were no museum relics for me to view.

But maybe that was a good thing. I could hold on to the image, with no proof to the contrary, of Étienne de Silhouette, deep in thought or denial, closeted away in his library, the shutters barred against the brickbats of the outside world, working away on his profiles. It would be fitting to leave him there, in the shadowy chiaroscuro of his declining years, with the corridors of the château at Bry echoing to the melancholy snip snip snip of his little gold scissors, until he, and his shadow, simply faded away.

CHAPTER 13

On the Trot with Harry Fox

"A Manhattan you always shake to foxtrot time,
a Bronx to two-step time, a dry Martini
you always shake to waltz time."
William Powell as Nick Charles in The Thin Man

I made a first tentative foray into the world of the foxtrot at the Goodman Dance Centre in Dartford, Kent. Driving southeast out of London, on the A2 heading into Kent, and executing a deft turn toward the town center within one of those one-way systems beloved of town planners, I found myself sashaying past the Mick Jagger Centre. Mick and Keith are two of Dartford's finest sons: their now legendary meeting, when the Glimmer Twins were conjoined by a mutual love of Muddy Waters, took place at the town's railway station.

This is also the home turf, the home parquet if you like, of Len Goodman, who recently acquired national fame in the UK as the senior judge on *Strictly Come Dancing* and international fame with the American equivalent, *Dancing with the Stars*. Len's studio has been teaching those with twinkling toes or two left feet for thirty years, the last quarter century in an airy room with arched windows overlooking a grassy square opening onto Dartford's Central Park, the town's war memorial and public library. Len Goodman was the reason I had booked an hour and a half lesson in the art of the foxtrot: I had never once thought about a person named Fox being the origin of the word "foxtrot" until I heard a radio interview with Len that mentioned that it was named after an American vaudeville artist of the 1900s and 1910s named Harry Fox.

My tuition was in the capable hands—and feet, of course—of

Len's colleague Sue Barrett, who had thoughtfully prepared a lesson involving a short routine combining half a dozen foxtrot moves. It was enough to give me a flavor of the dance, but not too much to retain at one go. In any case, she told me, she would normally expect a student to have first spent at least a couple of years mastering the basics of the slower foxtrot, the "social foxtrot," the one that allows couples to move around a dance floor without injuring anybody en route. I was—with absolutely no prior experience—being fast-tracked. All I knew was that I should bring along some snazzy patent leather shoes with minimal grip on the soles, because Sue had told me we would need to slide and glide. Apart from that one piece of knowledge, I had absolutely no idea whether I would have any aptitude for mastering the steps. Sue, a skilfully relaxed and cheerful instructor, had within minutes given me the impression that with some practice I could hack it on the ballroom floor—the sign of a good teacher.

Sue filled me in on the basics of the foxtrot, how the version we were going to attempt was very different from the original foxtrot of the 1910s, which had included jerky hops and kicks. She said the quickstep (a dance that evolved out of a faster version of the foxtrot) with its flicks and leaps was probably closer to the original. British dance teachers had disapproved of all those tricks and created a smoother, more flowing version in the 1920s.

The routine Sue had created included a number of gliding moves, starting with a feather followed by a reverse turn. A three-step walk moved into a natural turn and an impetus turn, kicked into off the heel, and then a "weave," a series of running steps that harked back most to that first foxtrot. A brief "hesitation" step would end this passage of steps before we eased back into the routine. That was the theory.

I learned a lot in an hour and a half. First of all—like leaping into the void on a flying trapeze—I had to learn to breathe. After we had tried the first movement, the feather, Sue suggested this would help. "There's no need to go blue." There is obviously some natural instinct in the body—or my body, at any rate—to draw and hold the breath while concentrating on learning a new task. Maybe I should take up pearl diving.

I learned about the body position of British ballroom dancing and the five points of contact—left hand holding the partner's hand, right hand on partner's back, partner's hand on my shoulder, the forearms and the abdomen touching—all the physical antennae by which an experienced gentleman could transmit his intentions and that the lady could follow. I understood—a little—about the high degree of balance required. Gradually we built up and practiced each element, adding more and more steps, repeating and repeating, until Sue felt we could have a go. We danced to songs by Frank Sinatra and Sammy Davis Jr., classic foxtrot numbers, but also to Van Morrison's "Moondance," as I tried to master the slow, quick, quick, slow rhythm of the dance.

In the foxtrot, one manual said, a couple should appear to be dancing on water, leaving the faintest of ripples in their wake. I suspect my version was like a two-year-old galumphing through puddles in galoshes, but in my mind I was skimming the surface with the best of them. Somewhat to my surprise, I absolutely loved it.

*

There is still a certain amount of dispute—I wouldn't go so far as to call it controversy—about how the name of Harry Fox came to be connected with the foxtrot. Not everyone is convinced he was even the originator of the dance.

For example, in his book *Modern Ballroom Dancing* the great Victor Silvester, the first-ever world champion of ballroom dancing in 1922 and later leader of his own much-loved orchestra, wrote of the foxtrot: "It has an eponymous hero in the person of one Harry Fox, who was among the first to introduce it to the vaudeville stage, but the suggestion that it was named after the gait or pace of the horse, known in the West as a 'Foxtrot,' is a much more plausible one."

There is indeed a diagonal, uneven, four-beat horse gait known as the foxtrot, connected particularly with a breed called the Missouri Foxtrotter from the Ozark Mountains. This foxtrot gait, in which the front legs of the horse appear to be walking while the back end trots, apparently makes for an easier, more comfortable ride that is suited to the terrain. And since this breed of horse was created in the early 19th century, long before Harry Fox made his debut, Victor Silvester's theory has some credence.

The king and queen of American ballroom dancing in the 1910s, Vernon and Irene Castle, and their bandleader James Reese Europe, were linked with boosting the foxtrot's early popularity, but none of them—in print, at least—pretended to have created it.

To help unravel a kind of truth, I consulted Richard Powers, a ballroom dance historian based at Stanford University in California, where he teaches dance classes alongside researching into the history of social dance. He happened to be in Europe for a week, running a series of workshops, so I took the opportunity to meet him for a beer as he wound down after his final London session.

Richard Powers added a new theory to the mix. He said that the version of the story he found more credible than any other involved a performer named Oscar Duryea ("but I wasn't there, so I don't know for sure"). Oscar Duryea—also a well-known dance teacher in New York—was at one point the main attraction at the Jardin de Danse, an alfresco rooftop cabaret set on top of the New York Theater. Downstairs in the main auditorium Harry Fox had a nightly show, and after his performance had finished patrons would head up to the rooftop Jardin.

"Oscar Duryea," Richard Powers told me, "had a fast trotting dance, which he performed on stage. One night Duryea was just too tired to trot, so he mixed walking steps with trots, and the audience loved it. He intentionally capitalized on his connection to Harry Fox's show in the theater below and named the dance after Fox. Some say that his original name was Fox's Trot, and then Fox-Trot."

It is highly likely that Harry Fox did not create the foxtrot. As Richard pointed out, Harry was a vaudeville artist, whose career thrived on publicity and self-promotion, and if he *had* been the creator of such a popular dance, he would surely have proclaimed the fact and loudly taken the credit.

There are genuine relics to support this theory, since some of Oscar Duryea's performances were preserved on silent films, but it is probably pointless to worry about who "invented" the foxtrot. "The Oscar Duryea theory is only one story about why the dance is named foxtrot," Richard said. "I believe that the dance itself more likely evolved simultaneously from multiple sources, because it is the most obvious way to dance to music of that tempo."

The point is that nobody knows. This is not a precise science. The foxtrot, unlike the Jacuzzi or the Frisbee or the Biro, was never patented, although the dance steps of the foxtrot as it evolved were eventually codified. There is no document like the grand patent for Adolphe Sax's saxophone that can be unearthed from the archives and flourished to settle the dispute.

A dance cannot be carbon-dated. It is living, moving, fluid. In general dances are not usually invented. Occasionally they can be—Richard Powers cited the Charleston, introduced in 1923 by bandleader James P. Johnson—but in general artificially devised dances fail to catch on in the long term; remember the lambada?

The most popular dance before the foxtrot was the one-step, which consisted of walking, one step to each beat. Almost everyone knew how to do it, even non-dancers. The best tempo for a walking dance was around 120 beats per minute, so with a 4/4 time signature that would be 30 bars a minute.

"Of course, the music that bands were playing was at a whole range of speeds. "But," said Richard, "if the music was much slower, simple walking would be too slow to be satisfying. Much faster, it would be too exhausting to trot that quickly for three minutes. So the most intuitive solution was to combine some slow steps with some quick steps, in a repeating pattern which was easy for a dance partner to follow." The beauty of the foxtrot was that it offered a straightforward combination of quick and slow steps that gave dancers the flexibility to respond to different tempi and to the syncopated music of ragtime and the blues. "We're not talking about choreographic genius here; we're talking about common sense. It's the only thing that works."

What is indisputable is that the foxtrot became popular in New York during the summer of 1914. Actually, "became popular" is far too tame a phrase. The dance absolutely ripped through the city, like wildfire through tinder-dry bush.

There was a genuine dance craze. Propelled by the rhythms of jazz and ragtime, each new dance would flutter forth like a mayfly to enjoy its ephemeral moment of glory. The faddish dance of the moment changed on a weekly basis. Such was the turnover of dances that people could barely keep up. Richard Powers had collected a contemporary cartoon that showed a man being stopped by a friend in the street: "Where are you off to?" "To dance," says the man. "But I can't stop. If I don't get there soon, the dance steps I've just learned will be out of fashion."

*

One of the earliest dance crazes was the arrival in Europe of the waltz, an import from southern Germany, which started becoming popular around 1780. With the development of the "modern" holding position in the 1810s, the waltz created a furor. Couples touching, swirling, a chap placing a hand on a lady's waist? Dear boy, it's positively immoral.

Byron saw a girl he fancied waltzing in the clutch of a rival and spluttered that she had been snared by a "huge hussar-looking gentleman, turning round and round to a d——d see-saw, up and down sort of tune, like two cockchafers spitted upon the same bodkin." Once George Byron and his contemporaries got used to this new level of familiarity, the waltz in 3/4 time became the dominant force in ballroom dancing for the remainder of the 19th century, seeing off the challenges of the schottische, polka and galoo. It offered a chance for couples to get as close and as intimate as they dared and provided a rather nice revenue stream for the Strauss family.

However, by the turn of the century dancers were looking for something to celebrate the new century and to replace the endless round of fast waltzes, which was still a staple of dance gatherings, along with the galop and the Lancers.

A variation on the waltz, called the Boston—danced to a faster tempo, and with more freedom to break out of the obsession with beat that characterized the waltz—briefly gave it a further lease on life, but the waltz's days were numbered. The final coup de grâce would be delivered from Argentina by way of Paris and by the new music of jazz.

The tango had evolved in the barrios of Buenos Aires, initially a dance-off between gauchos fresh into town from the pampas and their girlfriends for the night. It is said that the slightly crouching position typical of the tango dancer was obligatory because of the constriction of the gaucho's leather chaps, and that the couple's heads-apart stance was designed so the lady could avoid the lack of dental hygiene and general sweatiness of her partner. From these rough-and-ready beginnings, the more fragrant classes of BA evolved their own stylized version, a dramatization of a fight between gaucho and girl, which was demonstrated by Argentinian dancers in Paris in the very early 1900s.

By 1907 the French choreographer Camille de Rhynal was further developing the tango at the Imperial Country Club in Nice; he took it back up to Paris, and two years later it had become part of competition dancing. In 1911 the dance crossed the Channel to Britain following that year's summer season in Deauville and the other northern French resorts, and during the autumn in London there was a flurry of what George Grossmith, cowriter of *Diary of a Nobody*, described as " 'tango parties' in drawing rooms with an Argentine boy playing the piano." The tango craze also took off in restaurants, with couples dancing between the tables.

At the same time, a second prong of dance invasion left the United States, led by the advance patrol of "Alexander's Ragtime Band." The fresh, syncopated rhythms of jazz and ragtime—sanitized for white audiences—put New York at the epicenter of the frantic dance boom of 1914. The Rag and the One-step, straightforward walking dances that anybody could learn quickly, had led to a collection of canters and a positive menagerie of dances, including the Grizzly Bear, the Bunny Hug, the Camel Walk and the Turkey Trot. Among these a new vulpine arrival fitted right in.

*

I charted the progress of the foxtrot from a contemporary perspective, the London magazine *Dancing Times*, which by the very virtue of being based across the Atlantic was able to observe the foxtrot phenomenon with a certain amount of detachment. At the time the name of the dance was variously written as "Fox trot," "Fox-trot" and "foxtrot."

In the November 1914 issue of *Dancing Times* their American correspondent sent a dispatch from the front line in a column called "Gossip from the States." "In New York, and in fact throughout the States," she wrote, "the foxtrot has so infected the people that it has become known as the sleep hater's revel. Tango teachers may as well lie down and let the river run over them. At the tea riots, it is quite the vogue." One of the new dance's great appeals was its simplicity. "There's something in it for everyone—from the odalisque to the insurance agent, from the silly lily to the old girl who's been crouching for a year for a spring into the ballroom." The foxtrot, she reported, was sweeping all before it, including a clutch of dances that teachers and music publishers had tried, with limited success, to foist on the public, including the rouli-rouli, the ta-tao (based on a centuries-old Chinese dance) and the Portuguese-influenced lulu-fado.

By January 1915 "The Sitter Out," the magazine's opinion column, which each month offered a wry sideways look at the world of dance and which was written, I suspect, by its longtime editor Philip Richardson, was telling readers, "the foxtrot I cannot take very seriously." The writer reckoned that it reminded him of the Boston galop, or "as the Americans call it, the 'horse trot,' invented by Uriel Davis in 1913"—an observation that might give some reinforcement to Victor Silvester's theory that the foxtrot was named after the gait of the Ozark Mountain horse.

A teacher in St. Louis, Leslie Clendennen, had also been asked to report on the dance: "The foxtrot is not an exhibition, but a dance for everyone, a dance that can be learned in a few moments. It is not an imported animal, as many believe, simply a nerve-wracking movement arranged by a vaudeville artist named Fox." This was written only a few months after the dance emerged, so the Harry Fox theory was already in place. "He must have been a deuced clever chap, or had a big pull with the Associated Press, to get this simple little combination (that we have all done to death) put up in capsules that are so sweet to us." Clendennen whimsically describes the rapid number of variations on the basic steps that had been developed during one imaginary morning in November 1914. "By 11:49 a new variation has crept in, and by three in the afternoon the tango and one-step moves are being 'used by the stagy chaps.' "

And to clarify the foxtrot of 1914 and 1915, Leslie Clendennen provided a simple recipe: "There are but two things to remember.

First, a slow walk, two counts to a step; second, a trot of runs, one count to each step." That was it. No wonder it had caught on so painlessly. In a later issue an advertisement from one of the music publishers also explained the dance in two sentences: "Four long smooth steps on the ball of the foot, two beats each step. Eight short steps, one beat each."

By May 1915 even the previously unimpressed "Sitter Out" realized he was in a minority as far as the foxtrot was concerned: "We are to have a foxtrot year." That month, he noted, a Miss Harding was organizing a foxtrot competition at the Empress Rooms in London. "So the foxtrot has come." The following month *Dancing Times* organized a Foxtrot Symposium, a gathering of teachers, performers and composers adding their thoughts on the new craze and the tunes that bands were playing behind it: "The Fox Trot Ball," "Ballin' the Jack," "Goodbye Virginia," "Beets and Turnips" and "Hors d'Oeuvre."

All stressed the universal ease of the dance—even the elderly, one said, if they avoided too many hops, could "walk through it for hours." One composer, Tony Castle, who had written "The Elsie Janis Fox Trot" in tribute to a well-known American dancer and singer, said the key was not to play it too fast. The essence of the foxtrot was the repeating pattern of slow and quick steps, perhaps two slow walks followed by four quick running steps (Vernon and Irene Castle's preferred pattern). The dance was not syncopated, at least not until much later competition ballroom versions, but just as Tony Castle—no relation to the dancers—put it, "a quiet glide with a foxy movement" in 4/4. Uncomplicated and universal, but with those extra variations that made it more interesting than the one-step.

I tracked down a copy of "The Meadowbrook Fox Trot," published in 1914 and one of the first pieces of music to appear under the name. It was written by Arthur M. Kraus, who headed an orchestra at Rector's Restaurant on Broadway and 40th, a haunt of Diamond Jim Brady. The piece was dedicated to Hope

Loring, who later became a successful screenwriter, and published by Joseph W. Stern & Co. of West 38th Street. Sure enough, it was a 4/4, moderate tempo, suitably foxy.

The dance historian Charles d'Albert added his contribution to the Symposium. "I presume your readers know," he wrote, "that the name of the dance, though suggesting the Zoological gardens, has nothing in common with it. The name is derived from its inventor, Mr. Fox, a music-hall artist, of the United States."

★

There is precious little hard information about Harry Fox. Richard Powers, who has read and researched more than most in the social dance area, did not have much to tell me about Fox's life. According to the available sources he was born Arthur Carringford, in Pomona, California, in May 1882. In his mid-teens he performed with a circus for a while before trying his hand at professional baseball. His songwriting skills were noticed by a music publisher, who hired him, and either through that connection or his own efforts he appeared at the San Francisco Belvedere Theater in 1904 as "Mr. Frisky of Frisco."

Following the earthquake and fire that rocked San Francisco in 1906 he headed east, and we next find him in vaudeville in New York, notably in 1914. That May *Variety* announced his solo debut at the New York Theater—which the Ziegfeld Follies had recently vacated—performing a song-and-dance routine between film reels with his "American Beauties." By this time he had assumed a new stage name, the name of one of his grandfathers. The newspaper reported: "The debut of Harry Fox as a lone star and act amidst the films of the daily change at the New York Theater started off with every mark of success. The Dolly Sisters are dancing nightly on the New York Roof."

One source, although its grasp on history is rather flaky, is a film called *The Dolly Sisters*, released by Twentieth Century-Fox, appropriately, in 1945, a biopic following the fortunes of the act appearing at the same New York Theater as Harry. Jenny and Rosie Dolly—played in the movie by Betty Grable and June Haver—arrive in America in the early 1900s with their uncle Latsie and become huge stage stars. Jenny marries the vaudeville performer Harry Fox, and as a result Harry is the male lead in the movie, portrayed by John Payne.

In 1912 the girls, who have built up a reputation performing at the Little Hungary Restaurant in New York, are traveling to their first out-of-town engagement, in Elmira, upstate New York. On the train they bump into Harry Fox, in boater, bow tie and smile, who tells them he's a performer. "Are you an actor?" the sisters ask. "The jury's still out, but I think so," he says coyly. "Why are you going to Elmira if you've been on Broadway?" they ask. "I'm breaking in some new material." The girls, traveling in Lolita-ish schoolgirl outfits to avoid paying full fare, don't let on that they're artists too.

When Harry arrives in Elmira he finds the Dolly Sisters top of the bill and himself squeezed in below Elmer the Educated Seal. He's off to complain to the manager when he sees the Dolly Sisters on stage rehearsing and recognizes them from their train encounter. The girls are singing "Do the Vamp": "Vamp until you get a cramp. Then do a little foxtrot, do a little whatnot." Now, that is amazing, since we are in 1912 and the foxtrot was not created until two years later. I read that Rosie Dolly had overseen the production of the movie as a story consultant, but it constantly plays fast and loose with the sisters' story, not least by making the pair wholesome blondes, when in reality they were dark and quite exotic-looking.

The movie twirls on. Harry, dressed in boulevardier costume of Edwardian collar, belted jacket, bags and cane, does his routine, and inevitably he and Jenny hook up and start off along a rocky road of relationship, romance and marriage. However, in the end Jenny chooses her career as a Dolly Sister over life with

Harry, who in the meantime has found success as a songwriter through her Broadway connections (the song they give him in the movie, "I'm Always Chasing Rainbows," which John Payne sings like a McCartney ballad, was a hit for Harry Fox in 1918). Jenny's tours, fame and lifestyle conspire to pull them apart. "We're always saying good-bye," moans Harry. "I can't keep up this long-distance business forever." They get divorced. Later Jenny crashes a car while staying on the Riviera and is badly injured. She eventually pulls through, after cosmetic surgery, and at a benefit for her she and Harry sing a duet of "Rainbows." Harry's new fiancée leaves, saying she can see he's still in love with Jenny . . .

Although not much of the film is absolutely true, Jenny and Harry were certainly married. Jenny did have a serious car accident and needed extensive facial surgery. (What the film doesn't reveal is that she never got over this and committed suicide in 1941.) Harry went on to marry again after their divorce, and he and his new wife, Beatrice Fairfax, appeared in a number of minor movies in the 1920s and 1930s—one called *The Bee and the Fox*—but he lived a remarkably undocumented life, dying in Woodland Hills, California, in July 1959. It seems that Harry tapped, skittered and trotted his way through history without ruffling its surface unduly.

★

Unlike many of the dance fads of the 1910s, the foxtrot was lucky. It survived, primarily, says Richard Powers, because of timing. Evolved in 1914, it barely squeaked in before the outbreak of the First World War. Although dancing—and vaudeville—continued throughout the war, there was a natural cessation in dance fever, as the Allies got stuck in the mud of Flanders and America prepared its doughboys to join them.

After the Armistice of 1918, when America went back to dancing, the postwar generation did not want dances that smacked of a prewar mentality. They and their lifestyle had moved on. They wanted modernity, progressiveness.

The foxtrot made the cut. It was not considered one of the ragtime dances, now considered passé. The one-step was only a couple of years older, but for the new generation that felt like an *era* ago. The foxtrot, with its loose, relaxed mix of fast and slow walking steps, suited the mood of the moment, its easy freedom in tune with the spirit of an age that had overturned the old institutions. The Turkey Trot and the Grizzly Bear swiftly became endangered species, but the foxtrot lived on. It became, extraordinarily, an even hotter dance.

The name was so popular that it was applied to anything that moved. The same happened in the 1950s, Richard Powers told me, when "bop" became the term of the moment. "Foxtrot" was such a powerful selling tool that music publishers even started calling the tango the "Spanish foxtrot." As the 1910s turned to the 1920s, dance masters tried to resist this and said, "No, you can't call that a foxtrot." The dancers said they didn't care. Paul Whiteman's 1919 version of "Whispering" was called a foxtrot, even though the one-step was danced to it.

The foxtrot could also be speeded up, almost to one-step tempo, and this became known as the quickstep. To the non-dancer, the profusion and apparent cross-fertilization of dance names and techniques can quickly grow confusing. When describing the vocabulary of social dance, Richard Powers had a great phrase—he called it "a perfect mess," the same steps given different names, the same name applied to different steps.

The foxtrot survived all the subsequent dance crazes. The frenetic charleston of the late 1920s was so popular that the slogan "PCQ"—Please Charleston Quietly—was coined to avoid injury. The 1930s was a decade of British party dances, the Lambeth Walk, the hokey-cokey and the Knees up Mother Brown. The swing bands of the 1940s introduced the jitterbug and boogie-woogie, the latter somewhat too wild, so the professional dance powers took hold of it and controlled it as jive. Rock 'n' roll marked the beginning of solo dancing, most famously encouraged by Chubby Checker's "The Twist," which became an art form in its own right. Disco was the predominant force of the late 1970s—I can still remember the thrilling shock of the new when I saw the movie *Saturday Night Fever* in 1977. Line dancing, the lambada (vintage 1990), salsa and Bollywood dancing have all flared or flourished. And the foxtrot has tiptoed serenely past them all.

But as Philip Richardson, still editor of *Dancing Times*, noted in the 1930s, in the introduction to *The Text Book of Modern Ballroom Dancing* by Miss Eve Tynegate Smith: "If Modern Dancing is a living thing, it must obey the laws which govern living things. It cannot ever remain *in statu quo* for any length of time . . . All the historical knowledge in the world will not improve your Foxtrot."

⋆

As far as I can tell, the foxtrot is the only major dance form named after a person. The Lindy hop of the 1920s and 1930s was said to be named after the aviator Charles Lindbergh, but the dance predated his *Spirit of St. Louis* flight of 1927. By coincidence, however, aviation communication was responsible for rooting the word "foxtrot" even deeper into language across the globe: it is the international radio term for the letter F. And by coincidence the T is Tango.

The International Radio Alphabet, or the ITU Recommended and/or Standard Phonetic system, was created to overcome potential unintelligibility on unreliable radio or phone lines, which could easily lose single letters between the crackles. A first version drawn up for and adopted by the ITU, the International Telecommunication Union, in 1927 used a series of place-names, starting off with Amsterdam, Baltimore and Casablanca. The F was Florida, the T Tripoli. During the Second World War a new edition was created, the Joint Army/Navy Phonetic Alphabet: Able, Baker, Charlie (this is still familiar in some circles) with Fox for F and Tare, surprisingly, for T.

After the war and with the input of IATA, the International Air Transport Association, a third version was created, which is pretty close to the one we know today. Foxtrot and Tango were already in there, and by the time of its finalization in 1956, after extensive testing, only five terms, Coca, Extra, Metro, Nectar and Union, had been changed (to Charlie, Echo, Mike, November and Uniform respectively). This is the vocabulary of *Juliet Bravo*, *Bravo Two Zero* and the Wilco album *Yankee Hotel Foxtrot* (not to mention the Genesis classic *Foxtrot*), and of military slang, as in "Charlie Foxtrot" for "completely fucked."

It occurs to me that perhaps Foxtrot and Tango might not have made the list if it had been drawn up in a later era. If it had been created in the 2000s we might have found FT represented by Falafel Tae-kwondo, perhaps, or Four-wheel Tofu. As I packed up my patent leather shoes at the Len Goodman Dance Centre and made a resolution to come back and dance some more as soon as possible, I thought to myself that I was really, really glad that in radio language, as well as in the dance world, Foxtrot had, once again, made the cut.

CHAPTER 14

Welcome to Maverick Country

"Clouds of dust an' ropes awhirl, snubbin' broncs a-standing,
Bellerin' mavericks holdin' down, every outfit brandin' "
Jack Lee, "Powder River, Let 'er Buck"

Joe D. Hawes met me in Tivoli, Texas. "Turn right at the cross-roads with the traffic light. You won't miss it," he told me. "There's only the one light." Sure enough, on a foggy morning a single orange light blinked tentatively as I approached, after a 50-mile run from Corpus Christi out along the Gulf Coast. If this township was a tribute to the Tivoli Gardens in Copenhagen it had some way to go in the illumination stakes.

Joe's pickup was exactly where he'd said I would find it. A maroon Chevy Silverado pickup with an aluminium gun rack. Joe climbed down from the truck. He was all Texan. Tall, barrel-chested. Cowboy hat, work shirt, denim jeans and boots. A crinkled, weather-beaten, kind smile. "Welcome," he said. "Follow close behind me. We're heading out to the boondocks."

The boondock in question was Joe's ranch, Rancho Riacho—"we called it after a funny little creek"—where he lived with his wife Marjorie. They married in 1940, when she was seventeen and Joe was twenty, and now in his late eighties Joe was still keeping cattle. And more importantly, he was still running cattle out on the Matagorda Peninsula where, in the 1840s, a sometime rancher named Samuel Maverick had run cattle too, the cattle that carried his name into the English language.

From the turnoff to Rancho Riacho we lumbered over a mile

or more of rutted tracks, through muddy fords, over a timbered bridge crossing that funny little creek and past squat mesquite trees that looked as if their trunks were buried underground and only their highest branches had made it to the surface. Unfazed cattle watched us nonchalantly. As we drew up to Joe's house, a posse of wild turkey pottered across the track. In a townie kind of way, I ventured that up until then the only wild turkey I had ever seen was inside a bottle of bourbon. Joe laughed kindly as he leaned up against the gate to the ranch house. On top of the gate discolored metal letters spelled out J. D. HAWES. "All rusted up, just like me," said Joe sadly. He was getting ready for a hip replacement operation. "Been getting around on one leg for a while now. That's old age, I guess." But although his gait was a little stiff, he was still 100 percent prime rancher and, to my untrained eye, looked pretty damn healthy.

He and Marjorie had moved out here in the early 1970s, away from the coastline. A hurricane had wiped out one of their homes in Port O'Connor—"we never did found out where the house ended up"—and eventually they headed inland for a little more security. However, Joe knew the Gulf Coast, and the Matagorda area in particular, better than most. He was born on Matagorda Island, lived there until his twenties and was the locally acknowledged expert on the area.

First, a little geography. The Matagorda Peninsula, where Samuel Maverick kept his cattle, and the adjacent Matagorda Island are part of a ribbon of barrier lands that sweep along and protect nearly the entire arc of the Gulf Coast of Texas for more than 350 miles, from Galveston up near the border with Louisiana right down to the frontier with Mexico by Brownsville. The Matagordas form the central sector, the peninsula jutting out from the mainland near Sargent, some 40 miles south of Houston. The island lies immediately to the southwest and points the way down to Corpus Christi and onwards to the barrier's southernmost landfall, the hedonistic playground of South Padre

Island, America's very own Cancún. (The particular padre in question, by the way, was a Mexican priest named Padre José Nicolás Balli.)

The coastline is in constant flux, and winds and storms have determined the shape not only of the coast but also of the area's history. The weather is unpredictable, and hurricanes are an intermittent life-changing event. The impact that Katrina had on New Orleans in August 2005 has been acted out along the Gulf coast, but with less 24/7 news coverage, for centuries. In 1900, for example, Galveston, then *the* thriving port of east Texas, was shattered by a hurricane, and its role as a boomtown was picked up, but never handed back, by Houston. On Matagorda Bay itself the town of Indianola, a rival to Galveston in its own heyday, was wiped out in 1875.

Joe had lived through more than a few of these intense blasts and understood the realities of life on such a low-lying coast. "The island is quite high; our ranch house there always withstood the storms. But Matagorda Peninsula has a real low elevation. Figure on it. If you're gonna build on the coast on a little low place you're gonna git hit by those storms. It's one of the penalties you pay for living out there."

The worst experience in Joe's life had been Carla in 1961, a Category 4 hurricane that smacked into the area with winds of 120 mph and took out most of the houses in Port O'Connor, the town on the mainland opposite the peninsula "and half the cattle we had there. We didn't lose cattle on the island though. They were native, and went to the highest elevation they could find." There was little insurance when Joe was younger, and even if you were covered it could take from six months to a year for the companies to pay out on a claim. Even now it's hard to get insurance for any building on the barrier islands.

*

I had realized how vulnerable the Gulf Coast was to extreme weather conditions flying in, or trying to, the night before. The "Flight Delayed" messages were clicking up frantically by the time I landed at Houston for a connection to Corpus Christi. There was only a minuscule possibility of escape from Houston, and the airport corridors were full of frustrated businessmen downing beers, and overpepped-up college kids heading down to South Padre Island for spring break. On the TVs hanging in the full-to-bursting bar the chances of the Dallas Mavericks ball team were being discussed.

Somehow I managed to hustle myself onto the last seat available on an earlier, last-ditch flight south. Through the night sky, the plane rattled and bumped and juddered along the Texas coastline, hightailing it onto terra firma sometime after midnight in the middle of a spectacular storm. The weather in Corpus Christi was suitably biblical: viciously high winds, whipping rain, lightning jags strobe-lighting the sky for the next hour. Fortunately, things had calmed down by next morning, in time for me to find my way to Tivoli.

The Hawes ranch was full of Matagorda memorabilia. Faded photographs of Port O'Connor in its heyday. A wonderfully romantic shot of Marjorie and Joe around the time they got married in 1940, beaming out from a ranch house verandah. A table made from a slice of a huge mahogany tree that had flotsamed up on the beach at Matagorda Island. Joe settled back and told me some of his family history, which would set Samuel Maverick's experience into context.

Joe's great-grandfather, Hugh Walker Hawes, a lawyer by profession and already a fairly wealthy man, had come down from Kentucky to the Texas coast in 1839. He foresaw the area as a potential alternative to New Orleans. On Saluria Bayou, on the northeast shore of Matagorda Island, he built up a wharf and warehousing as a location for unloading deep-draft ships that did not want to venture into the shallow bay waters and for transferring the goods they bore onward to the cities of Corpus Christi and Victoria. By the late 1850s he and Saluria were prospering. "He was doing real good," said Joe, "but then the Civil War burned him out, and there was a storm in 1875 and that finished him off. It left him with only his ranching operation on the island."

A tall white stone marks Hugh Hawes's grave underneath the island's lighthouse, near where the Haweses and two other families set up isolated ranch houses. Because Matagorda Bay on one side and the Gulf of Mexico on the other provided two natural fences, the island was simply cross-fenced to demarcate areas where cattle could graze, alongside sheep, horses, geese and hens. The families grew crops and supplemented the produce with fishing and hunting.

It was a hard living, and even into the mid-20th century a pretty rough one, with primitive conditions: no running water or plumbing and no phones. But it was a wholesome existence: swimming on the beaches, riding the sand hills. "We worked hard with the cattle. Fresh air, and lots of it. It was real healthy. We ate a lot of fish, ducks and geese. I don't think you had all them dang diseases back then. Those doctors been busy inventing them ever since."

A coast guard station on the island and the lighthouse boat provided the principal link to the outside world, but a photo in Joe's house showed flat-bottomed barges bringing some Model T Fords out to the islands, the same barges that could transport the Matagorda cattle back to the mainland for sale. When the cattle were ready to ship it was all hands on deck. Breakfast was prepared for twenty or thirty hired workers, each with an unendingly hearty appetite. And before the roundups, the calves had to be caught, flipped, castrated and branded, twice a year, in June and late November, long enough before the cattle sales for the wounds to heal. It was a tradition in the Hawes family that all the kids and grandkids, especially the ones who'd moved away from the island, should come back and help, go in the pen one-on-one with the calves and try to flip them by hand the old way, something they'd never forget. This was real ranching and cowboy work. The heroic, stylized Hollywood version was an entertaining myth.

*

Samuel Augustus Maverick was a Texan by choice but a reluctant rancher. He was born in South Carolina, on 23 July 1803; his parents had moved out of Charleston to avoid yellow fever and settled in Pendleton, in the foothills of the Blue Ridge Mountains, to farm orchards and grow vines and dabble in cotton. Samuel's father had endured an education interrupted by the events of the Revolutionary War and did not want his son to miss out as well: Samuel went to Yale, after which he studied law at Winchester in Virginia, returning to South Carolina to practice in the late 1820s.

He departed a few years later, after getting involved in an argument at a public meeting called to discuss the Nullification Question, a bust-up between the state and the federal government of President Andrew Jackson that was one of the tremors presaging the earthquake of the American Civil War. The Mavericks were against the southern states seceding from the Union. When his father was speaking and being constantly interrupted, Samuel challenged the heckler to a duel, wounded him and promptly took the victim home to tend to his injuries.

However, to avoid inflaming the situation, Samuel clearly thought it was wise to leave South Carolina, heading first to Alabama to sample working on a plantation. That did not appeal, so he moved on to Texas, which was attracting adventure-seekers like moths to a storm light. In the 1820s the land developer Stephen Austin had promised to reclaim Texas from its Mexican overlords through the "enterprise and intelligence" of North American folk, with strict rules that there should be "no drunkard, no gambler, no profane swearer, no idler." Taking no notice of these criteria, they came anyway, in their droves from New York, Georgia, Kentucky, looking for a fortune (or fleeing bad debts). Samuel Maverick joined them and first arrived in San Antonio in 1835. The town, with its adobe and stone buildings, plazas and generally exotic Hispanic vibe, entranced him, and he decided to stay.

He found himself in the thick of Texas history after only a few weeks. The city, which was challenging Mexico's rule, was captured by a Mexican force, and Maverick was placed under house arrest, but somehow he managed to persuade his captors that if they released him he would leave the state. Instead, once clear of the city, he hooked up with the rebel Texas army and helped guide them back into the city, using his knowledge of its layout. The Mexican generals surrendered.

In the following year, 1836, Texas declared its independence; it's easy for a non-Texan to forget that for nine years the state was an independent republic, shrugging off the attentions of both Mexico and the United States. In that fateful year of 1836 Samuel was based at the Alamo but was chosen to be a delegate to the Independence Convention held in east Texas at Washington on the Brazos. Fate indeed—while he was away the siege of the Alamo took place, during which nearly all the Texan defenders were massacred. (Samuel later planted a garden nearby in memory of those who were killed.)

That year of 1836 was significant in Samuel's personal life too. He visited Alabama, where he had spent time on his way from South Carolina to Texas and met his wife-to-be Mary Ann Adams—she, helpfully, kept a journal for much of their married life. "Gus," as his family called him, was offered a property in South Carolina by his father, but his heart remained set on Texas, and Mary, with the couple's infant son, accompanied him back to San Antonio in October 1837. She recalled the trip as a particularly harsh journey and that during it they went close to Matagorda Bay, which Samuel wanted to visit "with a view of possibly locating there." However, they continued on to San Antonio and took up residence on the Plaza Mayor. Their second son, born there in 1839, was, she believed, the first child of pure American stock born in the city, and she the first American woman to make her home there.

By the autumn of 1841 Mary was reporting rumors that Mexican forces were again preparing to invade San Antonio, which they did by surprise attack in the following September. Maverick was again captured. This time, perhaps because of his earlier duplicity, he was sent with fifty other prisoners—"poor luckless Texians," as he described himself and his co-prisoners—on a long trek to Mexico, lasting two months. They finally arrived in Perote Prison in Vera Cruz, where Samuel was interned until his release in the spring of 1843. "Do not despond," he wrote in one letter to Mary Ann, reassuring her by describing his daily routine in the castle as one of monotony, although Waddy Thompson, the American minister to Mexico, who helped negotiate his release, recalled him as "a man of fiery and impatient temper, and chafed, under his confinement, like a chained tiger." Maverick had a particular reason for his anger. When the victorious General Woll had left San Antonio in triumph he commandeered Samuel Maverick's finest buggy, while his sidekick Colonel Carrasco helped himself to Maverick's best horse for the ride to Mexico. Apparently, Maverick never forgot this.

On the day he was released from captivity, his and Mary's second daughter was born; she was named Augusta in her captive father's honor. By May 1843 he was back in San Antonio, "in splendid health" his wife noted, "and happy as could be."

*

It was shortly after his release that Maverick relocated his family to Decrows or Decros (either way, pronounced "Deck-rose") Point on the very western tip of the Matagorda Peninsula.

Maverick had already bought some land at Cox's Point on the bay opposite Port Lavaca, but now they moved across the water to the thin, low-lying strip of land, "a dreary sandy flat," Mary called it, although she liked its proximity to the Gulf of Mexico and its "magnificent, calm, gently heaving water," and enjoyed the fact that every evening her husband would take her down to bathe in the sea.

They started making it as homey as possible, putting a fence up around the place and cultivating a garden. "What delicious watermelons! Flowers, grapevines and orange trees flourished luxuriantly." This was a period of relative stability on all fronts, and after its republican interlude, Texas voted to join the United States in 1845. There was a social life to enjoy in Matagorda City at the far end of the peninsula, which attracted the wealthy planters from the neighborhood, and the city even had an academy for young ladies.

But though their house was shipshape, the bay itself, treacherous for those unfamiliar with its tides and moods, was less manageable. On one occasion Samuel was in a small craft that capsized off Lavaca, but he managed to get rescued just before dusk fell. Another day fog fell in a blanket over a boat the Mavericks and some friends were traveling in; totally losing their bearings, they beached where they could and laid up overnight, huddling in the sailcloths for warmth. Mary's journals frequently mention the bodies of less fortunate neighbors washing up along the shoreline.

While living on Matagorda Peninsula, Samuel Maverick became a rancher by default. Owning cattle never interested him. Land acquisition and real estate were his real passions. "Mr. Maverick," wrote his wife, "was a most earnest and enthusiastic admirer of western Texas, and a firm believer in her future. What a grand home for the toilers of Europe, he would say. All men of strong imagination," she observed, "speculated deeply in land in those days." He carried on acquiring land for the next couple of decades and by the end of the 1860s had become one of the largest landowners in the west of the state. One of his wishes was to be able to travel from San Antonio to El Paso entirely on his own land, just as it used to be said that you could walk from Cambridge to Oxford on land owned by the Trinity Colleges of both universities.

Samuel Maverick was often away on business for weeks, even months. But on March 16, 1847 he was on Matagorda, and there is a significant entry in Mary's journals. She reports that "Mr. Maverick went to Tilton's place, 25 miles up the peninsula, and bought it and four hundred head of cattle at 3 dollars per head." In fact this was not a straight purchase but settlement of a debt. Samuel Maverick was owed $1,200 by Charles Nathan Tilton, and the 400 cattle at $3 canceled it out.

The property Samuel acquired back along the peninsula had an oyster bayou attached, as well as cattle pens. The family decided to move away from Decrows Point and up to the new house, an eight-room, three-storey frame house, built to resist the storms. "We lived well on the coast, had any quantity of fish, always fine, fruits fresh from New Orleans and splendid gardens. And still we were aware great storms might come and destructive cyclones at equinoxial times."

When Samuel's father heard that he was now a cattle owner, he reminded his son that one of his uncles had once taken a few hundred head of cattle in exchange for a debt and driven them to Pendleton. "Cattle, like an army of men, don't thrive," he warned gloomily.

I asked Joe Hawes what kind of cattle Samuel Maverick might have acquired in the deal. Joe reckoned that they would have been the common longhorn breed, the standard choice of the day, with a massive, distinctive handlebar of bone. The critical factor was that the cows could be turned loose on rough country and left to their own devices. Apart from sturdy cedar trees, the Matagorda Peninsula and island were covered in the thick scrub and brush that—from the Spanish *mata gorda*—gave the area its name; the peninsula was particularly rich in spartana grass, which grew along the water's edge and was high in protein, and the cattle would instinctively find their way to it, before moving to other areas and other grasses as the seasons changed.

Joe had told me that looking after cattle was "not too much trouble," and I'd thought he was being modest, but he insisted it was true. "We never did feed them cattle feed. They worked out where the best grass was; the cattle did the thinking for us." And when the mosquitoes came, the cattle would go down to the Gulf Coast, because the breeze off the water meant there were no mosquitoes around. At certain times the mosquitoes away from the water's edge were thick in the air. "I've seen it so bad, they even killed a deer; its windpipe got all choked up," remembered Joe.

Out on the peninsula Joe now ran the Beefmaster, a three-way cross of Hereford and Shorthorn cattle with the Indian Brahman bull, developed in the 1930s by the Lasater Ranch in south Texas. It's a good breeder and a hardy animal, "tough as a boot." Joe is dismissive of some of the more pampered varieties of cattle raised for life on less rugged ranches: "Cows today, turn them out on Matagorda, they'd starve to death." I had the feeling he identified with the old self-sufficient animals, especially when later on, he told me, "People today go through life so fast they don't know where they've been. The young people have never been deprived of anything. The older generation knew where money came from: a different kind of breed."

The style of ranching where cattle wandered free was the traditional way cattle were run in the mid-19th century. The huge Texan ranches (cue the theme tune of *Dallas*) were a later phenomenon, made possible only by the arrival of barbed wire, of which the most successful version was patented in the United States in 1874 by Joseph Glidden of Illinois. Barbed wire meant that huge tracts of land could be contained easily and quickly on plains where lumber and stone were in short supply and where fencing off vast acres would have been time-consuming and far from cost-effective. Landowners could swiftly divide up parcels of land huge enough to be measured in units known as RIs (Rhode Islands).

Before barbed wire, however, when cattle did run free, branding was an absolutely essential part of ranching, the only way to keep check on and track of the herds. Each brand was registered with the local cattlemen's association. The Hawes family's brand (a T overlaid on an L) was registered in 1873 and used long before that. But Samuel Maverick, although he had a brand mark of MK, failed to oversee its systematic use and gained a reputation for running unbranded cattle on the peninsula.

Shortly after acquiring the herd, he had in any case headed back to San Antonio. Both Samuel and Mary Ann had retained great affection for the place, where they had spent their early married life. They left behind both the cattle—in the care of Jinny and her son Jack, former slaves who worked for them—and the healthy lifestyle they had enjoyed out on the coast. The change of environment had immediate and fatal consequences for the family: within a year of returning to San Antonio one daughter, Agatha, died aged seven, the following year another daughter, Augusta, and an infant baby named John both fell victim to an epidemic of cholera.

While dealing with these personal tragedies—distraction enough—Samuel was receiving letters from acquaintances back in Matagorda reporting that Jack was finding it hard to manage the cattle on his own; others said that they were lost or stolen "from want of proper attention," or that other ranchers were simply branding them as their own. At one point Maverick was summoned to a meeting to discuss these cattle he had "abandoned and which had multiplied," the cattle that they had come to call "mavericks."

One former resident of Matagorda was Charlie Siringo, born on the peninsula, where he grew up enjoying much the same childhood as Joe Hawes a century later, catching crabs and rabbits, riding across the bush, swimming in the bay. Siringo was an adventurous soul—he spent some time on the Mississippi as a lad à la Huckleberry Finn, and later became a Pinkerton detective on the trail of Butch Cassidy and the Sundance Kid, among others. He was also a cowboy, and in 1885 published the first autobiography of a working cowboy, with a dull title—*A Texas Cowboy*—but a great tagline, "Fifteen years on the hurricane deck of a Spanish pony." Siringo was dismissive of Samuel Maverick, calling him a "chickenhearted old rooster" for not branding his cattle, but that seems unfair to me. Samuel Maverick was—as his real estate activities proved—a shrewd businessman, not a bumbling fool, but his heart was simply not in ranching.

Eventually, in 1854, Samuel had had enough. He hired some Mexican cowboys or vaqueros (from which the word "buckaroo" comes, as it happens) and, with his two eldest sons, Sam and Lewis, returned to Matagorda, rounding up the unmarked cattle and herding them off the peninsula to a stretch of the San Antonio River some 45 miles outside the town of San Antonio, a place they called Conquista Ranch. Two years later he got out of the cattle business altogether, selling the 400 head of cattle to a Mr. A. Toutant Beauregard. When it came time to collect them together, the freelance cowboys who did the job found some were branded and some not and again dubbed the unbranded calves "mavericks."

Joe Hawes remembered using the word "maverick" when he was growing up. "Maverick was the term for any animal where we didn't know who it belonged to or we found running wild. I never even connected it with Samuel Maverick, not until I started reading the histories, although I knew the family name from the old maps of the area."

With the help of itinerant cowboys, the ranching use of "maverick" spread away from its south Texan origin. The Maverick family, spurred by the appearance in one dictionary of a definition of the word as being after a "cattle thief named Maverick," tried to set the record straight. In 1942 Dr. Lewis A. Maverick, writing in the *California Folklore* quarterly, confirmed that it was the cowboys who herded the cattle for Toutant Beauregard who had spread the term as they moved on to other jobs and thought the word was disseminated during the big cattle drives from Texas up to Montana and the northern states. What is not certain, however, is how and where it crossed over to gain the further meaning of anyone who is nonconformist, and headed out into general usage.

Samuel Maverick did have a certain profile within Texas. Not only was he a noted landowner and a signatory of the Republic of Texas's Declaration of Independence, but he also held public office, as mayor of San Antonio and a member of the Congress of the Republic (an office he was voted into in absentia when he was imprisoned by the Mexican forces in 1842–3). And the Maverick name was sustained in the public eye in the next century by his grandson, Maury Maverick, a Democratic congressman who represented Texas in the 1930s and who is credited with coining the term "gobbledygook" and called his autobiography *A Maverick American*. His son, Maury Jr., having failed to get selected for the Senate seat vacated by Lyndon B. Johnson when he became vice president in 1961, became a well-known lawyer fighting civil rights cases.

Other branches of the Maverick family continued to do things differently and never followed the herd. I spoke to Robin Lloyd, who has plenty of Maverick blood in her veins: she is a peace and justice activist, a maker of documentary films about human rights. Robin's grandmother, Lola Maverick Lloyd, was a grand-daughter of Samuel's, who also kicked against the traces. Lola was a pioneer suffragist who married William Bross Lloyd (one of the founders of the Communist Labor Party of America). She was a moving spirit behind the Peace Ship chartered by Henry Ford during the First World War and became a founder of the

Women's International League for Peace and Freedom. Many of Lola's descendants have continued working for civil liberties and world peace; Robin herself had spent time in prison for civil disobedience, defending her beliefs.

Robin told me that even as we spoke three sisters, Maverick descendants, were trying to save the Maverick Ranch outside San Antonio from being flattened to make way for a new highway. "I feel lucky to have this heritage," said Robin. "It means I don't feel I'm the black sheep. We're all black sheep."

Although the Mavericks as a family matched the new meaning of their name, perhaps the reason the broader sense of the word caught on is that it so sweetly fits the Texan self-image of themselves as beings of independent thought and action and of rugged individuality, that "Lone Star State of Mind," as Nanci Griffith sang. James Michener put it another way: "Texans want to believe they're different, a reverberating quality that other places don't have."

And, of course, being a maverick is an image many of us like to convey. If you like to feel you're not a run-of-the-mill person, you say you're a maverick. It's right up there with "mercurial," a handy tag for anybody who zigs where others zag. When Robert Altman, the director of *M*A*S*H, Short Cuts* and *Gosford Park*, died in the autumn of 2006, damn near every obituary described him as a "maverick." Madonna called her record label Maverick. The Brazilian business guru Ricardo Semler titled his bestselling book *Maverick! The Success Story Behind the World's Most Unusual Workplace*. TV allowed James Garner to ensure that Bret Maverick was a household name. And of course, Tom Cruise, in *Top Gun*, had the call sign Maverick, because, hell, that's the kind of guy he was.

*

I was about to take my leave of Joe and Marjorie Hawes, who had arranged for their son Robbie to take me over to Matagorda

Peninsula. Joe has mixed feelings about Matagorda. He loves the island and the peninsula, but he and his family have been locked for decades in a legal wrangle with the U.S. government over the island, a Jarndyce vs. Jarndyce battle that has already clocked up sixty years and rising.

It revolves around an interpretation of the U.S. Constitution's Fifth Amendment: that no public property can be taken for public use without due cause or compensation. In 1940 the Hawes and the other families had been happily ranching on Matagorda Island for a hundred years. During the Second World War the island was identified as a suitably remote training base for gunnery and bombing practice by the USAF. But there was a population. The government rushed through a condemnation order. Joe's uncle was up a ladder putting shingles on the ranch house roof when a U.S. Marshal arrived, serving papers that gave them, after a century on the island, ten days to clear out and get themselves and their cattle off.

The families didn't mind giving up their land for the war effort, but they never got it back; after the war they were forced to accept $7 an acre for land (though they were allowed to lease it back) that later went for $1,200 an acre. And don't mention the mineral rights. The island is now a wildlife reserve, a refuge for the giant whooping crane, which stops off in Matagorda for some R&R. The battle has taken its toll on Joe and his family. Behind the Texan hospitality, I could see from the scars of cold anger and sadness that the saga has tainted the land he grew up on.

Leaving Joe at the gate to the ranch ("Anything else, give me a holler," he shouted), I drove on to Port O'Connor. Now, Port O'Connor is not somewhere you can swing by. It lies at the end of Highway 185, which heads on through the flatlands, past the occasional oil refinery and railway siding, on and on and on till you hit the sea. At the waterfront by 7th and Commerce, Robbie Hawes runs Boathouse Bait. He's one of the few shrimpers still working the waters here. Great shrimp too: Marjorie Hawes had whipped up a ginormous plate of them for lunch earlier. The day I arrived there was no bait in Robbie's tanks, where he might store, along with those shrimps, croakers and ribbonfish, mullet, sardines and squid. He pointed out old shrimping sheds across the quay, now reinvented as tourist fishing outlets.

Without much to-do, we dropped ourselves onto his flat-bottomed, two-man fishing boat, and he gunned up the outboard, sending us chop-chopping across scudding waves under a lowering sky, straight out across the wide bay toward Matagorda Peninsula. It was extremely exposed out here, and there wasn't much to hang on to. I remembered Mary Maverick's litany of corpses washed up on the beaches and gripped a little tighter. After ten minutes we closed in on the land of the peninsula and followed it down to the tip. Decrows Point was separated from Matagorda Island by the narrow Pass Cavallo, and through the pass the waves of the Gulf of Mexico were churning.

Robbie nosed the boat as close to the beach as he dared without damaging the propeller, and I leapt off the bow onto dry land. (Joe later told me, "I spoke to Robbie. He told me you jumped onto Decrows Point. Said you looked like Columbus!")

This was Decrows Point. A fishing shack was perched on stanchions a hundred meters or so away, but there was nothing much else to see. It was desolate, though not bleak, and reminded me of long empty stretches of shoreline in Suffolk or along the Atlantic coast of France. I found it very hard to imagine the Mavericks' house here or their neat garden of watermelons and oranges. And it was certainly bracing. At Joe's house I'd seen an 1851 ad for Huff's Hotel at Decrows Point—"the healthiest place on the bay"—but you could see just how fragile this place was and how vulnerable anyone living here would be. Joe had mentioned that the Decrow family lost their home in the storm of 1875: "They thought their fine house was strong, but it was destroyed, and twenty or so of the family drowned that night."

I paddled back out to the boat, and Robbie crossed the short channel to swing me around the edge of Matagorda Island—its landmark lighthouse proudly extant. The constant ebb and flow of the coastline was revealed by a bay that had been a channel to the ocean but was now closed in to form a sweeping beach where summer visitors set up their barbecues. On our way back to Port O'Connor, accompanied by a squadron of brown pelicans and, for a brief while, by a friendly dolphin, Robbie gestured to an empty shoreline—the ghost space of Saluria, where Hugh W. Hawes had built his wharves and warehouses and dreamed of fame and fortune. Matagorda felt like a landscape of ghosts. As I looked back at the peninsula, I almost convinced myself I could see one of Samuel Maverick's longhorns looking back at me munching on some spartana grass.

★

A Texan footnote. Just before I said farewell to Joe, I had remembered to ask him if he owned a Stetson. Many hats have been named after fictional characters—George du Maurier's Trilby, Robbie Burns's Tam o'Shanter and Dickens's Dolly Varden—and the bowler hat most probably took its name from the brothers Thomas and William Bowler, whose Southwark factory produced the prototype for Lock's of St. James's. But the Stetson is absolutely and undisputedly named after John B. Stetson, the son of a hatter, who set up his own business in Philadelphia in 1865. Although the design of the Stetson was not strictly his (he lost a lawsuit with Christy's of Frampton Cotterell in the West Country, who had claimed he lifted it from the hats they made for sugarcane plantations in the West Indies), the quality of his hats, their durability and their adaptability made the Stetson the hat of choice.

In *The Hell-Bound Train*, an anthology of cowboy songs collected by Glenn Ohrlin, I had come across a song called "My Stetson Hat," a tribute to a "walked-on, tromped-on old J.B.," which listed its many uses: "coaxing a smoldering fire, panning dust for gold, carrying oats to a spooky bronc, stopping wind in an open crack."

Joe had wandered off to look for his and returned with a hatbox, inside which was laid, as carefully as a Ladies' Day hat in its Bond Street box, an old original Stetson. He showed me its gray felt brim, its flat crown and the J. B. Stetson brand on its leather headband. Then he leaned right back, popped it on his head, and a slow wide smile creased his face. "This is it," he said. "This is the Stetson, the real McCoy." But who, I asked, was the real McCoy?

CHAPTER 15

The Reverend Guppy's Aquarium

"Whales have calves, cats have kittens, bears have cubs,
bats have bittens, swans have cygnets, seals have puppies,
but guppies just have little guppies."
Ogden Nash, "The Guppy"

The guppy was where this book first started. The instantaneous verbal and mental connection that was sparked by a single question on *University Challenge*—about a fish named after a Trinidadian clergyman—had set me off on a journey into areas, both geographical and etymological, that for me at least were uncharted and introduced me to some canyons, coves and creeks that I would otherwise never have had a chance to discover.

I was particularly pleased that the guppy was behind it all. As the dilettante owner and keeper of a tropical aquarium for ten years or so, I had enjoyed the calmness its presence added to a room, the gentle putter of the aerating pump as soothing as a Japanese water feature. The minor chore of cleaning the tank was a purification ritual, not just for the tank and its inhabitants but also for my own mental reservoirs. As the filters cleared the cloudy waters, so any personal murk dissipated in parallel.

My family grew very fond of the fish who came to stay. Some lasted only a short while: a Siamese fighting fish, magnificent in fiery vermilion, proved to be something of a wimp and was swiftly consumed by its more aggressive tankmates. Others were more tenacious. The neon tetras sought safety in numbers by ganging up in darting, flashing shoals. One angelfish started out as a cutie the size of a postage stamp, but over the years grew so large and out of proportion with the other fish that he or she (I never knew which) had to be relocated to a retirement home for gentlefish. Yet the guppies were always my favorites. They had tiny bodies but carried behind them a fabulous fantail that flickered and shimmered as they swam through the foliage, and they came in a rich palette of colors. The guppies seemed curious about their surroundings and wore, as much as any fish can, an air of intelligence.

My initial research into the naming of the guppy had thrown up the bare bones of a story that immediately snared my interest. The Reverend Robert Lechmere Guppy, I read, enjoyed an eventful life. Raised in the august surroundings of Kinnersley Castle in Herefordshire, he had shown little desire to inherit the family estate and fled to sea as a teenager. After various adventures—he was shipwrecked off the shores of New Zealand—he settled in Trinidad, married a plantation owner's daughter, sired nine children and, for relaxation, studied the local flora and fauna of the island.

He had sent one specimen of the small, brightly colored, frilly-tailed fish to the British Museum's resident fish expert, Albert Günther, who excitedly declared this a new species and promptly named it *Girardinus guppii* after its finder. Shortly afterward the eminent ichthyologist realized he had made a significant blunder and that the fish was, in fact, an already known species—but the name guppy has stuck ever since. It was an intriguing tale that promised plenty to explore, but, as I found, the story contained fragments of truth interleaved with figments of imagination.

*

Deep in the vaults of the Natural History Museum, or so I'd heard via an inadvertent tip-off—a throwaway remark on some mad fish fanatic's website—lurked Robert Lechmere Guppy's original guppy. Only nobody there seemed to know its whereabouts. Unable to offer any immediate help, the research staff, apparently convinced by my British Library reader's card and the smattering of knowledge I'd picked up from an afternoon on Google, invited me in to browse through their collection of Victorian documents.

Their instructions were precise and delightfully zoological: "Go past the dinosaur, under the turtle and turn right after the alligator." And sure enough, after walking around the museum's trademark diplodocus, beneath a rather tubby loggerhead and just past a lugubrious gator, there were the archives. Amid a hum of academic study and beneath the benign marble gaze of John Edward Gray, keeper of zoology in the mid-19th century, I was brought a volume of correspondence from 1858–75, E–F–G, the notes and letters bound into a mighty black leather, gold-banded case, between sky blue, sun-dappled endpapers.

Here was a snapshot—or I suppose a daguerreotype—of amateur naturalism during the Victorian era. This was a period when the young men of Britain, dispatched to the far reaches of the mother country's empire to administer, instruct and expropriate, found themselves with time on their hands and surrounded by exotic flora and fauna. And so, spurred on by requests for specimens to display at events like the Great Exhibition of 1851, that celebration of all things British and imperial, they painstakingly collected samples of the new and the rare and sent them back to London for identification and naming by the experts.

En route to G for Guppy I found myself swept away to foreign lands by these gossamer-thin, onionskin letters. In an age dominated by e-mail, I found myself bemoaning the decline of correspondence and wondering what resources the biographers of the future would be able to draw on, maybe a few perfunctory printouts or a cluster of memory sticks. Each of these letters carried within its fabric a lingering tang of the very air in which the writer's pen had inked his or her thoughts, mainly his. The embossed letterheads revealed sons of empire—minor aristocrats, civil servants in Calcutta, an early Crocodile Dundee from Carlton in Victoria listing the sharks he was about to supply— alongside specialists from the great European and American institutions, the Museo di Fisica e Storio Naturale di Firenza or the New York Society of Natural Science.

I paused briefly at a note from Arthur H. Gordon, dated 1875, from a rather less far-flung corner of empire in Sloane Street, beneath the Gordon motto "Forward without Fear." "I am afraid," he wrote matter-of-factly, "most of the sharks I brought are absolute rubbish, for I find my best collection has not yet arrived from Mauritius."

As I turned the page I found a letter—just the one—from Robert Lechmere Guppy. He had sent it from Port of Spain on August 31, 1868, writing in his capacity as secretary of the Scientific Association of Trinidad, and the letter was a rather formal thanks for information about West Indian fish and reptiles.

Guppy had addressed the letter to Dr. Albert Günther, the British Museum's resident fish expert. It was Günther, I knew, who had misidentified and misnamed the guppy. The librarian unearthed an archive box devoted to him. I hoped to get some insight into his mistake and into this man whose sons had bequeathed his entire family records to the museum, including the draft of an autobiography Günther had prepared toward the end of his life.

The biography never saw the light of day. I was amused to find a note tucked into the manuscript from John Murray, founder of the august publishing house that still bears his name. It was a model for any aspiring commissioning editor of what a rejection letter should be: terse, suitably disdainful—it was unlikely, said Murray, that the book would "gain much widespread public attention"—and discouraging any further contact.

Nonetheless, despite the dry prose, written in his adopted language, it was clear that Albert Günther, although proud of his establishment position and his eminent role as "the first ichthyolo-gist of the age," had loved nature as a boy in the south German countryside. Albert distinctly recalled his father's great love for animals, the aviaries and the tubs full of fish in their garden, and the wild martens he trapped. After her husband's death, Günther's mother had relocated to Brighton, and she wangled Albert a job at the British Museum (then the home of the natural history collections; the Waterhouse-designed Natural History Museum was not completed until 1880). The museum specifically wanted a German naturalist to help arrange and catalogue their collection, not just from a clichéd view of Teutonic efficiency, but because German naturalists were recognized as leaders in the field of taxonomy.

Albert arrived in Bloomsbury in the autumn of 1857 and set to for a decade of fourteen-hour days cataloguing not only fish but also snakes, frogs and the reptiles of British India. The first part of his six-volume fish catalogue was published in 1858. He admitted it was far from perfect but pointed out that he had been thrown in at the deep end. "I was deficient in the experience required for so extensive an undertaking." Dr. Gray, his boss, "was merely anxious to get the collection named and arranged and to obtain the necessary funds for the continuation of a catalogue." That said, Günther was picking up a neat monthly bonus for his troubles, and I suspected he hadn't rushed the job.

His working conditions were far from ideal. "Three long, half-subterranean rooms in which the spirit-collection was stored away. The light was dimmed by buildings outside, the floor was stone, and a rising well under the floor showed by large damp patches on the flags its desire of inundating the room. Non-inviting, rheumaticky quarters."

However, nowhere in the draft memoir, and despite exhaus-tive lists of his other achievements and discoveries, did Günther describe misnaming the guppy he had received from Trinidad. Some selective rewriting of history, perhaps, or shame at a pretty basic screwup? He had failed to pick up that a Venezuelan example of the fish had already been identified and named as *Poecilia reticulata* seven years earlier by a fellow German, Wilhelm Peters, curator of the Berlin Zoological Museum. An Italian zoologist, Filippo de Filippi, had also identified the same fish, but placed it within a different genus as *Lebistes poeciloides*. Clearly Albert Günther had slipped up.

During the period he would have been identifying Robert Lechmere Guppy's specimen, Albert was moving house, his wife was pregnant—she died ten days after giving birth—and he had been slaving away at his Sisyphean task with no vacations for over ten years. The error was probably a matter of simple exhaustion, and frankly I can't say I blame him, since the cataloguing seemed tedious beyond belief. Yet, however excusable a mistake, Günther certainly wasn't revealing anything about it for posterity.

I thought I might have reached a cul-de-sac in my search for Guppy's guppy. There were no further clues in the museum's paperwork, no matter how beautifully bound it was. Reluctantly I set the project to one side. Then a few days later there was a breakthrough. I heard back from James Maclaine, one of the museum's 21st-century fish experts. He thought he might have located the elusive guppy. I went back to meet him and the principal curator of fishes, Oliver Crimmen.

We convened in the Darwin Centre, the museum's brand-new research and storage wing. The specimen room was a vast, chilly space containing industrial-size stainless steel tanks and vats. Rails suspended from the ceiling carried hoisting gear to lift the larger samples, the coelacanths, sharks and dolphins. It felt like a morgue—and in fact, not long before the BBC had filmed some scenes here for its pathology-based series *Silent Witness*. On the shelves was an extraordinary collection of preserved animals huddled inside their original Victorian jars, each container bespoke, handblown to exactly the required size. This tableau of once animate animals frozen in time was unnerving. Over

Oliver Crimmen's shoulder, a trio of echidnas were crammed into their jar, like elephants in a Mini. A Komodo dragon eyed me mournfully. Apparently they'd had to remove the monkeys because visitors found them just too scary.

I'd wondered beforehand if ichthyologists came to resemble their charges, like dog owners, but there was nothing remotely piscine about Oliver or James. Oliver was jovial and enthusiastic (a boisterous bear cub, perhaps), James tall, patrician and eager (an alert Highland deer).

How big a mistake had Albert Günther made, I asked, by failing to recognize Robert Guppy's fish as an existing species? Was this a huge embarrassment, and was that why he had expunged any mention of the error from his life story? The fish experts shrugged; they didn't think it was that big a deal. "It's pretty common, a hazard of the job." But now there are filters and hoops—and computers—to catch the errors. Species are submitted to the ICZN, the International Commission of Zoological Nomenclature. They apply their regulations ("almost unfathomable," according to Oliver) and the niceties of their particular syntactic protocols, the first latinate term denoting the genus, the second, the "specific descriptor," traditionally named after the discoverer or in honor of an appropriate expert.

However, what had once been an immense privilege and accolade was now losing its cachet. "There's an institute in Australia," Oliver told me "that will guarantee to name a species after you as long as you fund its research. And do you know what they call it? The Immortality Project."

We had almost forgotten about the guppy. James disappeared to find the sample. He returned with a little glass vial, smaller than a traditional jam jar, protected by a painted yellow seal. Each time the vial, is opened the seal has to be repainted, the yellow signifying it as a Natural History Museum specimen.

With little ceremony James opened the jar and tipped the contents into a dish. Here it was, the guppy of all guppies, the syntype of *Girardinus guppii*, the one against which all other guppies are compared, measured and monitored. The very guppy that Robert Lechmere Guppy had, back at his Trinidad home nearly a century and a half before, tenderly wrapped in alcohol-soaked cloth before entrusting the package to one of the shipping companies for the slow voyage back to London.

With all that expectation riding on it, the guppy sadly failed to deliver. Historically, it was magnificent. Visually, to be frank, it was a disappointment: a pallid, pinkish, roughly fish-shaped object no longer than a little finger lay at the bottom of the dish. James took a wooden spill and poked it tentatively, maybe hoping to jerk the fish back into life. It rolled over and stayed put. When I thought of the gorgeous, flickering, flamboyant guppies that I'd left swimming in my home aquarium that morning, I was glad it wasn't my job to compare and contrast them with this bleached-out sardine.

We stood and admired the syntype as best we could before James poured it back into its jar for resealing, repainting and refiling. He seemed remarkably cavalier handling this precious relic, although I could tell that both he and Oliver were intrigued. The guppy obviously didn't get out much.

As James headed out of the door, he mentioned in passing, "Oh, Olly's got two species named after him." Oliver smiled modestly. What were they? "A catfish and a parasite." Which did he prefer? "I'm rather fond of the parasite, actually."

I left the fish men to their work. It was time to see the guppy in its original habitat and to find out if I could reach the end of my pilgrimage and locate the Reverend Guppy's aquarium.

★

I arrived in Port of Spain by boat from Tobago, where my BA flight had landed. This was at the sensible suggestion of my host in Tobago, Mark Puddy, a relocated Brit who, with his

Trinidadian wife, Zena, had built a wooden guesthouse called Mount Pelier Cottage high up off a dirt track in the hills overlooking Scarborough, Tobago's unpretentious capital.

Mark, a sage guide who was very good at explaining to me the differences between Trinidad and Tobago ("chalk and cheese," he called them) had pointed out that the maritime option was "more organic" than taking a shuttle flight and that it was certainly more authentic for the Robert Lechmere Guppy experience.

So very early one morning I had boarded the catamaran ferry, known as the Cat, at Scarborough docks and eased out into the Caribbean under a soft golden sun streaked with clouds. I was clutching a gift from Mark, an eponymous trophy he found for me as soon as he learned about my interest in people who had had objects named after them. He had rummaged in his larder and presented me with a large citrus fruit, a fresh shaddock, which he had happened to buy the day before.

I had never heard of the shaddock, but a copy of *Fruits and Vegetables of the Caribbean* from the guesthouse shelves filled me in. The shaddock, I discovered, was the direct ancestor of the grapefruit. Grapefruits had not evolved naturally, but from a hybrid between the shaddock and the sweet orange. And the reason the shaddock was growing in the Caribbean was thanks to one Captain Shaddock (possibly James, maybe Philip, the details were sketchy) who had brought the fruit to the West Indies on a merchant ship from Polynesia in the 1750s. The shaddock was larger than the average grapefruit—in fact it's the largest of the citrus fruits—and when I had it for breakfast a day or two later I uncovered a very thick pith, which is used to make candy in Trinidad, surrounding the distinctive segments of a grapefruit. The taste was strong and slightly bitter, but it seemed like good brain food and certainly set me up in an inquiring frame of mind.

Although Trinidad is less than 20 miles southwest of Tobago, the ferry trip took over two hours, since Port of Spain lies on Trinidad's far western coast, just under a finger of land pointing

toward a similar finger jutting out from Venezuela. To get there
we cruised all the way along the island's north coast. Through the
mist, wooded hills slowly emerged in ghostly blues and grays. As
the Cat swung around toward the city, Port of Spain sprawled out
beneath the hills framing the harbor, a large working port, full of
derricks, gantries and container elevators and all the kind of bustle
you would expect. The taxi I found in Independence Square
headed up toward my hotel on Lady Young Road, winding up a
hill just off the Savannah, the vast grassy expanse at the center of
Port of Spain. I had a chance to dump my bags, and my shaddock,
before meeting the first of my guides to the city and its environs,
Reginald Potter.

Reg, dapper in short-sleeved shirt and chinos, was the current
president of the Trinidad Field Naturalists' Club, and his pedigree
for the job was impeccable. His grandfather, Thomas Irwin
Potter, had been one of the founders of the Naturalists' Club in
1891, along with Robert Lechmere Guppy's son, Plantagenet, so
Reg offered a direct connection to the tradition of colonial
settlers. His family, like the Guppys, were British in origin and
had come to the island in the wake of the Spanish—the first
colonizers, hence the names Trinidad and Port of Spain—and the
French. He spoke with a Trinidadian accent, which still, though
of course it shouldn't, sounds weird coming out of a white man's
mouth, like a Caribbean ventriloquist act.

Our destination was the National Museum, a two-storey,
white-fronted, late-19th-century building on the far side of the
Savannah. Upstairs fans turned lethargically; outside purple
bougainvillea swagged a side gate. This had originally been the
Royal Victoria Institute, set up to celebrate that queen's golden
jubilee; Robert Lechmere Guppy was on the founding board. We
trawled its rooms, where exhibitions of calypso outfits and
mineral deposits rubbed shoulders. We turned into a gallery
devoted to the work of Michel-Jean Cazabon, Trinidad's first
painter of any renown; there was a scene of the St. Ann's River—

where Guppy had collected his sample and which I hoped to visit—under a shady covering of bamboo arches.

There had once been a large natural history section, but this was now reduced to a single, small upstairs space. On the wall a display paid tribute to the founders of the Naturalists' Club—there was a photograph of Reg's grandfather alongside Plantagenet "Planty" Guppy. But apart from a fleeting mention of his father and the guppy in Planty's brief biography, there was nothing else, no photo even of the guppy, no old Victorian nets, no aquarium. It seemed a shame that in the nation's main museum Robert Lechmere Guppy had effectively been eradicated.

Reg had called in a few favors to fast-track me into the National Archive, a few streets away from the museum, and we parked in a space splendidly reserved for "Researchers." The archive contained the original copies of local newspapers from the time of Robert Lechmere Guppy's death in 1916, and I leafed through them to see if I could spot his obituary. Among the First World War news reports and a vast array of gloomy medical advertisements (De Witt's pills to avoid "the worn-out look of the kidney martyr," and Minard's Liniment for "rheumatic misery") both *The Mirror* and *The Port of Spain Gazette* had reported his passing with some florid prose: "Hopes were entertained that he would have lasted a few years longer," intoned one. "Fate, however, had decreed otherwise, and the unrelenting hand of death was placed upon him." I also had a copy of his youngest daughter Yseult Bridges's book *Child of the Tropics*, in which she captured a vignette of life as one of the Guppies of Port of Spain, and between the two I was able to piece together something of Robert Lechmere Guppy's life.

*

Robert Lechmere Guppy was born in London on August 15, 1836. His family was already based in Trinidad, where his father, another Robert, had settled. Some later Guppys have suggested that the family was originally from Florence, where the family name was Guy Pigli (I can't help but think of "higgledy-piggledy" whenever I see that), and that they relocated to England via France, where they had been Huguenots, in the late sixteenth century. But this appears to be a fanciful, genealogically unsound tale, since Guppys had been based in West Country villages like Symondsbury, Chardstock and Farway for centuries.

The money in the immediate family came from Samuel Guppy, who with his wife had developed an efficient way to fix copper to the bottom of ships, slowing down the growth of barnacles and allowing the ships to remain at sea for lengthy periods. At a time when naval domination was critical, the government bought an exclusive on the technique for a hefty fee.

Robert Guppy senior, Samuel's son, was a civil engineer, and had settled in San Fernando, in the southwest of Trinidad, where he was repeatedly elected mayor, edited the local gazette and used his engineering skills to lay out the main drag, the Harris Promenade, and construct the first railway on the island, the Cipero Tramway, linking cocoa estates to the town's harbor front.

Possibly to differentiate him from his father, our Robert was known as Lechmere, a name honoring his maternal grandfather, William Lechmere, a naval higher-up who had been an admiral of the white and who had married one of the granddaughters of Sir Francis Dashwood, founder of the supposedly anarchic and libertine Hellfire Club. Lechmere—we'll call him that from now on—spent his childhood with his mother's parents on their estate, Kinnersley Castle in Herefordshire. His uncle John, who inherited the castle, took a shine to his nephew over and above his own off-spring, declaring that Lechmere alone possessed the Dashwood élan, and wanted him to take over the estate.

Lechmere was not at all so enthusiastic and planned an escape route. Using some inheritance money he decided to follow his father and study at Pembroke College, Oxford, but while he was there waiting for an interview a flurry of letters from his increasingly needy uncle, pleading with him to return, proved too much. He went AWOL, taking off for a life of travel, pitching up in Australia, Tasmania and New Zealand. For much of the time he was completely out of touch, refusing to respond to the advertisements placed by his parents and Uncle John, the latter threatening to sell Kinnersley Castle if he heard nothing (a threat he eventually carried out).

Lechmere found his way to Trinidad in 1859, apparently satisfied that he was no longer going to be sent back to England, with tales of shipwrecks and living with the Maori, exploring the hills and valleys of New Zealand, collecting specimens (and some tribal tattoos—a typical gap-year student), and claiming that at one point he was alarmingly close to being married off to a chief's daughter. He kept diaries of these travels, but, alas, the family mislaid them sometime during the Second World War.

After helping his father with the construction of the Cipero Tramway, Lechmere applied himself, as the rest of his family had done, to civil duties. He focused on education and became the chief inspector of schools, applying his keen intelligence to re-organizing and modernizing the island's educational system, including the introduction of regular exams, female teachers, teacher training, PE and modern furniture. He also met and married Alice, the seventeen-year-old daughter of one of the French families, the Rostants. For the Guppies, it was a case of opposites attract. Alice, according to her daughter Yseult, loved society and was elegant and vivacious (though "prone to ennui"). He was "a gentle, learned and rather remote English eccentric."

Alongside his educational duties, Lechmere Guppy was a passionate geologist, naturalist (particularly strong on con-chology) and astronomer, a very Victorian gentleman. His job, requiring him to travel around the island, allowed him to indulge these interests. Yseult wrote of him squirreled away in his study surrounded by books, papers, specimens, microscope and a telescope through which he observed the phases of the moon for the *Trinidad Almanac* he had set up in 1866 with his brother Francis. He would also disappear into a workshop first thing in the morning, where he constructed shelves for the increasing number of books, cedar-lined cabinets to hold his specimens and furniture for his daughter's dollhouse. Although the study was sacrosanct, he would invite Yseult in, and he had time to talk to her about his investigations; she remembered most his "learning and wisdom, gentleness and strength."

A. D. Russell, in a footnote to his collection of poems *Legends of the Bocas,* also portrayed Guppy's intellectual rigor but missed his intimate side: "A man of remarkable individuality. Tall, gaunt, white-haired, grey-bearded, rugged in speech, combative in his opinions. A whiff of cold air seemed to go with him wherever he went. Watching him stride over the Savannah, one imagined it a Yorkshire moor."

Although geology, marine fish, molluscs and especially shells were the areas Lechmere focused on, he had a general interest in all aspects of natural history, so although he might have found it odd to be remembered in perpetuity by a freshwater fish, it would also have seemed absolutely appropriate. "I think," wrote Yseult, "he would have been totally amazed and highly amused that this tiny fish could cause his name to become a household word."

Something that was puzzling me was that although I had intermittently found references to Robert Lechmere Guppy as a reverend, in none of the death notices or any of the brief biographies at the National Archive or his daughter's book did any life in the service of God feature. He was, on the contrary, it emerged, a great believer in civil and religious liberty, and as chief inspector of schools was strongly in favor of government rather than religious control.

I could, in the end, only put this reverend tag down to a photograph that often cropped up, in which he gazes over small, rimless specs at the camera, wearing a high-necked coat, with an even higher collared white shirt, his beard and baldpate and air of sanctity lending him the look of a clergyman. The reproduction quality of the photo was occasionally questionable, and the impression a viewer would have had was that he was sporting a clerical collar. Somehow this must have been incorporated in some biography or other and, as erroneous facts will do, had wormed its way into repeated histories, becoming a fictional factoid that would prove harder and harder to eradicate as the repetitions proliferated.

My theory was later vindicated when I managed to reach Nicholas Guppy via mobile phone. He was up a hillside somewhere in Bali, where he was now living. Nicholas is the grandson of Robert Lechmere Guppy, the son of Gareth, Lechmere's third son. All of a sudden, talking to him, the sepia-toned Victorian era of amateur naturalism seemed within tantalizingly close touching distance. Nicholas—who said that his grandfather had been "very much loved; he inspired those around him with a great deal of affection"—knew all about the clerical collar. "My grandfather," he told me, "was an idiosyncratic and inventive man, and he designed his own version of a clerical collar." I asked what would have prompted Lechmere to do that. "He hated tying ties!"

The obituaries of Lechmere Guppy mentioned the address of the house where he died, on Cipriani Boulevard, just off the Savannah, and as we drove back from the archive, Reg Potter diverted along it. Many of the original Victorian houses still fronted the boulevard, but number 85, alas, had been razed and replaced and was now some kind of IT company. I would dearly have liked to have seen the house, particularly the observatory Lechmere built there to house his telescope.

*

Reg hooked me up with a fellow field naturalist named Hans Boos, the former curator of the island's zoo, who was descended from a

German family and who had calculated that he was a sixth cousin of the Guppies. Hans had extensively researched both the Field Naturalists' Club and the Scientific Association, of which Lechmere Guppy had been the secretary. He told me that the Field Naturalists' Club had been set up in direct competition to the Scientific Association by a younger set who thought it unlikely that they would be invited to join that august body, or, as Hans put it, "You had to be an esquire to belong to the Scientific Association. The others thought, 'Bugger you, we'll form our own.'"

They chose the motto *Natura maxime miranda in minimus* ("Nature in its greatness looked at in close-up") and stated their aim as "getting at the truth of everything they enquired into." Their first president, Henry Caracciolo, told his colleagues that "the great and wonderful book of Nature is lying open before us, waiting for perusal." Lechmere Guppy—as a Scientific Association man—was not a founding member, though he wrote to them from England, where he was presenting a paper to the Zoological Society, to wish them well. But Albert Günther *was* an honorary member, sending over notes on the best way to capture and transport specimens to London. He was particularly keen to bag an example of the Trinidad otter, although any bats, mice and rats were also welcome.

The club prospered (the Scientific Association, in contrast, dwindled). Papers were presented on manatees, iguana ticks, cassava plants, parasol ants, butterflies and raccoons with, for light relief, a talk on alligator shooting. The members made occasional forays en masse, once heading down to San Fernando to Guppy Sr.'s house, where "after a capital breakfast, the party ascended the Hill and enjoyed the fine view," descending handily in time for lunch and the chance to toast their host as the Grand Old Man of Trinidad. These young naturalists were busy bees, and indeed the first paper Reg Potter's grandfather read to the club had been on the common honeybee.

His cofounder, "Planty" Guppy, Lechmere's son, a wonderful

illustrator of insects and fish, later retired from his civil service job and became a dealer in animals, especially tropical fish, helping to introduce the guppy to England, the United States and Europe and, perhaps in a shrewd piece of branding, using the name "guppy" for the fish. In 1909 the first living guppies, collected by a Captain J. A. M. Vipan, had been sent via the British Museum to Germany, where tropical aquariums were already popular. From these first live samples, breeders started selectively developing the brighter colored male of the species, producing a rich array of colors and tail shapes, from double swordtails to lyres and spears. As aquarium-owning grew in popularity after the Second World War, guppies were especially sought after, as they were—and are—an ideal fish for beginners, quick to adapt to a range of conditions and temperature ranges, sturdy, nonaggressive and good community fish. Captain Vipan, one booklet revealed, had been the first person to keep guppies in an aquarium. No wonder I hadn't been able to find a rusting example of Lechmere Guppy's aquarium—this was a 20th-century phenomenon.

Hans Boos was going to take me to the St. Ann's River, where Lechmere Guppy had found the specimen I'd seen in the Natural History Museum, but we also headed down to San Fernando, where Robert Guppy Sr. had lived. The obituaries said that after Lechmere Guppy's funeral, his body had traveled in a cortège, by train, to San Fernando, to be buried in the family vault in Paradise Pastures. If an aquarium didn't exist and his house on Cipriani Boulevard had been knocked down, maybe I could at least find his grave.

Hans, as it happened, had grown up in San Fernando. Although it was a sweltering Saturday afternoon he was relentless in the search. He spun us up around the Hill, the central feature of the town, which the Field Naturalists had climbed, now nearly quarried out of existence, where Hans had first gone out looking for specimens. He bounced us up and down past villas and bungalows on the switchback roads he had pelted down in

go-carts as a child. We visited the main town cemetery, just off
Guppy Sr.'s Harris Promenade, with its shady samaan trees, court-
house, town hall and a collection of churches. We drew a blank at
the cemetery, although Hans found the headstones of some of his
own former teachers and family friends. And although we found
another cemetery near the area called Paradise Pastures, the
graves were all far too recent. This Robert Lechmere Guppy was
proving elusive.

The journey, though, was far from dull. Hans was an entertaining guide, who knew some great tucked-away restaurants,
including Charlie's, an Indian-run café just outside Tunapuna
(close to where Lechmere Guppy had owned a plantation). He
introduced me to the divine rotis prepared by Sharon on her stand
just along from the famed bar of Smokey & Bunty's in St. James,
Port of Spain's best nightlife destination, teeming with clubbing
kids and rap-blaring cars. Hans was not only an observant
naturalist, he also had a keen eye for the local fauna—"Hey, boy,
there's a good-looking girl."

His local knowledge was handy. On one occasion he faced
down a sullen youth who followed us to one of the streams north
of Port of Spain in a vaguely threatening manner, which Hans
defused by asking if he was from the area, pointing out his own
uncle's house up the road, and by taking his Trini accent up a
couple of notches so that he made it clear we weren't foreign
tourists. The knife Hans held in his hand, albeit in a sheath, also
seemed to help. Crime is a problem in Port of Spain. Reginald
Potter and his wife, sitting on their balcony in the hills of Glencoe
above the city, had told me of a recent armed raid on the house
that had left Reg with a bullet wound in his leg.

★

The St. Ann's River, in the Fondes Amandes Valley, was less than
ten minutes by car from the center of Port of Spain. I was

surprised. Back in London I had imagined an intrepid Guppy risking life and limb in some mountain brook to uncover a rare species. The reality was that Robert Lechmere Guppy could have come here after a brisk walk, bike ride or an undemanding horse ride out of Port of Spain, and later even by tram. Any local naturalist could equally easily have trotted up here and captured a specimen to send back to London. Guppy just happened to be the first to pack one up and pop it on a cargo ship.

The guppy was rife in these rivers and streams; the local name "millions fish" made perfect sense. "I tell you, boy," said Hans, "these damn things exist in every watercourse and drain in the city." In one river down south in the toe of Trinidad's boot some zoologists he knew had netted a quarter pound of guppies with each dip of their net.

We clambered down from a high-arched bridge to the shallows beneath. This was drought season, and although there was water in the river, it was not gushing but calmly babbling over rocky basins to a broad pool, then on to a cascade beneath the bridge. It was the kind of gentle locale where I once collected frog spawn and tadpoles in England. Morning light filtered through the lush green trees and dangling vines.

I remembered reading in one of the Field Naturalists' Club journals an essay about an excursion to St. Ann's and the Fondes Amandes Valley in 1894. The description was as accurate a century and more on. "At my feet a crystal stream, fanned by the soft breeze, rippled through an agglomeration of white quartz. Immense trees, bending gracefully over the riverside, afforded a delightful shade, while through the interlaced branches the golden streaks of light distilling through the green foliage lent animation."

Hans had explored this stretch of river with his cousins when they were young, making risky descents down vertiginous, slippery climbs. All around were examples of nature that he could identify for me. A Trinidad stream frog, tiny but vociferous, called out. ("There used to be a chorus of them," said Hans, "but the population's been degraded.") Up on the top of the bank was an immortelle, the tree used for shading cocoa plantations. A toxic vine dangled from the bridge—"they call it the strangler, or the Scottish attorney." Butterflies fluttered by.

We looked down into the water. It took a little time to get your eye in, but there, as Hans pointed, I could see tiny, fresh-born guppies, translucent, miniature versions of the guppy that I had seen in the Natural History Museum, not the carefully bred, colorful tropical aquarium fish; this was the real thing, plain juvenile guppies feeding on small algae, foraging on the rocks, trying to avoid the predatory rainfish swimming close by.

As I sat in this natural amphitheater listening to Hans effortlessly explain the range of flora and fauna on display, in a wonderfully impromptu and alfresco natural history lesson, I realized that this moment was the essence of this book.

Robert Lechmere Guppy may not have been a reverend. The guppy should never have been called the guppy. And he would never have had an aquarium. But, you know what? It didn't matter. "Nothing is real," as the Beatles once sang, "and nothing to get hung about." Sometimes you are heading in one direction, and reality is sitting and staring out at you from a completely different angle.

The truth was that this riverbank I was sitting on, overhung by foliage, next to the water's gentle babble, this valley was what was authentic, a living, breathing, vibrant example of curiosity about things, about the willingness to go out and search for connections and to relish the strangeness and variety of what is there to be found. For Hans Boos, or for Roy Jacuzzi, Adolphe Sax, Robert Lechmere Guppy, László Biró or any of the questers and visionaries I had encountered, and for anyone who loves the richness and weirdness of life, the answer was the same. The whole world, our world, is the Reverend Guppy's Aquarium.

Acknowledgments

Many people helped to turn *The Reverend Guppy's Aquarium* into some kind of reality. For their faith, and for getting the whole project off the ground, I would especially like to thank my agent, Gordon Wise at Curtis Brown, Nigel Wilcockson at Random House Books and Erin Moore and Bill Shinker at Gotham. I also really appreciated the understanding and enthusiasm of the editorial team of Emily Rhodes, Lydia Darbyshire and John Garrett.

For all their time, advice, knowledge, contacts and suggestions, I would like to thank everyone who helped the book along its way at critical moments—in chapter order: Diane Bortone, Bonnie Campbell, Jim Campbell, Nancy Nickum Damtoft, Peter Frisbie, Farina Headrick, Scott Keasey, Mollie Keller, Lisha Rooney, Cliff Towne, Lisa Townsend, Elizabeth Van Tuyl, David Waisblum, Mary K. Witkowski, Stephen I. Zetterberg; Tony Bingham; Jacques Devos, Géry Dumoulin, Robert Howe, Michel Kellner, Barry McRae, Paul Mason, Michel Rossi Mori; Charene Beltramo, Luigi Caporal, Ida Galluzzo, Roy and DeeAnn Jacuzzi, Silvana Mulotti, Sean Ruck; Mariana Biró, Ben Donald, Maggie Ferguson, Eduardo Fernández; Kate Davey, Philippe Lepine, Paul McKenna, Nick Mason, Jacques Voinot; Titi Alvarez, Steve Gossard, Cathy Haill, Charlie Holland, Jenny Lister, John W. Marshall, Michèle Pachany-Léotard, Pauline and Jean Palacy; Anne Coco, John Cork,

Sondra Gilman, Barbara Hall, Keith from About Town Limo, Connie Lenzen, Ellis Nassour, Beverly Payne, Noreen Prohaska, Tim Rice, John Silberman, Libby Wertin; Piers Gibbon, Thomas Hoblyn; Sophia Gosselin, Erwin Haeberle, Christopher Star, Chris and Ana Stewart, Beverly Whipple; Paul Bocuse, Martine Bocuse, Nicholas Clee, Tara Corbett, Mark Gibbon, Orlando Montagu, Ian Schneider; Florijan Hadzic, Gordon Murray, Doug Nye, Wolfgang Rabus; Charles Burns, Yvette Cayrol, Michael Pierce; Sue Barrett, Kate Cleeland, Richard Powers; Forrest Hawes, Joe and Marjorie Hawes, Robbie Hawes, Robin Lloyd, Donald Ramsey; Hans Boos, Oliver Crimmen, Father Anthony de Verteuil, Frank Gray, Gerald Lechmere Guppy, Nicholas and Anna Guppy, Mandy Holloway, Cheryl Leekin, Helena Leonce, James Maclaine, Judith Magee, Rachel Perkins, Reg and Janice Potter, Lesley Price, Jeanne Ross, Burt Salvary, Polly Tucker. Thank you one and all.

The hospitality of Luigi and Jane Caporal, John and Nicole Cork, Agnès and Frédéric Espinoux and Mark and Zena Puddy offered welcome oases during the travel; IT support from Claud Binns and John Stack and good advice from Stuart Leaman kept me afloat; and the tolerance and laughter of my wife and daughters kept me sane.

Finally, a special thank-you to Peter Gwyn, executive producer of *University Challenge*, for digging out the definitive wording of that question that sparked the whole journey. It was, for the record, "Which small, brightly colored fish is found in North America and the West Indies, and is named after the Trinidadian clergyman who sent the first specimens to the British Museum?" Peter added: "It's always interesting [if you produce quiz programs] to find out that confidently asserted 'facts' are actually nothing of the sort!" Wise words indeed.

★

Promopub B.V. 2003. First published by Weidenfeld & Nicolson. By kind permission of the publisher.

Quote in "The Whirl According to Roy Jacuzzi" from *The Autograph Man* by Zadie Smith © Zadie Smith 2003. Published by Random House, Inc. By kind permission of the publisher.

Quotes in "A Hungarian in Buenos Aires" from *What A Carve Up!* © Jonathan Coe 1994.

Quotes in "A Hungarian in Buenos Aires" from *The Hitchhiker's Guide to the Galaxy*, by Douglas Adams, © 1979. Reproduced by kind permission of the estate of Douglas Adams.

Quote by Sir Alec Guinness in "The Magnetic Appeal of Anton Mesmer" from *Blessings in Disguise* by Alec Guinness © 1985. First published by Hamish Hamilton. Reproduced by kind permission of the estate.

"The Guppy" by Ogden Nash, copyright © 1949 by Ogden Nash. Reprinted by permission of Curtis Brown, Ltd.

From *Candy Is Dandy*, first published in Great Britain in 1983 by Andre Deutsch. Reprinted by permission of Andre Deutsch and Curtis Brown, Ltd.

Index